THE LEAN LAW FIRM

RUN YOUR FIRM LIKE THE WORLD'S MOST EFFICIENT AND PROFITABLE BUSINESSES

Larry Port and Dave Maxfield

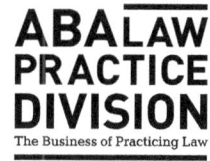

ABA LAW PRACTICE DIVISION
The Business of Practicing Law

Cover design by Lachina Publishing Services, Inc.

The materials contained herein represent the opinions of the authors and/or the editors, and should not be construed to be the views or opinions of the law firms or companies with whom such persons are in partnership with, associated with, or employed by, nor of the American Bar Association or the Law Practice Section unless adopted pursuant to the bylaws of the Association.

Nothing contained in this book is to be considered as the rendering of legal advice for specific cases, and readers are responsible for obtaining such advice from their own legal counsel. This book is intended for educational and informational purposes only.

© 2018 American Bar Association. All rights reserved.

No part of this publication may be reproduced, stored in a retrieval system, or transmitted in any form or by any means, electronic, mechanical, photocopying, recording, or otherwise, without the prior written permission of the publisher. For permission contact the ABA Copyrights & Contracts Department, copyright@americanbar.org, or complete the online form at http://www.americanbar.org/utility/reprint.html.

Printed in the United States of America.

22 21   5 4

Library of Congress Cataloging-in-Publication Data

Names: Port, Larry, author. | Maxfield, Dave, author. | American Bar
  Association. Law Practice Division, sponsoring body.
Title: The lean law firm : run your firm like the world's most efficient and
  productive businesses / by Larry Port and Dave Maxfield.
Description: First edition. | Chicago : American Bar Association, 2018.
Identifiers: LCCN 2018001110 | ISBN 9781641051385 (print)
Subjects: LCSH: Law firms—United States.
Classification: LCC KF318 .P67 2018 | DDC 340.068/4—dc23
LC record available at https://lccn.loc.gov/2018001110

Discounts are available for books ordered in bulk. Special consideration is given to state bars, CLE programs, and other bar-related organizations. Inquire at Book Publishing, ABA Publishing, American Bar Association, 321 N. Clark Street, Chicago, Illinois 60654-7598.

www.ShopABA.org

Contents

Foreword v
Acknowledgments ix

1   The Saga of Carson Wright 1

2   The Basics—Lean Thinking and Terminology 17

3   Systems Thinking 1—The Income Formula 31

4   Using KPIs—What, When, and How to Measure 49

5   Systems Thinking 2—Bringing Your System to Life 77

6   Lean Marketing 95

7   Locking It Down—Standardization, Written Procedures, and Checklists 125

8   Visual Communication, Meetings, and Rhythm 141

9   Getting Control of Technology 157

10   Goal Setting and the October Surprise 185

11   Buy In—General Adoption Tactics and Challenges Unique to Law Firms 205

Epilogue 223
Index 227

Foreword

We may be in the 21st century, but for many law firms, it's 1911.

That was the year that Frederick Winslow Taylor published his seminal work *The Principles of Scientific Management,* marking the dawn of a new age of "scientific" business management. It was around this time that visionaries like Henry Ford used these new management principles to accomplish feats of manufacturing never before seen. Manufacturing changed forever. But not so much for law firms. Even today, more than 100 years later, most law firms are operating as if they were in that time when the *Titanic* was being assembled in a Belfast shipyard and two world wars were still in the future.

Let me offer a bit more insight into this wild claim. When I first started observing the business side of law firms through my work with my software company Rocket Matter, I was struck by the reactionary nature of work in a law firm. It seemed as if the lawyers I observed were in a World War I trench with artillery shells constantly flying overhead. A request would come in from a client, a judge would throw a figurative grenade, or opposing counsel would file a motion requiring an immediate response. The lawyers and staff lurched from crisis to crisis, putting out fires and reacting to one emergency after another. More than 100 years after manufacturing started to really harness the power of systems, most of these lessons had yet to be translated for the legal profession.

Life in a law firm does not have to be utter chaos. As unique as law firms believe themselves to be, they are not unlike most of the business world. Most businesses face complex, long-term projects with uncertain outcomes. As with legal work, errors can result in disasters.

There has to be a better way. Lawyers and their staff deserve better lives, and their clients deserve better service.

Since the day I started my legal technology software company, I've believed that some of the techniques we use to run our operation could apply to the law firms we served. After all, if we in software—a much younger field than law—can leverage techniques from manufacturing industries, why can't a law firm? Isn't law a knowledge-based field like software?

I began my quest to spread the word about improved business processes for law firms, publishing e-books, speaking at continuing legal education (CLE) events around the country, and hosting countless webinars. Along the way I met other people who made the same observation I did and had pursued similar lines of inquiry. One of them was Dave Maxfield, my coauthor, who is a living embodiment of the Lean lawyer. Another, Nashville-based lawyer John McCormack, studies industrial engineering at Vanderbilt University. It was John who remarked to me that law firms were, from a managerial aspect, still stuck in 1911.

When Taylor wrote his seminal work *The Principles of Scientific Management* in that year, he exposed "the great loss which the whole country is suffering through inefficiency in almost all of our daily acts." As a remedy, he believed in "systematic management, rather than in searching for *some unusual or extraordinary man*."

In bringing science to the management of labor, Taylor sought to wring efficiencies from the American workforce. He sought to reduce process, and he maintained that it was up to management to identify the best method to complete each task. Today, Taylor is widely considered to be the father of the field of industrial engineering, and industrial management has never been the same.

As my friend John McCormack pointed out in commenting that most law firms exist in a pre-1911 world, most law firms have little to no awareness of **process**. Always running at 100 miles per hour, most firms do not step back to reexamine how they do things and what processes they've adopted over time. Instead, they do what they've always done: perform the client work, react to judges and opposing counsel, and hope for the best. Also, perhaps more than any other business, law firms can become overly reliant on the "unusual or extraordinary man" that Taylor referred to. A firm can be driven by the herculean capabilities of one or a few extraordinary lawyers. The fates of firms depend on these individuals.

Smaller law firms, where the lawyer must (in addition to practicing) wear the marketing and manager hats, suffer acutely from these problems. Lawyers are not taught how to run a business in law school, and there's enough to worry about with following the rules of civil procedure and knowing the law itself.

Here's the good news: The science of management has transitioned from the manufacturing world into knowledge and service industries of all kinds—including your law firm. That's what this book is all about. We will introduce you to methods that will increase your income, grow your law firm (if that's what you want), and allow you to live a less stressful life. We will be taking many of our cues from industrial organizations like Toyota, whose Toyota Production System (TPS) is more generically known as Lean. We also owe a huge debt (as do many modern businesses) to the groundbreaking work of the late Dr. Eliyahu Goldratt, whose Theory of Constraints (as presented in his book *The Goal* and elsewhere) we will reference repeatedly.

Some lawyers (and other business owners) hear the term *Lean* and equate it with the standard definition in the lexicon: being thin with no extra fat. This is a mistake. Becoming a Lean law firm does not have to do with a bare-bones operation or going through cost-cutting exercises. Those things may arise as a matter of consequence from Lean practices, but they do not constitute the practice.

Lean is not about cost cutting. Lean is about creating systems, then finding the constraints and inefficiencies that impede them. Lean lawyers believe in measurement, reducing waste, and producing as much value as they can for their clients. And more than anything else, Lean is about experimentation and continuous improvement. We will talk a lot in this book about measurement and key performance indicators (KPIs) because you cannot improve something if you can't measure it.

All that said, this is not a book of Lean business theory, but a prescriptive, real-world guide to using Lean to streamline your operations. It is also not an "orthodox" presentation of Lean (or Six Sigma, or Theory of Constraints, or anything else). You can find that anywhere. What we present instead is a hybridized system that we know works for actual law firms. If you decide to put what we show you to the test, your business will almost certainly improve.

Whether you apply all of what we present, or just what you think may work for you, the fundamental mindset you need before you embark on this journey is one of awareness. If you are willing to take a step back and contemplate the operations of your firm, you've already won half the battle. So, if you're no longer content to tread water and live in a constant state of reaction and interruption, continue reading.

Larry Port
December 2016

The year 2018 marks my 24th year as a practicing lawyer. Every minute of that time has been spent in a two-lawyer firm or as a solo practitioner. While I lack the perspective I might have gained from being a part of a "professionally managed" firm, I have had almost unfettered opportunity to engage in all kinds of experimentation. Some of my experiments and adventures in law firm management have been abject failures. The ones that have worked have a common root in the Lean methodologies about which you will read.

Along the route of my experimental journey into Lean, I've met fascinating, like-minded people like my friend and coauthor, Larry Port, who shares a passion for trying to find the best way, while realizing that there is no best, simply iterations of better.

Through years of experimentation, discussion, and thought, we bring you in this book principles and methods that will almost certainly work better than what you're doing now. If applied, they will make profound changes in the success of your firm. I hope also that they will profoundly change how you view your firm. If there's only one thing you take away from this book, it should be this: like any business, *your firm is a system*. When you start to see it that way, all the little levers and buttons that make it run better start to miraculously appear.

This takes us to the disclaimer: Only some of the methods about which you will read are truly original. As Larry says in his foreword, much of what we present comes from the world of manufacturing and industry, where people realized decades ago that all businesses are just systems that convert raw material into money and output. We have tried to attribute these practices to their rightful inventors as much as possible. However, what you will see in the following pages is a mash-up of so many sources that giving full credit everywhere is impossible.

In closing, if I can persuade you to have a second takeaway from this book beyond the realization that your firm is a system, it is this: *do your own experimenting*. Your law firm is a laboratory. Borrow and try ideas not only from other firms, but from different industries entirely. Repurpose. Reinvent. See what works and what does not work for you. Fear not failure, nor change, nor being different. Different begins when you turn the page and realize you just bought a "graphic novel about management science." So, without further ado, on to our story.

Dave Maxfield
January 2017

Acknowledgments

The authors would like to thank our wonderful peer reviewers:

Debbie Foster, Partner at Affinity Consulting Group, who saw this book through from beginning to end, always with an eye towards what really matters to our readers based on her decades of experience in improving law office profitability, technology and function. Debbie—we could not have done this without you.

Britt Lorish, Partner at Affinity Consulting Group, our great peer reviewer whose support continues even after publication.

Professor Carrie Queenan of the Darla Moore School of Business at the University of South Carolina, whose wealth of knowledge in engineering, systems, and management science—and explication of Little's Law—tied our systems chapters together. Carrie—thanks for your patience (and gentle mathematical corrections)!

The authors would also like to thank the great people at Lachina Publishing who made this book possible (and dragged us across the finish line) including **Jenni Claydon, Morgan Ewald,** and **Molly Montanaro.** Thanks also to **Lauren Thompson** of the American Bar Association for helping us get the book to market, and finally to **Lisa Pansini** at Rocket Matter for her great graphic design eye—and 11th hour illustrations.

Dave Maxfield would also like to thank Kristen Maxfield for her patience and support as I worked on this book on vacations, at home (and in the end everywhere) and his grandfather, Wayne C. Smith, MD, his father D. Richard Maxfield, and his law partner of 17 years, Gene Trotter, all of whom taught me that knowledge is meant to be shared, and to never stop learning.

Larry Port would like to thank Dina Roth Port for being an inspiration as a published author and an amazing, understanding wife. And Samantha and Zachary, who gave up time with their father to work on this book. Thank you also to Neil and Mickey Port for raising me to appreciate education, to think big, and for their unlimited love and support. And big thanks to all of my teachers along the way who pushed me to write, especially Edna Neely.

CHAPTER 1

The Saga of Carson Wright

November

Carson Wright sat at a conference table with five of his fellow lawyers, high above the streets of Central City, waiting for his team leader, partner Virginia Radcliff, to start the meeting. He was ready to get the holiday started but, like the rest of his team, he had had his mood dampened a bit by rumors of big changes coming to K&M. As a key member of the product liability team with nearly ten years under his belt at K&M, his job should be secure. Shouldn't it?

Virginia began, "As some of you may have heard, there is a possibility of our firm merging with a larger, national firm. I want to emphasize at this point that all of this is speculative. No agreements have been reached and, at this point, it's all just talk. Now, let's move on to the General Bearings Multi-District litigation.... When we return after Thanksgiving, we are going to need to focus on...."

"Carson," whispered Cindy, "is it true we're getting merged into Aquino, Haverford & Meyer?"

Carson replied, "I know just as much as you, Cindy—nothing. But it's hard to imagine what working for a megafirm like that would be like."

Cindy looked pensive. "Do you think we'll still have jobs?"

"I'm sure you and I will be fine," Carson said. "We've

been on the General Bearings case for two years. They need all hands on deck for that." But inside, Carson felt less certain than he sounded.

As Thanksgiving arrived the next day, much the same as ever, Carson had mostly forgotten his worry. Full of turkey and content, he sat at the table with his wife Pamela drinking coffee as their kids, Jamie and Sarah, attacked a pumpkin pie. Not forgetting the point of the holiday, Pamela asked, "Jamie, what are you thankful for today?" As Jamie rattled off an impressive list, "our house, our neighborhood, my school," a brief panic flashed through Carson's thoughts. All of those things—their nice house, Jamie's private school, and even Sarah's day care—cost money. And not just a little. A heavy dread fell over Carson the next morning when, unexpectedly, Virginia called and asked him to come by the office. Even for a firm like K&M, the Friday after Thanksgiving was semi-sacrosanct. What could she want? As he got off the elevator at K&M's building, he thought it even stranger that Virginia wanted to meet him alone in one of K&M's small conference rooms. He entered, found Virginia seated at the opposite end of the table, and sat down.

Virginia began, "Thanks for coming in on Friday, Carson. I'm sorry to interrupt your Thanksgiving holiday. But things are happening fast, and I wanted you to know what's going on as soon as possible."

"What do you mean?" asked Carson, a gnawing uneasiness starting to grow in his stomach.

"I mean the rumors are true. We're being folded into Aquino, Haverford & Meyer. Effective Monday. Which means, unfortunately, that General Bearings—who does not have the best relationship with AH&M—is pulling the case from us."

Carson sat in stunned silence.

Virginia continued, "As you can imagine, since the case is being pulled, we are not exactly indispensable to AH&M. They've agreed to pay two months' severance, career counseling, outplacement, though. The usual."

"I can't believe it," Carson finally managed. "I've got over ten years in here. What am I supposed to do with that?"

"I wish I knew what to tell you," Virginia said. "I suspect I'll be asking myself some of the same questions pretty soon. Hopefully not, but you never know."

A FEW WEEKS LATER

December

As it was every year, downtown Central City in December was decked out in holiday lights, beautiful in the crisp early evening. More light from the store windows streamed onto the sidewalk, which was thick with holiday shoppers.

None of this registered with Carson, though, as he walked along the sidewalk lost in thought.

"Not going to be much of a Christmas this year," he thought. Pam had taken the news of his being sacked by K&M pretty well, but they still hadn't told the kids anything. "Just get through Christmas, act normal, keep your head down, keep going," Carson kept telling himself. The kids thought Daddy was just "on vacation" from work. They loved it. But Carson was starting to really worry.

As Carson continued along the sidewalk lost in thought, he felt his shoulder ram a fellow pedestrian and watched shopping bags fall to the ground.

As the man's packages tumbled to the ground, Carson looked up into the startled face of Ambrose Gray. Awake now, Carson scrambled at the sidewalk to retrieve Ambrose's packages.

"Ambrose!" said Carson. "I'm so sorry! I wasn't paying attention."

Ambrose Gray laughed. "It's not a problem, Carson. Takes more than your lanky frame to knock me off a sidewalk! How's your father?"

Carson laughed too, relieved that Ambrose was unhurt and unperturbed. "He's fine. Retired to Florida, playing a lot of golf."

"Glad to hear that, Carson," said Ambrose. "Sometimes I think about hanging it up myself. But I'm a terrible golfer. Plus, I would go stir crazy after a month of retirement, I think. Being a lawyer is all I know."

Ambrose continued, "Speaking of lawyers, how are things with you? You know, I always wish you would have come and talked to me before taking that job with K&M. How long has it been, now, eight years?"

"Almost 11," said Carson. It was funny Ambrose should say that. Carson had almost gone to see Ambrose about a job when he graduated from law school ten years ago. Ambrose and his father had once been close friends, and Ambrose was kind of like a distant uncle—someone his family revered but did not see much despite living in the same town. However, even 11 years ago it seemed clear that Ambrose's practice was past its prime. Ambrose could wrap things up and shut the door at any time, and that would have been it for Carson. So he never seriously considered working for him. Besides, the K&M offer to him out of law school had been too rich to pass up. Carson wondered now if that had been a mistake.

He thought about fibbing to Ambrose that everything at K&M was great. But you didn't lie to Ambrose Gray. Plus, he probably already knew as much as any K&M associate about the AH&M acquisition. Ambrose had a way of doing that.

So Carson said, "Well, not so great actually. In fact, terrible. I was let go about three weeks ago."

"I'm really sorry to hear that, Carson. Especially this time of year." Ambrose looked thoughtful for a moment before asking, "So, what's your plan?"

"I'm hoping to move laterally into another job in litigation with one of the other big firms in town. I've had some talks, but nothing concrete yet." Carson hesitated before adding, "Truthfully, I think they are just being polite. It's strange, because from time to time when I was at K&M, partners at other firms would say things like 'If you ever think of making a move, call me.' But now that I'm actually calling, they don't seem so interested."

Ambrose gazed at Carson, staying silent a moment. "Well," he finally said, "I might be interested."

Carson started to laugh but remembered himself. "Ambrose, that's very kind but ... how ... ahhh...." He didn't know how to say what came next, so he just blurted it out. "How can you afford that? Everyone thinks you're struggling yourself."

Ambrose's gaze into Carson's eyes intensified, and Carson saw just the slightest trace of pain and fear. "Those are not just rumors, Carson. It's true. Things are not what they used to be. I still know how to try a case, maybe better than ever, but all the things that go with running a law firm.... I just can't seem to make it work as a business anymore. I was never great at that part, honestly. But when the money and good cases were coming in as fast as we could handle them, it didn't seem to matter. As my father used to say, most problems go away if you rub enough 'green salve' on them. Ironic, because he never had two dollars to rub together. But now, there's not much 'green salve.' We still have cases. I still have my reputation. And I can still try a case. But that's just not enough anymore."

Ambrose continued, "Last year I hired the smartest young law school graduate I've ever met—Briana Reyes—naively thinking that she would help turn things around. She works hard, and she knows technology. But Carson, she's 25 years old. She's had some real-world experience, and she will be an amazing lawyer one day. But really, she's as lost as I am."

"Maybe," Ambrose mused, before turning his intense gaze back on Carson, "maybe, Carson, running into you tonight wasn't an accident. You're a good lawyer. You have a business degree. I know you're a hard worker. And you're right in the middle of where I am and where Briana is—not too old or too young. You've been working in a professionally managed firm for more than ten years. And you have a family to feed and you need a job. So, I think you might be exactly what the Gray Firm needs right now. What would you think about that?"

Carson was in near shock. But what did he have to lose? "Umm ... sure. I think I can help you, Ambrose. I say yes."

"Excellent, Carson!" exclaimed Ambrose, offering his hand before Carson could change his mind. "It's a deal then. Come in after New Year's and we'll figure out the details. Now, if you'll excuse me, I've got some shopping to do." With that, Ambrose turned on his heel and walked away.

"What have I just gotten myself into?" Carson wondered, watching Ambrose walk down the sidewalk and disappear into the night.

Later that night...

As they were finishing putting the kids' presents (which seemed fewer than last year) under the tree, Pam looked up at Carson and asked, "What are you going to do, Carson?"

Carson replied, "I don't know. There's no lawyer I respect more than Ambrose. He had one of the best practices in town once upon a time. But it's been in decline for a long while. And I'm not sure I'm comfortable with—or even understand—what he's asking of me. I've never worked in a small firm. I'm not sure why he'd choose me, or if I'm even the right choice. The last person in the world I'd want to disappoint besides you is Ambrose Gray."

Indeed, every lawyer in town knew the story of Ambrose Gray. He was basically a legend in Central City, growing up the son of poor mill workers, earning his way through State on a football scholarship, then working his way through law school as a night manager in the very same mill his mother and father had slaved away in.

Sickened by the workplace accidents he saw with appalling regularity, almost immediately after graduation Ambrose hung out his own shingle and began representing the same injured workers he had once supervised. He filed workers' compensation claims, personal injury cases, and product liability cases against the makers of the same mill equipment  that he worked on and around. By the time he was 32, Ambrose had over 100 jury verdicts, including some record breakers. As business grew, so did his firm, eventually employing 7 lawyers and 15 support staff who handled everything from injury cases to divorce to bankruptcy and criminal defense.

But now, 45 years after it began, the firm was down to just two lawyers, Ambrose and newly minted Briana Reyes. The firm still handled every kind of case under the sun, but it was known to be struggling financially. Everyone thought of Ambrose as an elder statesman or lawyer emeritus with not much actual gas left in the tank. And while those who knew her thought Briana was brilliant and had a bright future, they assumed that her future would be with some other firm eventually. However, Briana clearly idolized Ambrose and appeared willing to stick with him to the bitter end. The only question was how far away that end was.

Pam broke Carson's reverie. Thinking about the kids, she said, "Carson—we don't have a lot of choices. If you trust him, maybe you should trust his reasons for believing in you."

Carson agreed, "You're right. I told Ambrose I'm going to do it. So I'm going to take it. How bad can it be? It's Ambrose Gray!"

January

So, a few days after New Year's, Carson found himself sitting across a desk from Ambrose and heard himself promise not to let Ambrose down.

Later that night, though, as Carson reviewed the Gray Firm's troubling financials on his computer, he wondered if it was a promise he could keep.

"This is a nightmare. Ambrose has been losing money for years, and I can hardly see anything on the horizon that is going to change that. I just CAN'T do this…."

January

Things were not much better a few weeks later. Carson had been working nearly nonstop since starting at the Gray Firm. He was on his way there right now, in fact. But it was an unseasonably warm and bright Saturday morning. Carson, a lifelong bike geek, found himself drifting to the bike shop next door. As he stood admiring a new C² Tsunami 6 racing bike, he thought about how simple things used to be in his competitive cycling days when the sole focus of his life was racing.

Train more, pedal harder, and get from point A to point B before anyone else. When did things get so complicated?

Carson felt a hand on his shoulder. He turned to see an older but very fit man with an intense but friendly expression that Carson would recognize anywhere. The man asked, "You like that one? 100% titanium. 16.5 pounds with the pedals. Like riding a feather; you can just about steer it telepathically."

"Guy!" Carson said, turning. "Guy Chaplin! Wow. How are things with you? How are things at the bike factory?"

"Never better, never better," said Guy. "How are things with you at that big-time law firm? They make you partner yet?"

"Oh … umm…," stammered Carson. He hesitated, thinking of the best way to spin the story for his old cycling coach—and owner of one of the most successful bicycle factories in the country—a man he respected completely. In the end, respect won out, and he simply said, "I got fired, Guy."

"What? Why?" exclaimed Guy, shocked.

Carson filled Guy in on the details of the merger, and concluded with his new job with Ambrose Gray.

"Well," said Guy. "Sounds like you really landed on your feet there, Carson. Lots of folks think Gray's the best lawyer in Central City. He's a legend."

Carson hesitated again, wondering how much information he should share with Guy, who was not only his old cycling coach but also mentor and former employer. Besides Pam, there was no one he trusted more. And he really needed to talk to someone.

Finally, he said, "I don't know about a legend. Maybe more of a myth, these days. He's still got the courtroom chops and the razor mind. But his business is basically a wreck. I know because I've been through all his financials. Ambrose brought me in thinking I would know how to turn it around. But, honestly, I don't have the first clue. I don't know where to start, or what to do. It's only been a few weeks, and I can't imagine I'm going to even last a year there—if the firm itself can last that long. So, overall, not so good."

Guy looked intently at Carson before saying, "You look like you could use a cup of coffee. Let me buy you one. I've got a story to tell you. One I've never told you before. I think you'll find it interesting."

Guy began, "You've known me most of your life, Carson. And you know all about my bike factory. Heck—you worked there for a while. But you only know half of the story.

"By the time you were in high school, Carson, when you were racing and working for me at C² Cycle, we had figured out a lot of things at the factory. It was running well by then. We still make little changes and improvements all the time, but by the time you came around, I'd already figured out the big picture. But getting there wasn't easy."

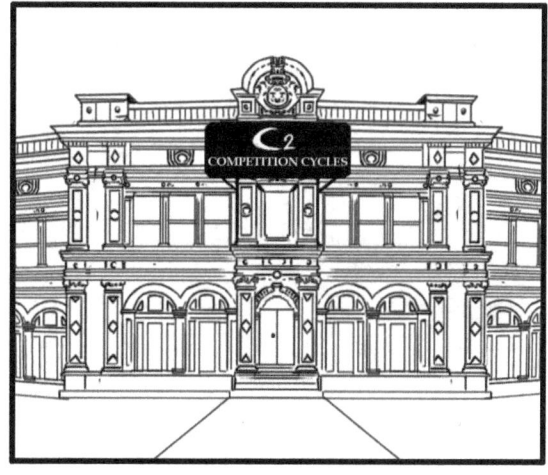

Guy's eyes grew distant as he remembered. "My dad started the company as Chaplin Cycle Company in 1960. Things were different then in a lot of ways. There were a lot of manufacturing businesses and factories in Central City, but very few of them were black-owned. My dad didn't have the opportunities that I had growing up, but he was smart and he had an amazing work ethic. He was fascinated by all kinds of machines, and he loved working on them. Even more, he loved people and treated everyone fairly.

"And back then—when there were no big-box stores or foreign competition here—that was enough. He risked everything he and my mom had to start the factory. And it paid off. In five years he was the biggest bicycle manufacturer in the state. In ten, one of the biggest in this part of the country.

"We built every kind of bike you can imagine—racing bikes, tandems, unicycles, and just bikes for kids to knock around on. It was a great time. And for a wild little kid like me, growing up around the bike factory was like being in a candy store."

Guy continued, "It was 1974 when I left home. I was 19. Leaving my mom, dad, and the factory to race professionally was one of the hardest things I've ever done. I knew my dad wanted me to stay and learn the business, and one day take it over. He even talked about renaming it Chaplin & Son Cycle. But in the end he knew my dream was not the same as his. And he was, after all, the one who put me on a bicycle.

"So, just before I left home, Dad called me into his office. And he pulled a little sheet off the finest racing bike he ever made—to this day, one of the best I've ever ridden. He called it the Tsunami because I was headed to Japan to join my first racing team. Then he put into my hand a one-way plane ticket to Tokyo. He said, 'Don't come back until you've made your dream come true.' We broke the bike down together and he shook my hand. A few days later I was on a plane over the Pacific. Neither one of us knew how much things would soon change.

"Professional bike racing—even in 1975 Japan, which was not exactly Europe—was tougher than I ever imagined. I landed there thinking I was Eddy Merckx, but almost as soon as I got there it became clear I was going to be the low man on the totem pole of Team Miyoto Manufacturing. I was a pretty good racer for around here—maybe better than you, Carson. Or almost as good. I had won the City Cup every year since I turned 16. Heck—I was beating the pants off 25-year-olds. But in Japan? There I was just another rider in the back of the peloton trying to hang on for dear life.

"They paid me almost nothing. The only perk, if you could call it that, was that they gave me a day job at Miyoto Manufacturing's factory making microwave ovens. Which were cutting-edge technology back then!

"The best part of going to Japan for me, as you can probably guess, was meeting Kumiko in '77. Next year, we'll have been married almost 40 years. The second-best thing wasn't the bike racing, although I loved that. It was actually that job at Miyoto. Because what I learned on the factory floor at Miyoto would turn out to save my family's company."

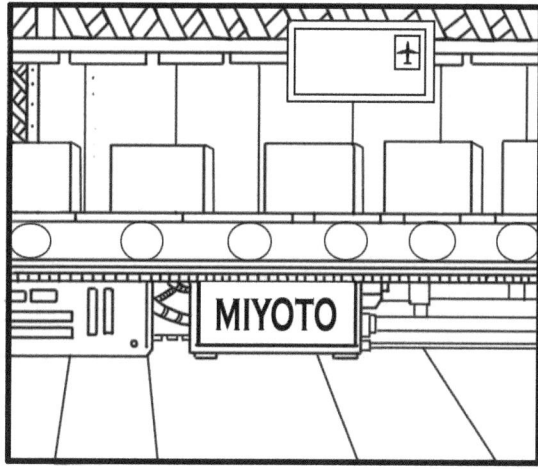

"What are you talking about, Guy?" said Carson. "What do you mean *saved*? I've known you for more than 20 years, and C² has been absolutely killing it the whole time. You build some of the best racing bikes in the world; your employees are happy, the factory runs like a Swiss watch, and I know you're making good money. I don't know that I've ever even seen you really stressed—at least not about business."

Guy's brow creased for a moment. "What do you mean 'some of' the best bikes in the world? THE best. Or at least, the best for the market we choose to own. Anyway, though, it wasn't always like that. Let's have another coffee and I'll tell you the rest of the story."

"OK, Guy," said Carson. "But we'll have to make it quick. I know it's Saturday and all, but I've got to get into the office pretty soon."

Guy said, "Sit tight for a moment, Carson. I want you to hear this. So, it was November 1980. I was living and racing in Kyoto then. Kumiko and I were still just newlyweds. My riding was improving to where I could almost make a living as a pro. My Japanese was even getting pretty good, and Mr. Aoki, who ran the Miyoto microwave factory, had kind of taken me under his wing, showing me all about how the factory worked. Things were going great. Then one morning I get a call from my mom—Dad had suffered a stroke. My mom told me to get home now. Kumiko and I packed the few things we had, got on a plane, and said goodbye to Japan. I thought Kumiko and I would be coming back in a few weeks after Dad recovered. But he never recovered. He died a few weeks later.

"So there I was, only 25. The only child. My mom had never really worked, and everything that my family had was in that bike factory. Not to mention a lot of employees who counted on the factory to feed their family. It was just assumed I would step into Dad's shoes and run things.

Business as usual. But when I finally got in there to figure out where things stood, and got a look at the books and outstanding orders, I could tell pretty quickly that it wouldn't be business as usual for very long. We were losing money and customers, and the profit margin for all the different kinds of bikes we built was shrinking almost monthly.

"So I decided to do what I always did, and what my dad had always done—work harder than anyone. Without any clear understanding of where we were headed, I put my head down and tried to just do more of everything. We made at least 18 models of bicycles then, everything from cheap steel kids' bikes to 4130 chromoly BMX racers, mountain bikes, unicycles, and of course our super-light aluminum and titanium racing bikes. And I was all about just producing more of everything. Ramping up production. I thought if I could make more, I could sell more, especially to the big-box department and sporting goods stores that were popping up all over the country.

"It was a disaster, though. We had six separate production lines. We made 18 bikes, and each line was making at least three different bikes, with different components. Most of the bikes came in different frame sizes, and our really high-end stuff was spec'd with different custom components. So, really, we weren't making just 18 bikes, but several hundred different kinds of products.

"And each time a production line needed to change what it was making, we had to stop the line, change out some of the tools, bring up the materials, and restart. All of these changeovers, all of the different products we were trying to make—and me pushing everything harder, faster all the time—created a lot of opportunity for errors. Equipment breaking. The wrong components being put on bikes. And so forth. It got to where about 15 percent of what we made was so flawed we couldn't in good conscience sell it. Just waste. My dad, who was about quality first, would have turned over in his grave to see it.

"And of course, some of what we made just sat there because we had no buyers for it. In the meantime, some of our bikes that we had existing orders for took weeks or even months to build because we had no way of producing them quickly on demand. Customers who ordered racing bikes, for example, just had to wait until a production line was changed over to build those.

"And my only solution was to work even harder, to build even more. I didn't know it wasn't working because I didn't really think about how or what to measure. I set sales goals for our managers that were not grounded in any reality. The 'goals' were just wishful thinking. When those goals of course went unmet, I started one company initiative after another. One month it was all about sales. The next month it was quality control. The next, everything was focused on upgrading our equipment. There was no consistent theme as I hopped from thing to thing, always looking for the magic bullet that would fix things. It seemed I was spending half of my life on the factory floor and the other in staff meetings. And despite all the meetings, my staff was more confused than ever.

"My final initiative was to reduce the workforce. As Chaplin Cycle started to circle the drain, I started cutting employee hours, furloughing, etc. Some of the employees who had been with my dad from the beginning started leaving. It was a really dark time.

"By the end of 1987, we were literally on the doorstep of bankruptcy. I was exhausted. It made me sick to even look at a bike, let alone think about riding one." Guy smiled a half-smile, raised his eyebrows and whispered, "And that's when something finally clicked."

Carson was intrigued. He had never known Guy to struggle. But he was also growing impatient. As much as he wanted to hear Guy's story—which Guy obviously meant for his benefit—he had a lot to do today. And as much as he respected Guy, he didn't see any parallel between his law firm's situation and the plight of a company that manufactured bicycles. He interrupted, "Guy, this is fascinating. Truly. I would love to sit here and listen to the rest, but I'm meeting our associate Briana to look at some new software for the firm. I don't want to keep her waiting."

"Of course, Carson," said Guy graciously. "We can finish some other time. But do call me if you ever want to talk."

"I will," promised Carson, walking out the door. His mind was already turning to the meeting with Briana and wondering how they could even consider investing in new technology when he was trying to cut firm costs across the board.

CHAPTER 2

The Basics
Lean Thinking and Terminology

February

The winter sun had long since set, as Carson sat at his desk in a dark office at Gray Firm. He squinted his eyes and looked at the spreadsheet on his computer screen. There was lots of red on the spreadsheet that even his half-closed eyes couldn't hide.

"I don't understand this," thought Carson. "Things are not getting better. They are actually seem to be worse! Everything I try to change causes some new problem. I increased our advertising, and the business that comes in the door isn't any good. We can't even handle it because we don't have the resources. Briana is too busy figuring out the new software to help, and every week we have less money than the last even though I've cut expenses to the bone. It's like I have the opposite of the Midas touch."

As Carson looked blearily away from the screen, his focus alighted on a photo of himself from long ago after winning his second state amateur championship. He sat astride his bike, with Guy standing next to him, arm around his shoulders. He dialed Guy's number from memory. "Guy? It's Carson. Sorry to call you so late.... I'd like ... I think I need to finish our talk."

Guy, never one to waste time, replied, "Meet you at the coffee shop in 45 minutes."

"Guy," said Carson, "I've been thinking about something you said last time we were here. You said that something 'clicked' with you at the bike factory. What did you mean? Because it sounds to me like nothing that happened to the factory back then was your fault. Times had changed, and lots of manufacturers in America were going through exactly the same thing. You inherited the situation. What else could you do? You made huge changes to every single part of your business."

"That was just it, though!" said Guy. "I was trying to improve each part in isolation, without considering the impact each change would have on the whole. What I had forgotten—and what I finally realized—is that the bike factory was just a *system*. All the parts—marketing, production, etc.—had to interact toward a simple, common purpose: turning raw materials and parts into bicycles and money. Like a bike and its rider—or a team of riders—it all has to work together toward a common goal."

Carson looked skeptical and disappointed. "That's it? That's what 'clicked'? Because that's not exactly earth-shattering information, Guy. It seems kind of obvious, really."

"Yes, and no," said Guy. "Or, as my Japanese teammates used to say, 'simple, but not easy.' Let me give you an example. In bicycle racing, think how obsessed teams get with their equipment and mechanical efficiency. Think about a team time trial stage of the Tour de France or the Gir d'Italia. Each team of riders races against the clock. The team that gets from point A to point B in the shortest time wins the stage.

"Every second matters, and the team has to function as a unified system. Each rider takes a turn at the front of the line while his teammates draft behind him in the slipstream. After his turn, the lead rider swings over, allowing the next teammate to take the lead, while he moves to the back.

"Since wind resistance plays such a big part, all the equipment—bikes, clothes, helmets—is wind-tunnel tested to reduce drag coefficient to create the least wind resistance. Less resistance equals faster times.

"Now imagine a team where one of the riders was unfit. Just hopelessly out of shape. And it's his turn to ride at the front. What happens?"

Carson replied, "Obvious. The whole team has to slow down. He's their weakest link. They can't ride any faster than he can, even if they are much more fit."

"Exactly," said Guy. "So how do you fix that?"

"By focusing everything on getting him fitter or replacing him," said Carson.

"Right again," agreed Guy. "That's exactly what you should do. But what if instead of doing that, the team's coach viewed the entire problem as an equipment issue? He sends all the helmets back to the wind tunnel and makes some more changes to reduce the drag coefficient of the helmets by 2 percent. Would that fix the problem? Absolutely not. It would be a meaningless improvement, because he's not focusing his efforts on the actual constraint in the system."

"So what does all this have to do with saving Chaplin Cycle in 1988?" asked Carson.

"Everything," said Guy. "Because until then, I was just like that coach. I was focusing on everything that did not matter instead of focusing on what did: *making something that people really wanted, as perfectly as possible, available when and how they wanted it. And relentlessly hunting down and improving everything that slowed down or got in the way of that.*

"After I finally realized that, I took what I knew about systems—every kind of system from cycling teams to car manufacturers. I remembered what I had learned at Miyoto. I read everything I could get my hands on about Lean manufacturing. And that's when things finally started to change."

Guy continued, "After immersing myself in all things Lean, I returned to the core concept, or mission, that I now clearly saw for the business: Building something that people really wanted, as perfectly as possible, available when and how they wanted it. I started to think about how I could measure progress toward that overarching goal. We were measuring all kinds of metrics in the business, and I had stacks of reports. More than I could even read. So I decided to boil it all down to just a few Key Performance Indicators, or KPIs, that could tell me if I was headed in the right direction. I used those KPIs to take the pulse of the business. While the pulse was pretty weak, and the overall picture was dire, the KPIs started to reveal exactly how and where we were getting stuck. From this, we came up with a simple *Income Formula* that could help get us unstuck and return us to the black. That formula was this:

Income = Throughput Rate × Average Unit Value

More about that later, though, because I want you to get the overall picture before we dive into specifics.

"With that in mind, we began to rethink the entire process—not as disparate parts, but as an integrated system. With our system mapped, we could tease out the constraints—blocks and bottlenecks in our process—that were hampering the rate at which we could complete finished bicycles, a.k.a. units. In Lean-speak, we call the number of units completed over time our Throughput Rate. We knew if we could improve our Throughput Rate, everything would change. But how to do that? Well, the biggest determiner of Throughput Rate is something called Cycle Time, which is simply the amount of time, on average, that a unit spends between the start and finish lines of a system. If you can shorten the amount of time that it takes to turn a lump of titanium into a finished bike, you've shortened your Cycle Time. And when bikes get made faster, naturally you can produce more of them in a given amount of time. Throughput Rate naturally increases. But how to decrease Cycle Time? The answer is to find the places in the system where bike building is blocked or slowed down, where the bikes in various stages of production just sit waiting for the next step of production. That 'just sitting there' time we called, naturally enough, Wait Time. And we figured out that by doing whatever we could to reduce this, we would reduce Cycle Time, and thus speed Throughput Rate. By increasing Throughput Rate, provided we were building the kinds of bikes for which there was constant demand, we could sell more of them. And by doing so, we could earn more income. And we'd make our customers happy by having the bike available almost immediately for them. Which would improve our reputation, and bring even more business.

"So, after we made some initial progress increasing our Throughput Rate, I returned to the question of how to make what people actually wanted to buy. We had been making every kind of bike, but what we all really loved to make were the high-end racing bikes. We were still good at that, and even when things were at their worst, we could sell them as fast as we could make them, which wasn't very fast, unfortunately. They also had a high profit margin over our cost to manufacture them.

"So, in 1991, in the boldest and hardest decision we had to make, we decided to turn all our efforts toward the entry-level segment of the high-end racing bike market. And that's when Chaplin Cycle became C^2. I took my inspiration from the Tsunami my dad built for me. We rebranded the company as C^2: C-squared—like the speed of light. All of our marketing could then be directed toward our core market. By 1992 or so, things were starting to get pretty good again. We were starting to grow.

"But one problem we still had was that our long-time employees were retiring and, with our budding growth, we needed to hire more. In order to ensure continuity, and not lose track of all we learned, we focused hard on standardizing all of our processes, continually refining and improving them and, most importantly, putting everything in writing so there was no possibility for errors.

"Then, to further enhance communication, we began using a system of visual controls, including a Kanban board on the factory floor, like ones I had seen years before at Miyoto. The Kanban board as we use it is basically a big digital sign that shows where a unit of work (like an order) is located in the system, in real time. In our system, each unit is represented by a digital card. You can look up at the board and see where that card is in the overall workflow. Everyone on the factory floor can see what they need to focus on right then, and where each unit is in our process—and what may be blocking progress.

"Our Kanban system is a pretty high-tech visual control. But look, Carson, you could do the same thing with sticky notes on a whiteboard. Like this." Guy took a napkin and with his pen marked a few columns on it, then drew a few sticky note "units" in each column to illustrate.

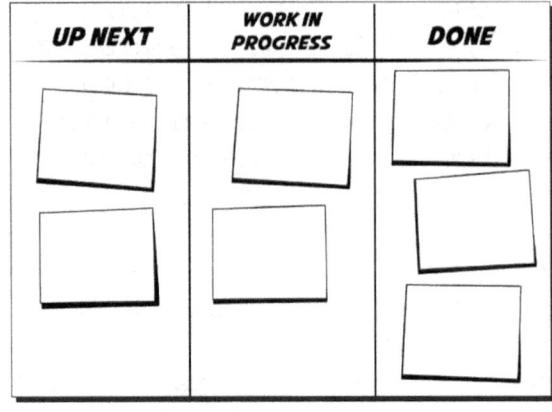

"Pretty simple, really. So, Kanban was an important piece of the puzzle for us, because for the first time we could see our progress in real time. By October of 1992 we were fully out of survival mode and thinking about the future. That was when we instituted our first 'October Surprise'—a one-month period when we focused on system improvements, re-examining all of our processes to find kinks and little opportunities to improve—part of what the Japanese called *kaizen*.

"As part of this process, we looked at our production and information technology. Whereas I once viewed technology as a solution or savior and thought that by sinking enough money into it I could fix things, now I saw it for what it was. Simply a tool that enabled the system to flow faster and better. So, it was only after remaking the system that we started really pushing things in the high-tech direction you saw when you first came to work for me."

Carson said, "That's amazing, Guy. I had no idea that you had gone through so much. As a teenager working for you, I guess I thought things had always been smooth and easy."

"Far from it," said Guy. "And I don't want to give you the impression that all of these changes were easy, or that everyone just got in line and agreed with me. Not so. Not everyone bought in to the vision at first, especially the guys on the unicycle and tandem line. It took a lot of effort to sell. The fact that we were in crisis mode, trying anything to survive, probably didn't hurt, though. People knew things could not remain as they had been. As Winston Churchill once said, 'Never let a good crisis go to waste.' In the end, though, it worked out."

Carson laughed, somewhat ruefully, and thought, *Guy, I sure have a good crisis for you now.* But savoring the memory of a time when life seemed to come easy, he said instead, "Well, things sure seemed simple to me back then. All I had to do when I was riding for you was think about school and cycling. No disrespect, Guy, but I think I won one more City Cup than you, if I'm not mistaken."

Guy chuckled. "You did. You got me beat, Carson. Truthfully, you were a better racer than I ever could have been. Everyone around here thought we'd be watching you on TV one day winning the Tour de France. Especially with all the training you put in when you were at college. You just got stronger and stronger. We called you The Terminator, remember? It was like you were indestructible. Well, until . . ." Guy trailed off.

"Until the accident?" Carson finished. "Yeah, I thought so too."

The silence lingered momentarily until Carson said, "Guess neither one of us exactly had the career we thought we were going to have, huh?"

"Guess not," said Guy. "But I have no regrets. You shouldn't, either. You were the best rider the C^2-A team ever had. But the world is full of good riders. If you hadn't had the accident, you wouldn't have ever gone to law school after college. You probably wouldn't have met Pamela, had those beautiful kids, or have the opportunity you have right now."

While Guy sipped his coffee, Carson asked, "What opportunity is that, exactly?"

Guy looked up from his coffee. "To remake your law firm. To help Ambrose become Ambrose again. To build something great for the future. For your future."

Carson was silent.

Guy continued, "I miss hanging around with you, Carson. And I could use a new project. So, I've decided that I'm going to be with you on this. We'll meet every month. I'll give you some ideas—and homework— and you'll do the rest. Rest assured, none of what I'll tell you is stuff I invented in my own head. But I know it works. It worked for C^2 and it will work for the Gray Firm. I know you don't see how the bike shop and your firm are similar right now. But in time, you will.

"So, here is your first month's homework: I want you to take some measurements." Guy scribbled down a short, bullet-pointed list on a napkin. "Here. Measure these things. We'll meet back here, same time, first Saturday in March, and we'll talk more. For today, though, let's talk about some core Lean concepts that are the same whether you are making microwaves, bikes, or law."

"I don't make law, Guy," Carson said. "Law comes from appellate cases. And I still don't really see how a bike shop is like a law firm."

"Just listen, Carson. Just listen."

LEAN THINKING AND TERMINOLOGY

As Guy says, a major premise of this book is that whether you're manufacturing microwave ovens or putting together cases, Lean concepts can optimize your process, and hence the results you get for your clients and your profitability. This is true because at the most basic level, all businesses do the same thing: they get raw material and put it through some kind of process to create *something* (whether it be bicycles, appliances, or completed legal solutions). From that completed product output comes money. For lawyers, the money may be paid up front (flat fee), as you go (hourly), or at the end (contingently), but it still comes from producing something. Some of this money will be kept as profit, and the rest will be reinvested in getting more raw material or improving the process.

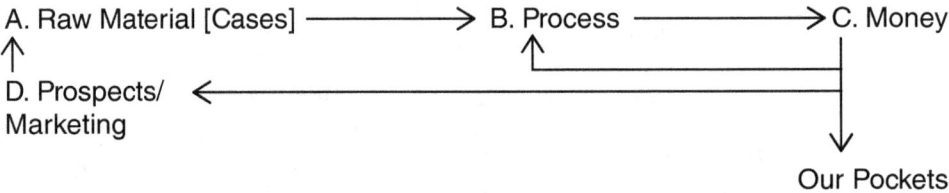

So, while the complexity of the process that creates the output (and money) may vary, the overall system is actually simple. While all of this seems obvious on paper, this basic systemic truth is easily lost in the complexity of the daily demands placed upon us: the need to be constantly available, a seemingly endless stream of to-do's, and the complexity of legal work itself. However, it's when we see our practices for the simple systems they really are that the real magic can begin.

There's a lot that goes with this basic mind shift. Giving you the details and helping you to turn your practice into a system is the purpose of this book. Before we do that, though, we need to give credit where it is due: to the people and industries that made this mind shift long before most lawyers, specifically, the pioneers of Lean Manufacturing and the Theory of Constraints, the two pillars upon which much of this book rests.

The phrase "Lean Manufacturing" first appeared in MIT professor James Womack's 1990 history of automotive manufacturing and assembly, *The Machine That Changed the World*. While the phrase was new, many concepts Womack described were decades old. And some—like Eli Whitney's use in 1799 of interchangeable parts for muskets—were much older than that. With the rise of industrialization in the next 100 years, the idea of applying science to manufacturing strategy, and the view of manufacturing as a system, took root.

Where it really flowered was in the automotive industry, with Henry Ford's conscious arrangement of all elements of his manufacturing process into a contiguous system. General Motors adapted and improved many of Ford's methods, which, with the coming of World War II, became critical to Allied arms manufacture. Ford is still considered by many to be one of the first practitioners of Lean, at least on a large scale.

Ironically, it was the Allied victory that brought many of these concepts to Japan, and eventually to Toyota, which improved and expanded on Lean concepts to create the Toyota Production System (TPS). The many enhancements pioneered by Toyota included just-in-time inventory management, huge decreases in setup and changeover times, and, perhaps most importantly, empowering employees on the factory floor to contribute directly to quality control. The TPS also introduced us to Kanban boards and the concept of *kaizen*. In this book, we borrow these and many other Lean concepts—now standard operating procedure in manufacturing—and show you how to use them to make your law practice run better.

The second pillar for the ideas in this book is Eliyahu Goldratt's Theory of Constraints (TOC). In his 1984 book *The Goal*, Goldratt proposed that the flow, or "throughput," of any system was always restricted by one or more constraints that dictated the speed of the entire system. By identifying and optimizing the identified constraint, the entire system could be made to flow better and faster. Once a constraint was removed, a new one would arise at a different location. The process of identification and optimization was repeated, over and over, to continuously improve the overall system.

In this book we borrow from, alter, and hybridize Lean and the TOC to create something useful for law firms. The relationship between Lean and the TOC is illustrated by Guy's central tenet: You become profitable by making something that people really want, as perfectly as possible, available when and how they want it (Lean), and relentlessly hunting down and improving everything that slows or gets in the way of that (TOC).

Since our work is based on Lean and the TOC, we borrow much of their terminology. Because these terms can have different meanings (even among manufacturing systems experts), we define how they are used in this book next.

> **Lean Manufacturing (Lean)**: The science of finding better, more efficient ways of producing a product that a customer wants to buy. The focus of Lean is on creating value for the customer (Client) and increasing efficiencies by eliminating anything that does not add value to the end product (Waste).
>
> **Theory of Constraints (TOC)**: The practice of finding and improving the most important limiting factors (i.e., constraints) that stand in the way of achieving the related goals of production and income so that the constraint is no longer the limiting factor.
>
> **Backlog**: An accumulation of undone work; for lawyers this means especially cases accepted but not yet at the starting line of the system, and instead held in a sort of buffer. Backlog can also refer to an accumulation of work behind a constraint in the system.
>
> **Brand Basket**: A collection of complementary niche practice areas organized around a firm's central theme or competency.
>
> **Buy-In**: The willingness of employees to embrace Lean techniques and other improvements, and the cultural shift in the firm that comes with it.
>
> **Changeover**: In a manufacturing process, the delay caused by stopping a production line to change tools to produce a different part. Toyota discovered years ago that the time it took to build each car was greatly increased by long Changeover. Every time the production line switched from building one model of car to another, the line had to be stopped to change stamping machine dies. Cars in process waiting for the machine, meanwhile, piled up in the line. As the process of changeover improved from 12 hours to less than one-half hour, the bottleneck was reduced, and the cycle time for each car build dropped. Over time, this simple change paid massive dividends. While a law firm does not require tool changeovers, it has to similarly switch gears (and slow down) when it handles too many varied practice areas. A premise of this book is that handling fewer, similar practice areas results in fewer changeovers, greater standardization, a faster, better process, and thus more income.

Client: As used in this book, a person or an entity who has formally retained or hired a lawyer or firm. A Prospect or Prospective Client is simply a potential Client who may have a case but who has not been converted formally into a Client.

Case, Matter, or Case Unit: Lawyers often think in terms of Clients, who have Cases or Matters. As will become clear in our Systems chapters, however, this can actually make things tricky to measure. One Client may have multiple cases if he or she is involved in separate and independent lawsuits. But you may also represent a single Client against three opposing parties in a single litigation case. Is that one Case, or three? Since those Cases can resolve at different times—and may be at different stages of our system at any point in time—we propose that from a systems standpoint you think of this as three "Case Units." Thinking this way will give us a truer picture of how much Work in Process (WIP) we have and the average value of each Unit. Thus, think of Case Unit in your system like a bicycle in Guy's: a piece of Inventory that can move through the system independently.

Constraint: In the broadest sense, a constraint is any limiting factor that prevents us from achieving our twin goals of production and income. Practically, constraints include anything that blocks our progress or slows it down, thereby increasing Cycle Time (and decreasing Throughput Rate). The way we make a system flow faster is to find and optimize its constraints. While we use the term *constraints* liberally throughout this book in a general sense, we can divide them into two types: External Constraints and Internal Constraints.

External Constraints are things outside of the firm that limit the speed at which a process can move. For example, the Rules of Civil Procedure generally give a party 30 days to respond to a Request for Production of Documents. If a necessary part of your litigation process involves the review of documents in possession of the other side, the Rule slows your overall process by 30 days. Some kinds of External Constraints can be improved (e.g., hand delivering a complaint to a court for filing and obtaining a filed copy immediately, rather than by mail). With others, particularly those governed by rules or court calendars, there may be little you can do about it (although we will discuss how it may be used to your advantage). Thus, External Constraints may include things that Block us outright (waiting on a ruling, for example) or mandatory Wait Times (court rules, etc.).

Internal Constraints, on the other hand, are much more within your control. As the name implies, they are not imposed from the outside but come from inefficiencies inside your firm. Internal constraints may include not only internal Blocks (i.e., waiting for another team member to complete work), but also places in your system where work backs up, waiting for work ahead of it to be completed (Bottlenecks). Diving deeper on these two terms:

A **Block** is a full-on constraint that brings a process to a standstill. A simple example would be that a paralegal cannot file a complaint in court because a lawyer has not yet signed it. While this minor detail can be fixed in a matter of minutes, a major premise of this book is that *anything that slows down your process unnecessarily is reducing your income.* Using visual controls that alert team members to Blocks—so they can be addressed immediately—is a key to minimizing them. Better still is to design processes that minimize their occurrence.

In contrast, a **Bottleneck** is an Internal Constraint where workloads overwhelm a part of the production system, causing the whole system to run slower (because a chain is only as strong as its weakest link). To return one last time to our complaint example, a traditional bottleneck in a plaintiff's small or solo litigation firm often occurs near the beginning of the process, where accepted but unfiled cases pile up in a queue awaiting complaints to be drafted or some other affirmative action. *A Bottleneck is a symptom of a less-than-optimal process at the point where the case units start to pile up.*

Blocks (whether internal or external), Bottlenecks, and all other types of constraints increase **Wait Time**. Wait Time is simply the time a unit spends with no active work being done on it as it waits to move forward. Since it is (mostly) caused by constraints, you can decrease Wait Time by identifying and optimizing constraints. However, there is also a particularly sinister subcategory of Wait Time that we call **Waiting for No Reason (WNR) Time**. In contrast to a situation where a case gets stuck by an external or internal Block, or behind other cases in a Bottleneck, WNR Time accrues when a case just sits for no good reason at all. As with Blocks and Bottlenecks, good visual controls alert you to WNR Time, and all good systems minimize it. Whatever the cause, all Wait Time increases Cycle Time, which we will talk about next.

Cycle Time: In this book, we define Cycle Time as the amount of time a Case Unit spends between the day you accept it formally and the date that case is considered done (i.e., matter fully concluded, money in the bank). **Reaction Time**, as we use it in this book, is the time in weeks from the date a prospective case or client first appears in your consciousness until it is converted into a Client. **Lead Time** is simply Reaction Time and Cycle Time added together.

All of these affect income. If our average Cycle Times and Reaction Times are getting shorter over time, that is a good indicator we are headed in the right direction. While we have more direct control over shortening Cycle Time (because the case or client is fully inside our system), we measure Reaction Time, too, because the longer it takes to convert a Prospect into a Client, the less profitable that Client is to us.

Just-in-Time (JIT) or Pull Scheduling: This term has broad application, and it is sometimes used synonymously with Lean Manufacturing or the Toyota Production System. Here, however, we apply the term in the context of deadlines that confer no benefit when we beat them, and we recommend that you don't begin work on them any earlier than necessary.

Kaizen: The philosophy and practice of gradual but continuous improvement.

Kanban Board: A visual control where (for our purposes) each Case Unit is represented by a "card" on a board that depicts the firm's production system as a left-to-right flow. As the Case progresses through the system, it is moved to the right toward completion. Anything that impedes progress (Blocks, Bottlenecks, WNR Time, etc.) and the total work in progress can be seen at a glance on the board.

KPIs (Key Performance Indicators): The most important measurable values that show whether a firm is meeting its key objectives.

Multitasking: Trying to do more than one thing at the same time; it is technically not possible and generally produces waste because it increases changeover from task to task.

Process: A series of actions or steps taken to achieve a particular end; in this book, "process" generally describes taking a case from the client stage through completion.

Income Formula: The formula that determines how much income your firm will make: Throughput Rate × Average Case Unit Value. Improvement of either element of the formula—especially Throughput Rate—increases income for flat-fee or contingent cases.

Throughput Rate (a.k.a. Average Flow Rate): The amount of raw material "units" (Cases or Matters for our purposes, or bicycles for Guy's) processed through your system and completed in a given amount of time. For example, if we complete 60 cases in six months, we could say Throughput Rate is 120 per year (or ten per month).

Average Case Unit Value (ACUV): The income to the firm derived from a Case or Matter. Most often, we talk in terms of ACUV, which is simply the average income to the firm derived from a Case Unit as defined earlier.

Work in Process (WIP), a.k.a. Inventory: The number of Case Units or Matters within the boundaries of the firm's system at a given time.

Visual Controls: The communication of information using visual signals (rather than text), allowing the condition of the system to be monitored and allowing constraints to be quickly identified.

Waste *(Muda)*: Any futile work (including especially having to redo work previously done incorrectly) that does not add value to the case or process.

CHAPTER 3

Systems Thinking 1
The Income Formula

March

Carson entered the bike factory with a lot on his mind. He had started trying to think about the Gray Firm in the way Guy described, as a system. He could see that what Guy said was indeed true. And he could finally see parallels in the way that the firm—like the old Chaplin Cycle—was trying to do too much of everything. And worse, how a lot of those cases seemed to be stuck in neutral, not going anywhere soon.

More cases or more kinds of cases—even all the tech Briana was obsessed with—were not the answer. But what was, then? Carson needed some kind of unifying principle to start to tie it all together. He was interested to hear what Guy said next.

"So, Guy," said Carson. "Why did you want to meet down here? What's wrong with the coffee shop?"

"Because I want you to really understand that your law firm is just like my factory," said Guy. "I don't think you believe me yet. I want you to see that, as complicated as both of our businesses appear, they are really just simple linear systems with a limited number of components."

"What do you mean exactly, Guy?" Carson asked, returning to his earlier argument reflexively. "There's nothing simple about practicing law. Do you know how many things I deal with on a daily basis? Even when I was just an associate with K&M—where I didn't have to think about the business at all—I had to answer hundreds of e-mails every day, crank out briefs and pleadings, plan and prepare for court appearances, keep up with the latest changes in the law, and be on call for any sort of client question or problem."

Carson continued, "And now at the Gray Firm, I have to do all of that while worrying about bringing in clients, controlling costs, dealing with employee issues and about five million other things. I can't see how you can call that simple, really."

"We'll get to that later, Carson," said Guy. "For now, I want you to think in really basic terms. First, let me ask you: Why does the Gray Firm exist?"

"What do you mean?" asked Carson. "Ambrose founded the Gray Firm to stand as a bulwark against injustice and...."

"I know all that, Carson. Go more basic. Ambrose Gray became a lawyer for two reasons: first, he cared about helping people; second, he came from nothing, had nothing, and he wanted to earn a decent living. To answer the question bluntly—his firm exists to make money by solving people's problems."

"Doesn't sound very idealistic," said Carson. "I doubt Ambrose would say it that way."

"Probably not," Guy replied. "But he knows it. He knows it, even if he's gotten deep into the weeds and the routine of daily practice. Sometimes you get so bogged down in the details of the work that you mistake busyness—answering e-mails, etc.—for business. But somewhere Ambrose knows that to continue to fulfill his firm's moral mission of helping people, he can't ignore the practical reality that he needs to be profitable. Why else would he take a chance on bringing you in?"

Carson thought this over as Guy continued, "I love making high-end racing bikes that people can actually afford. I love the joy that people get from flying down the road on them. And from winning races on them. But I couldn't keep filling that need if I was losing money, could I? So I have an obligation to my customers, and my employees, and my family, and myself to be profitable."

"Now to the point, Carson," said Guy. "Every business exists for the same purpose—to make money by filling a want or need. That's pretty obvious. What's less obvious is that at root level, every business does it the same way: by putting Raw Material A through a Process B, out of which comes Money C, part of which is kept and part of which is reinvested. A-B-C." Guy went to a whiteboard in the room and sketched:

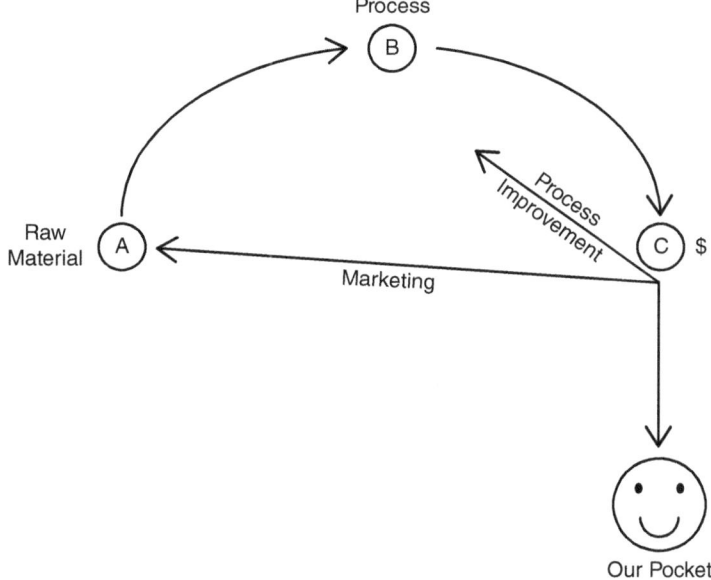

Carson rolled his eyes. "Guy, you're right about one thing. This *is* really obvious. Why did you bring me down here to show me this?"

Guy replied, "Yes. It is obvious. But think about what happens when we look at things this way. It becomes immediately apparent that only two things, A, Raw Material, and B, Process, stand in the way of getting money. So, anything that impairs the function of A or B—a block or bottleneck, for example—will hurt C. More important, though, is the converse: Anything that optimizes A or B will increase C. Which means not only more money in your pocket, but the opportunity for more reinvestment, whether it be made in marketing or buying additional Raw Material, or in improving the Process.

"An example for you. At C^2 we build all of our frames from titanium; we cast the frames here at the factory, and they are turned into our finished product, a high-end racing bike sold for $999. Assuming consistent demand for our product—which there is, because we've focused on that single product line, and it's the very best—we can sell them as fast as we can build them.

34 The Lean Law Firm

"So, Carson, if we can acquire the same high grade of titanium for less money, what happens?"

"You make more money because your cost of production drops," replied Carson.

"Right," said Guy. "Or you could buy more and increase the number of bicycle units made. Now, hypothetically, what happens if we sold each unit for $1,100 instead of $999?"

Carson replied, "Assuming your demand wouldn't drop—which it wouldn't because it's still an amazing price—you would make more money."

"Yes," said Guy, "that's an easy one. You've increased the Average Unit Value, and assuming the same rate of production and constant demand, you make more money. But in most businesses—yours included—the market dictates price, and you don't have that luxury. So, again, assuming there's constant demand, what do you do instead? You increase Throughput Rate; that is, you increase the number of units you produce over a given period of time. And the way you do that is not to try to build more units at the same time (which tends to overwhelm your system with inventory) but to put each unit through the system faster. You decrease the Cycle Time that each unit spends on average between start and finish of production. So, what happens if we increase Throughput Rate by decreasing the time it takes for each unit to go from being a lump of titanium to a finished bike? That is, assuming we could continue to sell them as fast as we made them."

"More money."

"Yes," said Guy. He turned back to the whiteboard and wrote a formula:

Income = Throughput Rate (R) × Avg. Unit Value (AUV)

"Now, let's talk about your law firm. Instead of making bikes, you handle cases. Problems—what you lawyers call cases—are your Raw Material. You process these by getting from the beginning of the case to the end, solving the problem (hopefully) by getting to some result. Let's assume you are handling them on a contingency, and that you get paid based on a percentage of the result. With these assumptions, let's plug some numbers into our formula.

"Let's say you have a Throughput Rate of 100 Units

per year. Since you deal in cases, let's start calling them Case Units. So, 100. That's how many Case Units get to the finish line in your firm each year, on average. And let's assume the Average Value of each Case Unit to your firm, in terms of what net fees it will yield when paid, is $1,000."

Guy went to the board and wrote:

$$\text{Income} = \frac{100 \text{ Case Units}}{1 \text{ year}} \times \$1{,}000 \text{ Avg. Case Unit Value (ACUV)}$$

He explained, "In this example, our Throughput Rate is 100 cases per year. We could also express that as 8.33 per month. Throughput Rate is just like miles per hour in a car; it's a measure of speed over time. Here, since we're trying to calculate the Income over a specific period of time—in this case one year—we put our time measure in the bottom of our formula. On the top, we leave the number of case units. Then, to find our income for the given period of time, we just multiply the number of units by the average value of each. Working through the math here, our income in this example is 100 × $1,000 = $100,000 per year."

"Still obvious," said Carson, flatly.

"Yes," said Guy. "So, it should be equally obvious to you that if we improve either variable, your Income will increase. If we increase Throughput Rate 10 percent to 110 cases per year, annual Income goes to $110,000. If we increase the Average Case Unit Value 10 percent, the very same thing happens: $110,000 per year. If we increase both 10 percent, it goes to $121,000.

"So," said Guy, turning from the board to Carson. "We can improve either variable for the same result. Does that make them equal?"

"Obviously it does," griped Carson, getting bored.

"Nope," said Guy. "Wrong."

"What do you mean, wrong, Guy? You just showed that, mathematically, an equal improvement to either variable yields the exact same result."

Guy replied, "It's wrong because you have more control over one variable than the other. You have far more control over improving Throughput Rate than you do over increasing Average Case Unit Value. While there are things you *can* do to increase Value—which I'll show you later—it's far easier to improve Throughput Rate.

"Example," said Guy. "Like we talked about a minute ago, I could probably increase my unit price per bicycle to $1,100 and get away with it. But there is an upper limit to that. If I arbitrarily go to $2,000, I'm going to start losing customers and selling fewer bikes. The market—not me—dictates price. And there's only so much the market will allow before it punishes me. For you, even though the 'market value' of your cases is far more variable (not to mention dependent on your skill), in the end—even if you take a case to trial—someone else besides you gets to decide its value.

"Thus," concluded Guy, "the lever of change that you can most easily grasp—and more or less fully control—is Throughput Rate. Putting most of your efforts there, that's what will make the biggest difference."

Carson had more questions than he could vocalize coherently, and they flowed out stream of consciousness. "What about hourly billing—this wouldn't work for that, and we do a decent bit of hourly billing? Doesn't turning the case over faster hurt us there? And it kind of sounds like you're talking about trying to settle everything on the cheap, Guy. Is that what you mean? And how do I increase Throughput Rate when we are at the mercy of the courts for scheduling? This sounds great in theory, Guy, but I just don't see how it all fits together."

"Good questions, all," said Guy. "Let's walk out to the factory floor and talk some more."

BUSINESS IS JUST BUSINESS

Is a law firm different than a manufacturing organization? Sure. Do those differences really matter for purposes of creating a Lean law firm using lessons from the manufacturing world? No, not really. But just to make sure you're really convinced, let's talk about those differences.

One difference is **output.** Manufacturers output tangible goods. We, on the other hand, are in the business of making and selling something less tangible: a legal result. That result may be a drafted and consummated contract or closing. It may be a favorable litigation outcome such as a verdict or settlement. It may even simply be well-researched and reasoned advice. While intangible, what it has in common with a tangible manufacturing product is that it is built by *a process*, and the results (and some or all of the money) generally come at the end of that process. Moreover, it's the quality and speed of that process that (just as in manufacturing) will determine the quality and Cycle Time of the end product. For our purposes, then, output is really not so different.

Another difference between lawyers and manufacturers is that we don't hold tangible inventory. Inventory in manufacturing presents two huge challenges. First, manufacturing organizations must store enough raw material and parts along the key points in their processing systems to avoid running out. But that's a tricky balancing act. There must be just the right amount on hand to keep the system flowing; any more than that must be stored at the manufacturer's expense. Much of the Toyota Production System is dedicated to solving this problem through Just-in-Time delivery of materials or components immediately before they are needed; this keeps inventory storage costs down. Second, manufacturing organizations must accurately predict the demand for their finished products. Unsold, aging product for which there is no demand is waste (*muda*) by definition.

Law firms, fortunately, don't face the same inventory challenges. We don't have unsold products because we don't begin work on a case or matter until someone asks for it specifically. And we don't have to physically store much of anything. But that's not to say we don't have inventory problems. Ever feel like you have too many matters or cases backlogged that aren't going anywhere? That's an inventory problem. And having too many cases or matters as Work in Process (WIP) can clog the flow of your system, which can be a Throughput Rate killer. The good news is that while we don't have exactly the same kinds of inventory problems that manufacturing industries face, many of their inventory solutions will work for us, too.

What manufacturing calls customers we call **clients**. The main difference is that manufacturing generally creates products before any specific customer asks for them, hoping that if they build it (and market it properly) the customers will come. We do the opposite: We market for the customers and then create the product or output based on what they need. Regardless of the order of things, though, we both face the same core marketing issue: *We have to tailor our product to what people really want or need.* For both lawyers and manufacturers, that generally means we must find and exploit a niche, catering to (or creating) demand.

Both manufacturing and law firms require skilled **employees**. While we may think of a factory worker on an assembly line as possessing a limited amount of skill—and think of our own employees (and certainly ourselves!) as legal "artisans"—the lines between the two are not (and should not be) as solid as you think. First, as Toyota and many other manufacturers realized, workers in the line should be empowered to make decisions and suggest improvements—even to the point of allowing them to bring the entire production line to a halt to prevent production mistakes. While their training is specific, most industrial workers are highly skilled for their jobs.

In our law practices, we want to empower our employees in a similar way. At the same time as we value creativity, though, we need to embrace standardization. We want our employees to be highly trained to do things in a very specific—and repeatable—way, because standardization and repetition are key to improving the quality and speed of throughput. Finally, and for the same reasons, we want to embrace automation in our practices, just as manufacturing did long ago.

Least importantly, in contrast to manufacturing, we have the luxury of not having to be tied firmly to a physical location. More and more, cloud-based and mobile apps allow us to work wherever we want. So while most of us still have one or more physical locations, much of our work can be done anywhere. We can also work whenever we want. But does this advantage come at a price?

BUSYNESS IS NOT BUSINESS

Being able to work anywhere and anytime is, unfortunately, as much a curse as a blessing, and not just in terms of what it does to quality of life. It can also be toxic for productivity.

> **Dave:** When I was a young lawyer trying hard to figure out how to manage a law practice, I read all of the law firm management books I could get my hands on. One of my favorites was a hardbound book written around 1955 about how to establish a thriving law practice. It suggested that a lawyer's typical day should look something like this:
>
> **Typical Day, circa 1955**
>
> | 9:30 a.m. | Arrive at work. |
> |---|---|
> | 9:30 a.m.–10:30 a.m. | Read local paper and recent court opinions. |
> | 10:30 a.m.–12:00 p.m. | Dictate correspondence and pleadings. |
> | 12:00 p.m.–2:00 p.m. | Lunch at club (no more than two martinis, though). |
> | 2:00 p.m.–3:00 p.m. | Meet with clients. |
> | 3:00 p.m.–4:30 p.m. | Place phone calls; general office work. |
> | 4:30 p.m. | Home. |
>
> Thankfully, with the addition of computers, cell phones, and various mobile technologies, our day can now look like this:
>
> **Typical Day, circa 2017**
>
> | 7:30 a.m.–8:00 a.m. | Drive to work (get there earlier by shaving in car while listening to voice mails). |
> |---|---|
> | 8:00 a.m.–9:30 a.m. | Answer 143 e-mails that came overnight. |
> | 9:30 a.m.–1:00 p.m. | Type correspondence, draft pleadings, answer discovery while being interrupted by 6 cell phone calls, 48 e-mails, 16 text messages, and 14 landline calls. And meetings. |

Typical Day, circa 2017, *continued*	
1:00 p.m.–1:15 p.m.	Lunch (Hot Pocket standing at firm microwave while reading about Kylie Jenner's latest project on iPhone).
1:15 p.m.–4:30 p.m.	Answer more e-mails; more writing and typing. More meetings.
4:30 p.m.–5:00 p.m.	Drink two Red Bulls; read advance sheets and hope to not be in them.
5:00 p.m.–6:30 p.m.	Phones stop ringing; time to focus on what you didn't finish this morning.
6:30 p.m.–7:30 p.m.	Take kids to soccer practice; continue to work on iPhone, answering e-mails and texts.
7:30 p.m.–9:00 p.m.	Pick up family dinner at Wendy's drive-thru; get kids to bed.
9:00 p.m.	All is finally quiet; time for more work.

To quote David Byrne, you may ask yourself, "Well, how did I get here?" In a nutshell here is what's happened to us:

1. **Technology is running us (instead of the other way around).** Obviously, the biggest change in the world between 1955 and now is technology. Sixty years ago, prospective clients chose a lawyer based on reputation or personal recommendation. Then lawyers began advertising, which gave rise ultimately to Internet marketing, search engine optimization, and social media marketing. Today, Internet marketing is no longer an option for small firms. It's a business reality and a survival necessity to make yourself as "findable" as possible.

   Since we are all doing it, though, it means that prospective clients can go online and find 100 local lawyers claiming to do exactly what they think needs doing. We have succeeded through advertising at turning ourselves into commodities. If we are not available to prospective clients (who, because of their own use of mobile technology, expect to reach us on short notice), it's on to the next lawyer down the list of their Google search result. We are compelled (and over time, conditioned) to respond immediately, at the expense of getting real work done. The more general your practice is, the more interchangeable you will be viewed by the public, and the worse this problem will be for you. We talk extensively about how to fix this in Chapters 6, 7, and 11.

2. **We don't know what to do right now (or which hat to wear).** The paradox for small firm lawyers is that, even if we know we should only do one thing at a time, we don't know what that one thing is. This is where classic law firm management really fails small firms. Big firms are managed. Lawyers in them (associates at least) know what they are supposed to be working on because someone has told them. Their work is further delineated by set hourly billing goals and the limited stable of clients bestowed upon them. While they are responsible for (and their ultimate success depends upon) some rainmaking, they are not the only rainmakers in the firm. While their schedules are less flexible, they are more predictable. Thus, Big Firm lawyers are better at knowing what to do "right now" because there are fewer choices and less freedom.

Ironically, perhaps, as lawyers advance through a big firm, their roles may become less defined by others. Partners do billable work, rainmaking, and marketing; they mentor associates, help with firm management, serve on committees, and may become involved in community projects that boost the profile of the firm. With increased freedom may come decreased clarity. So partners, particularly those responsible for overseeing teams, can actually benefit greatly from the techniques in this book.

But, generally speaking, Big Firm lawyers wear fewer hats than solos and small firm lawyers. Associates have one job: to produce work. Higher-ups have more jobs, including some management and marketing functions. But nobody must wear *all* of the hats in a big firm. Smaller firm lawyers are responsible for marketing, prospecting, networking, working on actual work, and going to court, and they may be making the mistake of trying to handle their own accounting and web design. Because no one tells small firm lawyers what we should be doing, we flounder around in our freedom of choice and get nowhere.

The answer to the question of "What should I be doing right now?" is, as you may be starting to guess, found when you can visualize your practice for the system that it is. Note by *visualize* we don't mean merely to accept the concept that your firm is a system, but to use tools to actually map and see that system in action. When you can see the system as a whole, identify the constraints that hinder it, and measure the results of your attempts to improve it, you and everyone on your team will always know what to do next. We talk more about how to do all of this next and in later chapters.

3. **We are trying to do too many things at once.** The irresistible urge to check our inboxes and feeds for new business and other communications (once they hire you, Clients *really* expect to get you), plus the information bombardment we are all subjected to, creates a culture of **multitasking**.

We don't have to tell you this is bad, do we? All of the studies tell us we are far more effective when we only focus on one thing at a time. You know from your own experience that, when you really have to knock out a brief, the best way to do it is to shut down all communications and distractions and get into the flow until it is done. We have to go out of our way to create space for this kind of focus. And we have to guard against its antithesis, multitasking, if we want to be truly productive instead of merely feeling busy.

Don't believe us? Here's what the American Psychological Association found:

> *[A]lthough switch costs may be relatively small, sometimes just a few tenths of a second per switch, they can add up to large amounts when people switch repeatedly back and forth between tasks. Thus, multitasking may seem efficient on the surface but may actually take more time in the end and involve more error. Meyer has said that even brief mental blocks created by* ***shifting between tasks can cost as much as 40 percent of someone's productive time***.[1]

It's the "shifting" that really hurts us. We think when we are multitasking that we are handling several things at once. But we're fooling ourselves. We're not handling multiple things at the same time; we're just shifting back and forth serially.

And it's in all the shifting that the time is lost because shifting is really just an individualized form of **changeover.** As Toyota discovered years ago, when it reduced the die changeover time on its production line from 12 hours to less than 30 minutes, cutting changeover time results in massive productivity gains because it increases the speed of the system as a whole. You can do the same thing by focusing on one thing at a time.

But how do you figure out what that one thing should be?

---

1. American Psychological Association, *Multitasking: Switching costs*, 2006. Available online at http://www.apa.org/research/action/multitask.aspx; D. M. Sanbonmatsu, D. L. Sanbonatsu, N. Medeiros-Ward, Strayer, and J. M. Watson, "Who multi-tasks and why? Multi-tasking ability, perceived multi-tasking ability, impulsivity, and sensation seeking." *PLoS ONE* 8(1): e54402, 2013.

THE SYSTEM IS THE SOLUTION

Systems thinking can help us in many ways, not the least of which is to make clear to ourselves what we should be focusing on right now. As we will discuss later, once we learn how to visualize our practice as a system, our focus will generally be on finding the constraints that impede the flow of the system and optimizing them so that Throughput flows freely. Focus may sometimes be on marketing to get more "raw material," as well.

Before we get into all of that, though, we have to get more basic. Why does your firm exist? What is your purpose?

For lawyers (and all for-profit businesses, really) our purpose is invariably twofold: We want to help clients with a certain type of problem (mission), and we want to earn a living doing it (income). And no matter how altruistic our mission, we must remain profitable to accomplish it.

Every business makes money the same way: by putting Raw Material (A) through a Process (B), out of which comes Money (C), part of which is kept and part of which is reinvested. A-B-C.

This all seems obvious at first. But think about the implications of viewing your firm this way. First, it becomes apparent immediately that two things, Raw Material (A) and Process (B), stand in the way of getting the Money (C). So, anything that impairs the efficiency of (A) or (B) (that is, any constraint) will hurt (C). Conversely, anything that increases Raw Material (A) (that is, increases the number of cases or improves their quality) or improves Process (B) will increase Money (C). Which means not only more money in your pocket, but the opportunity to invest in marketing to further increase the number of Raw Material "case units" (Inventory) and the quality (Average Case Unit Value) of new cases. You can also invest in Process (B) that enhances the average value of the case and the rate of speed at which the case can be turned into money (Throughput Rate).

THE INCOME FORMULA

This basic truth—if you want more Income, focus first on improving Throughput Rate and second on improving Average Case Unit Value—leads us naturally into our **Income Formula**. Before jumping into the formula, however, some Warnings and Disclaimers: This formula does not work well or at all on an hourly billing model. Why? Because an hour is always an hour. And no matter how much you improve the efficiency and speed of your Process, that fact will never change.

If you are billing by the hour, improving your process may improve the results you get for your clients (and hence their happiness). However, it will not add directly to your bottom line. Perhaps (assuming unlimited client ability and willingness to pay and ethical "flexibility" by the lawyer) *less* efficiency is actually preferable (we don't counsel this, of course, but, from a pure numbers standpoint, it might be true). If you do work mainly or exclusively on an hourly basis, focus most of your efforts into marketing and results improvement.

Why? Because with hourly billing, there is a fixed limit to the amount of work you can take on, which means there is an inherent ceiling that prevents you from producing more revenue. The only way to add more hours is to add more hourly billers. You are increasing inventory, but you are increasing costs. There is nothing wrong with this method of growth, and it is a proven Big Law formula, but your ability to scale throughput is sharply curbed.

What we are interested in is a formula for firms that works well for contingent and flat fee cases. Our formula is:

Income = Throughput Rate × Avg. Case Unit Value

In our story, Guy helped us plug in some numbers to see how proportional increases in Throughput Rate or Average Case Unit Value have the same positive effect on income. Going from completing 100 cases in a year to 110 cases is the same as staying at 100 cases and making each case 10 percent more valuable.

But as Guy also explained, the fact that an increase in either Average Value or Throughput Rate has the same effect does not make them equal, because we have far more influence over Throughput Rate than we ever will over value. As Guy said, Throughput Rate is the lever we can more easily grasp. But, as we will see next, Throughput Rate itself is not really a single lever but something we can improve by working the two related levers—Inventory (WIP) and Cycle Time—upon which Throughput Rate depends.

LITTLE'S LAW: THE RELATIONSHIP BETWEEN CYCLE TIME, THROUGHPUT RATE, AND INVENTORY

In 1961, MIT professor John Little proved a mathematical relationship between Cycle Time, Throughput Rate, and Average Inventory (WIP) in a stable system. In simplest terms, Little's Law states that *Average Inventory equals Throughput Rate times average Cycle Time*. The formula looks like this:

Average Inventory (WIP) = Throughput Rate (R) × Average Cycle Time (CT)

Before we talk about what this means for lawyers and law firms, let's relate these terms to our practices. Let's talk first about what Little calls **Inventory.**

You might recall that earlier we defined Inventory as the number of matters your firm is working on at a given time. We use the term Case Units to more closely mirror system-thinking concepts. A matter in this context is one you're actively working on—that is, it's not a potential matter—and if you're representing multiple defendants, each claim is its own Case Unit.

Throughput Rate, as we've discussed, is simply the average flow rate (or speed) at which case "units" cross the finish line of your system (i.e., completed, money in the bank). Note that a rate is a measure of velocity, in the same way that a car going 60 mph is simply "completing" 60 miles every hour. A law firm might complete 12 cases per month (or 144 cases per year), and that's a measure of its velocity.

Finally, **Cycle Time** is simply the amount of time, on average, a Case Unit spends between the start and finish lines of your system.

With our terms defined, let's look at an example. Imagine a bicycle road race, with an "inventory" of five riders lined up at the start. The gun goes off and the riders commence pedaling. The five riders finish in the following times:

Rider 1: 60 min
Rider 2: 90 min
Rider 3: 120 min
Rider 4: 180 min
Rider 5: 240 min

If we take an average of these times (adding them together and dividing by 5) we get 138 minutes. This is our average **Cycle Time.** Since we know our Inventory (5) and average Cycle Time (138 min), we can use Little's Law to find our Throughput Rate. We start with the formula:

$$WIP = R \times CT$$

We arrange that through simple algebra, to solve for R, like this:

$$R = \frac{WIP}{CT}$$

Plugging in the numbers:

$$R = \frac{5 \text{ riders (WIP)}}{138 \text{ minutes (CT)}}$$

Doing the math, 5 riders divided by 138 minutes gives us

R = 0.036 riders per minute.

To convert this to hours, we now need only to multiply our Throughput Rate of 0.036 riders per minute by the 60 minutes in an hour; this gives us

R = 2.17 riders per hour.

Our Throughput Rate (R) is 2.17 riders per hour.

While the preceding example is basic, don't be deceived by the simplicity of Little's Law. Not only does it allow us to find the missing variable when we know only two (e.g., we can calculate average Cycle Time simply by knowing how many case units we have in Inventory and reviewing how many have closed over a specific time [CT = WIP / R]); **Little's Law also tells us that increasing Throughput Rate depends on reducing Cycle Time and regulating the flow of Inventory into the system.** How's that? Let's return to our bike race example. In our earlier example, the Throughput Rate of bike racers is 2.17 racers per hour. But what would happen if we cut our average Cycle Time down by about 25 percent, from 138 minutes to 104 minutes? What would that do for our Throughput Rate?

$$R = \frac{5 \text{ riders (WIP)}}{\cancel{138} \, 104 \text{ minutes (CT)}}$$

Doing the math, we get an R value of 0.048 riders per minute. Multiplying this by 60, our Throughput Rate jumps to

R = 2.88 riders per hour.

What we get by cutting Cycle Time is, of course, what we expect—a proportionate increase in Throughput Rate. That's great news because Cycle Time is a lever we can really get both hands on. Because, in a law firm, almost all of what we call Cycle Time for a Case Unit is actually time the case spends *waiting* for something to happen. That is, most of our Cycle Time for a Case Unit is spent just waiting, with no active work being done on the case at all. And there are lots of things we can do to fix that.

Think about it in your firm: When a case is within the bounds of your system, how much of the time is it being actively worked on? Not very much. You have lots of cases, and you can only work on one at a time, really. The same for your staff. So, most of the time, the case is just sitting, waiting for you to finish whatever you're doing on some other case. Wait Time.

Other times, progress on the case is internally blocked by someone else in your firm—one firm member (who may be ready to act on the case) cannot do so because someone else has not finished an earlier step on which progress depends. Sometimes these blocks are External Blocks, where we are waiting on our client or even opposing counsel to complete a step. Court rules present another kind of External Block or limiting factor and (assuming the case proceeds to trial) may impose a kind of speed limit on the case. But, truthfully, most of the waiting is caused by our own faulty processes (or lack of any process).

So how can we solve this? First, we find the constraints in our own system that are blowing up our Cycle Time (and thus hurting Throughput Rate). Second, through technology and standardization, we can improve our process so that—in those times that we are actively working on the case—we are moving faster and with fewer errors. Finally—and most counterintuitively—we regulate (and most likely reduce) the Inventory of cases coming into the system at any one time so that we have more time to actively work on the cases that are within the bounds of the system (and each case spends less time waiting).

In the chapters that follow, we'll talk at length about locating (and improving) constraints and using technology and standardization to speed active work. Before closing out this chapter, though, a bit more on the most counterintuitive step: reducing the Inventory of cases in the system at any one time (WIP). While, mathematically, decreasing Inventory would appear to decrease Throughput Rate, in the real world it results in a shortening of Cycle Time that more than offsets the smaller Inventory. Over time, the increased Throughput Rate results in your completing far more cases. Best of all, because you are concentrating more work in a shorter time on each case, there's less changeover, better quality, and very likely an increase in the Average Case Unit Value of each case you handle. So, wins all around.

CHAPTER SUMMARY

Despite the formulas shown above, you really don't have to worry too much about the math in this chapter. Just remember this: The point of the system is to increase Throughput Rate, which you do by decreasing Cycle Time through reducing constraints, standardizing your active work, and regulating the flow of WIP into your system, finding a level that allows you to move as fast as possible. In the chapters that follow, we'll show you how to visualize your practice as a system so you can optimize it. And in Chapter 10, we'll give you a way to calculate a starting point number for finding your ideal WIP level. Before we get to all that, since you can't improve what you can't measure, let's first talk about what you should be measuring.

Terms we learned:

Term	Definition
Output	The result of a process; in manufacturing this is a tangible good. In law it is a legal result.
Inventory	Unsold product; in manufacturing these are physical goods, in law these are matters that are not closed or collected.
Changeover	In manufacturing, changeover is when a production line switches from producing one thing to another. In legal firms, changeover occurs when you switch tasks.
Throughput Rate	In manufacturing, the rate at which a system completes units. In legal firms, it's the speed at which a case can be turned into money.
Average Case Unit Value	How much, on average, your cases are worth.
Cycle Time	Amount of time something takes between the start and finish lines of your system. In legal firms, this corresponds to the time it takes for you to open a case and close it.
Income Formula	Throughput Rate × Average Case Unit Value

CHAPTER 4

Using KPIs
What, When, and How to Measure

April

As he sat on a bench outside the coffee shop Carson wondered, "Where's Guy? He told me to meet him at exactly noon. It's ten minutes after. He's never late. Ever. I wonder . . ."

Carson's cell phone rang and lit up with Guy's number. Carson picked up. "Hey Guy, where are you? I'm here."

"Running late, Carson. Be there in a few minutes. How about you go on into the café and get us a couple of coffees. One large. One small. Tell Sandra to put it on my tab."

Guy clicked off. Carson went into the coffee shop. He was returning with two steaming coffees of different sizes, as Guy had instructed, when Guy rode up on a vintage electric blue Tsunami 2.

"Thanks, Carson," said Guy, taking the large coffee. Carson looked annoyed. "What?" Guy asked innocently. "You're too wound up already these days, Carson. You get the small."

Carson, badly needing the caffeine but not wanting to appear ungrateful, mumbled his thanks.

Guy laughed and handed the large coffee back to Carson, taking the small for himself. "Measurements don't seem so important until they affect you personally, huh?" he chuckled, before continuing, "That's today's lesson. Measurement.

"You ever hear the saying 'what gets measured gets done?' Well, the reverse is true, too. Whatever you decide to measure you have to actually do. And since measurement itself takes time and effort, you have to understand what things are critical to measure in your business, and what is simply nice to know. That's sub-lesson one: Only measure what really matters."

"How do you know what that is?" asked Carson. "What really matters?"

Guy answered, "To me, only four things matter: Quantity, Position, Speed, and Deadlines.

"**Quantity:** How much do I have of something? That could be how much money do I have in the bank? Or it could be how many bicycle units do I have in process right now, my Inventory or WIP? And, of course, how much money, on average, am I getting for each unit, my Average Case Unit Value?

"**Position:** Where is that unit of inventory in my production system right now? More on that in a minute, because it's very important from a systems perspective but hard to measure numerically. Much easier to see visually.

"**Speed:** What's my Throughput Rate? That is, how many units are getting to the finish line over a given period of time? Related to this is Cycle Time: How much time, on average, is a unit spending between the start and finish lines of my system? Also, how much time is it taking for a prospect to become a client, and thus get to the starting line, or Reaction Time?

"Finally, I measure **Deadlines.** What's due when? And that's about it. I try to keep it very simple. So, within each of these broad categories, Q, P, S, and D, I have just a few KPIs—Key Performance Indicators.

"Let's talk a little more about Quantity. First, I track Inventory—WIP—so I know how many units I have within the boundaries of my process. Second, I track money: How much do I have in the bank right now, and how much do I have coming into the business from completed orders that have not yet been paid? I call what I have right now **Cash Quantity.** What I know I have coming in I call **Cash Pipeline,** or just Pipeline. This is going to sound too simple, but if the amount of money we have increases over time, that's a pretty good indicator that things are going like they should. Our goal is to make money, after all. So I check those measurements just about every day.

"I have another Quantity measurement I check, but less often: **Average Value per Unit.** I review metrics like how much a bike costs to make versus what we can sell it for, to see what bikes are winners for us—which ones are profitable—so I know which kind to focus on. That's how I first realized that we needed to focus on the niche racing bikes that no one else was really making—ones just under $1,000.00 that could compete with the bikes costing three times more.

"Years ago, a little while before the rebranding into C^2, we had a huge debate at the factory about what bikes to build. I'll tell you more about that later when we talk about marketing. Some of my managers wanted to saturate the low end of the market with a lot of volume. Others said that was crazy, and that the very high-end bikes—four- or five-thousand-dollar carbon fiber racers—was where the profit was. But our margins were very small on the low-end stuff. And the high-end bikes were extremely expensive to make because a lot of the work was custom, and very time-consuming, and involved reworking entire production lines already geared toward titanium frames.

"It was the numbers that told the tale. The greatest margin for us was in titanium racing bikes costing around $1,000.00. And just inside that number was a very exploitable place in the market. When we finally put our egos aside and looked at the numbers, the path became clear.

"Now for Position. Unlike Quantity, Position is hard to measure on a spreadsheet. You kind of have to see it in real time. Watch this," said Guy, taking out his smartphone. He pushed a button for an app that brought up a map. On the map were several dots—each with a name label—moving along a road in a rural part of the county. Guy explained, "That's the C^2 Junior Women's team on a training ride. See that gap opening up between Christine and Brittany? I'm not liking that." He tapped at his phone and spoke into it. "Brittany!" A breathless voice came back through the phone. "Sir?" Guy replied, "Tighten my line up, please, Brittany." The voice croaked back, "Yes sir!" Guy closed the app.

Carson was impressed. "Coaching sure has changed."

"I miss yelling at them in person," griped Guy. "Anyway, back to Position. Just like the GPS app here for my riders, I need to see where things are in real time to determine where gaps are opening because of Wait Time or constraints. In the factory, I'm interested in where each unit is in the system. Our goal is higher Throughput Rate. For me to increase Throughput Rate, I have to know where things are getting hung up. Is a prospective order hanging up on the verge of being converted to an order? Is a new order languishing without moving into production, not really blocked but just not being worked on? (By the way, we call this Waiting for No Reason or WNR Time.) Is a completed sale stuck waiting for payment? If we can see where every unit lies in the system, there is a good chance we will spot sticking points immediately, and we can put our focus there so that the whole system continues to flow.

"And speaking of Speed, we've already talked extensively about Throughput Rate. Super easy to measure. You just pick the finish line of your system and note when each completed unit crosses it. For me, that's when the bike goes out the door. For you, I would imagine, it's when the money hits the bank. If you count how many cases cross that finish line for any given period of time, you have your Throughput Rate for that period. And like we talked about last month, Cycle Time is also very important; it's simply a measure of how much time, on average, a unit spends within the boundaries of the start and finish lines of your system. The starting line, for you, might be when the retainer agreement is signed by the client; the finish line is simply the same one you use for Throughput Rate. A shorter Cycle Time—less time spent in the system— means faster Throughput Rate. You should also measure Reaction Time, which is just the time it takes between first contact with a prospect and their conversion to full-fledged retainer-signing client. Less time is better here, too.

"The last measurement is Deadlines. We know we can't miss them. You know me, I hate being late. But when I showed up late, you noticed, right? Customers—and clients—they hate to wait. So we can never miss appointments or deadlines. At the same time, what your mom told you about starting early on that term paper is wrong. Work has a way of expanding into the time we give it to get done. And many kinds of deadlines have no upside to early completion. Example: The IRS wants me to file my taxes by April 15. I'm never going to be late with that, ever. Conversely, though, I'm usually going to owe them money, so there's no upside to me getting them done by February 15. It just means I have to pay it sooner! For deadlines like this *with no performance incentive*, we track them, of course, but we schedule their completion as late as possible, or ASLAP. This is related to what we talked about a month or two ago,

Just-in-Time scheduling. Long story short, we have to track our deadlines so we never miss them. But putting our focus there first, instead of on the constraints, slows our entire system down to no advantage.

"Now," Guy said, "let's talk more about what Quantity, Position, Speed, and Deadlines you would want to measure in a law firm. I bet they're not too different than mine. And maybe some other things that you could track as well, once you've mastered those...."

If you're in the minority of attorneys that loves working with numbers, consider yourself lucky. You're a Numbers Ninja.

If, on the other hand, you have a natural aversion to numbers, note that you have a lot of company. Many attorneys pursued political science, history, and other liberal arts majors, sidestepping mathematics whenever possible. We'll refer to these individuals, to borrow loosely from *Seinfeld*, as Anti-Numbites.

Fret not, Anti-Numbites. Our goal here is to transform you into a Numbers Ninja. This chapter is going to tell you exactly which numbers to pay attention to, why they're important, and how often you need to look at them.

It's helpful to reframe the idea of numbers in a more favorable light. For instance, heated, ego-driven arguments can be a thing of the past when firms agree to make decisions based on data. Numbers allow you to settle debates—competing ideas can be tried, results can be measured, and the best one wins.

Numbers are not the dull and boring purview of accountants and mathematicians. Rather, numbers are your glorious mountain peak, upon which you can survey the expanse of your operations and see them in plain light. They are beacons that help you navigate turbulent waters. They are a mirror that reflects how you're doing, not just as a business, but as a client advocate. Instead of being a nuisance or, worse yet, PTSD-trigger-points from your days as a math student, numbers will help you sleep well at night. Without them, you have no idea how your law firm is truly doing or how well you're likely to do in the future.

- ✔ **DO:** Use numbers to discover more about your business and what you can improve.
- ✘ **DON'T:** Engage in arguments about hypotheticals. Use data or data gathering to chart the best way forward.

✗ **DON'T:** Try to measure anything that is not really important to your business. It's easy to get carried away with cool, Star Trek–like "dashboards" that measure every metric known to humankind. But remember: What gets measured gets done. If it's not something you need to be doing, then don't bother measuring it. Measure only what matters.

Numbers that tell you information about your business are referred to as **Key Performance Indicators (KPIs)**. KPIs are also commonly referred to as **metrics**. You measure KPIs not just once, but as an ongoing activity. Some are best measured once a year, others monthly, others weekly, and some daily.

The first accurate measure of a KPI is known as its **baseline**. When you examine a KPI over time, comparing it against the baseline is a fundamental part of tracking progress.

As a Numbers Ninja armed with the following KPIs, you will stand metaphorically atop the Rock of Gibraltar, wind and sea whipping at your face, gazing upon your firm with the authority of one who commands the elements.

Note that this is not an exhaustive list of KPIs, but a collection of what we believe are some of the foundational ones you need to run your business with confidence. They are also fairly representative of different aspects of the business, such as financial management, marketing, sales, operations, and HR, and as such they serve as good jumping-off points for your own further explorations of those subjects.

QUANTITY KPIs (HOW MUCH/MANY DO I HAVE)?

KPI: Cash Quantity (CQ)
Monitoring Frequency: Daily
Importance Level: Critical
Why It's Important: Helps you focus on the number-one resource for your business
Ninja Level: Absolute Beginner

Cash is king. It is oxygen for your business. You need to know *on a daily basis* how much money you have at your disposal, right now, because it is the most critical element for your business's survival. That's the reason why this KPI takes the number-one spot.

Your CQ (also known as Cash Balance or Cash Position) is comprised of all of your liquid assets, that is, money that you can use to quickly pay people or vendors. This includes money in your operating account, lines of credit, or any immediately available CDs or bonds. It does not include money in your trust account, of course (although money in trust that is headed for operating may be tracked in your Cash Pipeline, as described next).

How do you measure this? Look at your accounting software or current online banking balance and see how much money you have in your operating account. Just be careful to note if you have cut any checks by hand, as these won't be reflected in your online cash position. Cutting checks online, on the other hand, will be reflected.

KPI: Cash Pipeline (CP)
Monitoring Frequency: At least weekly
Importance Level: Critical
Why It's Important: It's the forecast for what cash *should* be coming in.
Ninja Level: Beginner

Your CP is simply the *money that is supposed to be coming in*. It includes money earned from completed work (e.g., cases settled but without final payment, or billed work) as well as short-term CDs or bonds that may be available for use in the immediate future (60 days, for example).

How do you measure CP? The easiest way to get started is to simply track it on a spreadsheet. For lawyers working on a contingent fee basis, CP is simple. You've settled the case and you're just waiting on the check, but you don't yet have it. So you make an entry in your journal or spreadsheet (1) identifying the matter, (2) showing the gross settlement proceeds, (3) showing the firm's expected net, (4) showing the date that the matter was settled, and (5) identifying the associated practice category (e.g., Workers Comp.).

Of course, in the spirit of Lean, you can iteratively improve your CP tracking by graduating from spreadsheets to dedicated legal time and billing software. These programs help you track accounts receivable (money you're owed), pending billing activities, trust account management, and work-in-progress reporting. Because they are tied in to your activities and accounting, they make it easy to stay up to date with the work you've performed and the money you can expect to come in. However, we suggest understanding the process manually first before you dive in to a sophisticated system. Only by understanding the fundamentals will you be able to leverage these powerful tools.

For hourly billing, it's only a little more difficult. You've completed the work (or at least completed your billing cycle), the money is in trust, and it only remains to be rolled into operating. (Later, we'll talk more about billing clients for whom you do not have money held in trust.)

What both of the preceding items—settled contingent cases and completed hourly work against money in trust—have in common is that they are, if not a sure thing, about as close as we lawyers get. Just like that short-term CD, we can be relatively confident that this money will indeed be coming in soon. So we count it in our CP, too.

Adding all the preceding "coming soon" items together (net fees and recovered costs from contingent cases, earned fees from money in trust, and short-term instruments like CDs) gives us our CP.

Before we talk more about how to track CQ and CP, and how to handle hourly billing when the money is not in trust, a short word about flat-fee cases. As we discuss in more detail later, there are several advantages to flat fees. They are predictable for the client and (unlike an hourly billing model) allow the lawyer's efficiency and Throughput Rate gains to increase profit (e.g., a lawyer who charges a flat fee of $500.00 for a service that he figures out how to do in half the time has just doubled his money).

> On our companion website, you'll find the world's simplest spreadsheet for tracking CP, CQ, and the financial health of your firm: leanlawfirmbook.com Use correct terminology and show the categories at bottom.

For accounting purposes, the beauty of the flat fee is that it is paid up front. As long as ethical rules are followed in the collection of this fee and handling of the case, the flat fee goes immediately into CQ. It's money in the bank. And moving the collection of the fee from the back of the case to the front shortens an often-lagging aspect of the case (collection). The take-home lesson is when you get a flat fee, go ahead and include that in CQ.

Benefits of Knowing Your CQ and CP

Knowing your CQ and CP intimately means a variety of other good things can happen. First, you can take the temperature of your business any time. You can see how things stand, right now.

Secondly, tracking this over time allows certain trends to become clear. Are there times of year, year after year, when money is tight? When you are flush?

Even more importantly, are certain practice areas far more profitable than others? If so, you should consider doing more of those (and less of the others).

And perhaps most importantly, is the amount of money coming in increasing from year to year? Because if you're doing things right, shouldn't it be?

Tracking also means that you will manage money well. You will know when you should pay outright for new computers or furniture or if you should finance your purchase. You will get good at scheduling your largest payments so they don't coincide at the same time, such as rent, your primary business credit card, and payroll.

✔ **DO:** Actively schedule your payments so that your CQ doesn't get hit all at once, and push payments out as long as is acceptable to your payee.

Paying attention to your CP will also focus your attention on when money should be coming in, leading you to put more significance on the collections part of your business. For contingent fee cases, collections are as simple as taking action when the CP tells you payment is lagging. From a systems thinking perspective, you now know that this "lagging" payment is making Cycle Time longer. So you take swift action to collect, perhaps filing a motion to compel settlement.

Note that collections—whether we are talking about recovering promised settlements or collecting on invoices for time billed—is usually the weakest yet most critical aspect of a law firm's business. Making sure you get paid for the work you perform, as we will see, is one of the most significant improvements you can make to your practice, and it will likely have more dramatic effects than an improved marketing operation. Uncollected money = longer Cycle Time. And we know that's bad.

"Constantly improving the cash flow of the company—and better understanding how cash moves through the business—is a powerful driver for improving the firm as a whole," says business growth expert Verne Harnish in his book, *Scaling Up*.

We can't count unpaid hourly invoices (which are not billed against trust) in either our CQ or our CP. Elsewhere in this book, we recommend against hourly billing models for a variety of reasons (even though we still talk about best practices for hourly billers). Finally, if you are billing a flat by-the-job fee, and you don't get the payment up front, we should not have to even tell you why that's a bad idea. Needless to say, if you are using one of these models, it is critical that you track—through your accounting program or otherwise—unpaid and aging balances, and:

✔ **DO:** Constantly strive to collect on invoices as quickly as possible (more on this in a moment).

✔ **DO:** Track Firm Collection Percentage (see the discussion that follows).

Even though it's not really a Quantity measure, we'll talk about tracking collection percentage as a KPI later in this chapter. But, as a final parting shot against hourly billing (especially where no money is held in trust) and "back-end" flat fees, note that the tracking and collection work required by these billing models is taking up precious resources, either your own or your staff's, that could be used instead to actually produce something.

KPI: Firm Collection Percentage (FCP)
Monitoring Frequency: Monthly
Why It's Important: Critical in hourly and deferred flat-fee models
Ninja Level: Intermediate

Collections refers to the cash you receive on your invoices. *FCP is simply how much of what you are supposed to get you are actually getting, expressed as a percentage.* You should be aware of the percentage of your invoiced work that you receive payment for, or your collection percentage. The reason your collection percentage is number two on the list is because it ties closely to cash management and is almost always overlooked by attorneys, Numbers Ninjas and Anti-Numbites alike.

> **Key Stat: 71 Percent**
> According to a Georgetown Law study, on average law firms only collect on 71 percent of the work they perform.
>   Source: http://www.law.georgetown.edu/academics/centers-institutes/legal-profession/upload/FINAL-Report-1-7-15.pdf

For any lawyer handling cases by the hour, focusing on improving the percentage of collections can radically transform everything about the business for the better. It means more cash will be available. It also will result in work getting wrapped up and invoiced, especially for non-litigation-dependent attorneys. Some attorneys tend to let administrative work pile up once the principal legal activity is done. This is a rookie mistake. Closing work out and sending prompt invoices avoids lingering receivables. The same is true for hourly litigators. Bills need to be fresh, processed crisply every 30 days. The longer you wait to bill your clients, the bigger the haircut you'll receive on your payments.

Finally, if you are billing hourly, realize the advantages of credit card or e-check processing, both of which improve Cycle Time by speeding collections.

- ✔ **DO:** Invoice within 30 days of legal activity. The longer you wait, the more of a haircut you'll receive on your bill.
- ✘ **DON'T:** Work on collections yourself. Task it out to a staff member, who will prioritize it better than you.
- ✔ **DO:** Explore more frictionless payment methods, such as recurring billing, payment plans, and pay by credit card.

> **Why Switching to E-Billing Is a Must for Cash Management**
>
> When you send out paper bills, you have to print your invoices, fold them, stuff them into envelopes, address the envelopes, purchase stamps, affix stamps to the envelopes, and then await payment in the mail. Hopefully your client pays on time, in which case you process mail, deposit the check, and record the payment in your accounting program.
>
> This is a slow, laborious process that is largely unchanged from the days when John Adams and Abraham Lincoln practiced law.
>
> With e-billing, you can e-mail your invoices to your clients or allow them to view them through a secure portal. None of the preceding steps is necessary. Your clients can then pay through a secure web page, and if you're using a good system, your ledgers will be updated automatically.

KPI: Inventory/WIP

Monitoring Frequency: Weekly

Importance: Critical

Why It's Important: Per Little's Law, WIP directly affects Throughput Rate and Cycle Time; too much inventory in process at once chokes Throughput Rate and lengthens Cycle Time. Too little hurts Throughput Rate (because too few units cross the finish line). You're looking for the sweet spot.

Ninja Level: Intermediate

This is still a fairly easy one for the Anti-Numbites. WIP refers to the number of Case Units within the bounds of your system during a given time period. The Income Formula tells you that if you can increase Throughput Rate, you can generate more income (provided your average unit value doesn't decrease). Maybe you're not looking to maximize income but are looking to achieve a specific income to achieve work–life balance. In any case, you're looking for that certain sweet spot where cases flow through your system, your clients are happy, and you're not fighting fires seven days a week.

Measuring WIP is straightforward. You simply count the number of Case Units between the start and finish boundaries of your system at any point in time. (You can do this manually, but if you are using Kanban software, this is generally handled automatically.) The point of monitoring your WIP inventory "levels," of course, is to see which level allows the best Throughput Rate and average Cycle Times.

In Chapter 10, we will give you a way to calculate a rough number of what your average WIP *should* be. But finding the right WIP number is more subjective than objective, and finding how to adjust it is like a pilot learning how to use a throttle: It involves experimenting with different inventory levels over time and seeing which level provides the fastest Throughput Rate and the shortest Average Cycle Times.

KPI: Average Case Unit Value (ACUV)
Monitoring Frequency: Quarterly
Importance Level: Critical
Why It's Important: Helps you target profitability and guides future marketing
Ninja Level: Intermediate

ACUV refers to the profitability of an individual Case Unit and, as you probably recognize, it's one of the elements of our Income Formula. To measure it, you simply note the income that the case brought in when you're totally finished with the case and, importantly, the *type* of case (practice category). Why? *Because your ultimate goal is to identify the kinds of cases that have the highest return and do more of them.*

This measurement becomes valuable when you've got enough data to spot profitability trends in practice areas. Another thing: Since you're already entering data into a spreadsheet showing the value and case type, why not also add:

> Date of first contact (i.e., date prospect first contacted you)
> Start date (date prospect became a client and entered system)
> End date (date the Case Unit crosses the finish line to "done")

If you've graduated from your KPI spreadsheet to a sophisticated legal practice management system, you can likely automate this KPI.

By simply adding these three data points you can, over time, calculate average Reaction Times, Cycle Times, Throughput Rate, and, of course, ACUV (and ACUV by matter type). By using Little's Law, moreover, you can calculate your WIP levels for a given time as well. In short, you have all the key metrics in one place.

You can find a sample spreadsheet at leanlawfirmbook.com.

KPI: Average Net Case Value
Monitoring Frequency: Quarterly
Importance Level: Important
Why It's Important: Helps you target profitability and guides future marketing
Ninja Level: Intermediate

This is just an analogue of ACUV, but an important one. In addition to tracking the average (gross) value of cases, you may want to dig deeper to see not only how much money a case has brought in, but how much it has cost you to provide service for that case.

Note that to calculate net fees (as opposed to gross fees), you still need to know how much it costs you to provide legal services. If you're tracking your time (which you should be even if on contingency), you can see how many attorney and staff hours went into the case.

A warning for Anti-Numbites: We now must take a look at a mathematical equation. Do not skip this, or the way of the Numbers Ninja will elude you. Think of mastering this equation as your first rite of passage as a young numbers grasshopper. The good news is, it's easy to understand, and the even better news is that it is powerful.

As we've discussed before, one of the reasons that a contingent or flat fee model can be superior to an hourly fee model is that the per-hour return is not fixed, and it can be enhanced by improved efficiency and process. A case that brings in $1,000 but takes five hours of work is inferior from a business standpoint to one that returns $1,000 but takes only two hours. At the end of the quarter (or year), if you are tracking your returns by case type (and you should be), the cases with high profit potential (relative to their required resource investment) will become clear. Do more of these.

But be careful in your assessment. Do not ignore the importance of Cycle Time. Those variables—Value and number of hours invested (V, h)—are helpful in determining the profitability of a case, but they don't tell the whole story. That's because they don't factor in Cycle Time (CT).

Let's look deeper. We have Case 1, which returns $1,000 and takes five hours of lawyer or staff resource hours to complete. Its average hourly rate is $200.

Case 2 also returns $1,000, but it takes only two hours of resource time to complete. Its average hourly rate is $500.

Case 2 may look like it's much more valuable. And that would be absolutely true if we could practice forever. But we can't. Even lawyers with long careers have a finite time to make whatever money through their practice that time, fate, and industry will allow. Like pro football players, we have a limited (albeit hopefully longer) shelf life. So, to be very blunt, from a purely business standpoint your objective is to make as much as you can in the time that you have.

Let's look at Cycle Time again for these two cases. If it is equal, Case 2 is of course more profitable. But let's say Case 2 takes one year from start to finish to complete and Case 1 takes only one month. Which is the more profitable? If you were to divide your hourly rate of return by the number of months it took to receive it, Case 1, which appeared to return only

$200 per hour, is actually more valuable to you. You made $1,000 in one month in Case 1, versus $1,000 in 12 months ($83.33/month) in Case 2.

While both ways of looking at profitability are important, given our goal of Throughput Rate and the fact that Cycle Time affects it directly, we prefer Case 1—in and out in one month—to Case 2. The point of identifying Average Net Case Value, then, is to find which areas you can truly exploit: cases that have high value relative to the resources required to realize them. Because when you identify a more valuable Case 2 (two hours to handle for return of $1,000.00) and can collapse its Cycle Time to Case 1 levels (one month), you're really on to something.

Even when we return to an hourly fee model, and reflect on the KPIs for cash and collections, you can see now why processing invoices and collections in a timely manner has a significant impact on your business: It shortens your Cycle Time, thus boosting profitability by increasing Throughput Rate. Thus, even if you do not boost your inventory of cases, you can still boost profitability by increasing value (or your rates) or reducing the time it takes you to process a case.

KPI: New Leads per Month
Monitoring Frequency: Monthly
Importance Level: Nice to know
Why It's Important: Serves as a leading indicator for future business and keeps marketing accountable
Ninja Level: Intermediate

If you're not measuring, you're not marketing. Whether your operation includes billboards or simply networking with a small group of people, you're not going to get very far without being a Numbers Ninja.

A lead is a prospective client. Monitoring new leads per month is the first step in getting your marketing house in order. These should be qualified leads, meaning legitimate ones that fit your practice, not incomprehensible rants you receive on your answering machine at 2:00 a.m.

Leads are a leading indicator of the health of your business. As you track them over time, along with new clients per month (covered next), a pattern of conversion percentages will emerge, which will allow you to build predictability into your practice.

Ideally, they should come from a variety of sources such as networking, word of mouth, online, or other sources. In the business world, your marketing sources are referred to as your "channels." As you gradually become more comfortable as a Numbers Ninja, you can dive infinitely deep with your marketing data to determine which channels are more lucrative than others. For this reason, tracking referral sources is key. If you do things right, you'll be able to calculate the cost per lead (CPL) for your different lead sources.

> Beware the "vanity metric." It is a danger that can seduce and destroy a Numbers Ninja. A vanity metric is one that tells you very little about your business but is something you track anyhow, eating up valuable time and emotion.
> Marketing is rife with these worthless sirens.
> For example, your number of Twitter or Facebook followers does not have a predictable effect on your business. It doesn't matter if you have ten or 10,000 followers if you are not generating new business at a satisfactory rate. A slightly more valuable metric, for example, is the number of shares or retweets of an article you posted. The gold-standard KPI would be leads originating from any articles you shared.

KPI: New Clients per Month

Monitoring Frequency: Monthly

Importance Level: Nice to know

Why It's Important: Indicates ongoing health of business and helps with seasonal and year-over-year trend spotting

Ninja Level: Beginner

Here's an easy slam dunk for the Anti-Numbites: Calculating your new clients per month is a piece of cake—if it isn't, the rest of this book will help you iron out your processes and tools so that it will be easy to do so. Remember that a client is simply a prospect who has signed a representation agreement. While Inventory (WIP) is one of our big Income Formula drivers, if you can't turn a prospect into a client, it never becomes WIP. So it's nice to know how well you're converting.

If you have compiled these numbers in one place, you will start to see some trends and establish sanity in your practice immediately. In fact, it's possible that you have accurate data to build out a history that goes back 12 to 24 months. If you do, it's very worthwhile to gather that data into a spreadsheet. You will spot the effects of seasonality by comparing year-over-year (YoY) numbers. If you can identify when you implemented marketing campaigns, you can look for correlations in new client growth.

In addition, when you track new leads compared to new clients in a given time period, you establish a conversion percentage. Once you see your conversion percentage, you will understand that you can acquire more new clients through better lead generation *and* better sales techniques.

- ✔ **DO:** Measure the number of legitimate inquiries that come into your law firm across all marketing channels.
- ✘ **DON'T:** Spend time and energy tracking vanity metrics or KPIs that have no discernable direct impact on your business.
- ✘ **DON'T:** Track too often. Your data will vary greatly on a week-to-week basis, and it might prompt you to investigate red herrings.
- ✔ **DO:** Compare the same period in one year to the same period in a previous year, as opposed to comparing sequential months and quarters.

POSITIONAL KPI—WHERE IS IT?

KPI: Stage/Kanban
Monitoring Frequency: Daily
Importance Level: Critical
Why It's Important: Tells you where in your process a case unit is right now and pinpoints anything that is blocking progress
Ninja Level: Intermediate

This KPI is not so much a numerical measurement as it is a bird's-eye view of where a Case Unit is in your process. It's more of a GPS than a calculator, but it's no less important. While law firms handle different kinds of cases in different ways, all cases have in common a left-to-right motion from a matter being merely a prospect to that matter being a finished, completed case. Tracking where that matter is in your process, whatever your process may be, is absolutely critical. We've written already (and will write more, don't worry) about the importance of shortening Cycle Time. We'll talk more in Chapter 10 about the enemies of short Cycle Times—constraints—and what to do about them. For now, know this: You need to be tracking where a Case Unit is in your process.

SPEED KPIs

KPI: Throughput Rate
Monitoring Frequency: Weekly
Importance Level: Critical
Why It's Important: Together with Average Case Unit Value, determines Income
Ninja Level: Easy

As we've discussed at length, improving Throughput Rate is likely the single most important thing you can do to become more profitable. So of course we have to measure it. Fortunately, doing so could hardly be simpler.

Once you have determined the end point of your system (case done, money in the bank), you simply note the date upon which that end is reached. We can note this in a spreadsheet. Even easier, most Kanban software programs can track this automatically. As long as we know when a Case Unit has crossed the finish line, it is easy to pick a time frame (e.g., a year) and see how many cases crossed it in a given length of time. If 100 Case Units conclude in a year, for example, our Throughput Rate is 100 per year.

Whether that's a good Throughput Rate number or not is relative; the real reason we measure Throughput Rate is to see if we are increasing it over time. If we are, we know we're headed in the right direction.

KPI: Average Cycle Time
Monitoring Frequency: Weekly
Importance Level: Critical
Why It's Important: Under Little's Law, together with WIP, determines Throughput Rate
Ninja Level: Intermediate

Remember that Cycle Time is simply the amount of time that a given Case Unit spends between the start (taken in as a client) and finish (money in the bank) of your process. Measuring is not difficult because you simply need to note and track the start and finish dates of all of your Case Units and figure out how much time in days each takes to complete. When you have enough cases, you can add all the time together and divide by the number of cases to get an average. It's not difficult, but it can be cumbersome to keep up with. Fortunately, most Kanban software has features or add-ins that will handle this calculation for you so that you can watch the trend. Remember that shorter Cycle Times lead to greater Throughput Rate. If your average Cycle Time is decreasing, that's a clue you're doing things right.

Note to Mathletes: If you really want to geek out, remember that if you know any two elements of Little's Law (WIP, Cycle Time, or Throughput Rate), you can always calculate the third.

KPI: Average Reaction Time
Monitoring Frequency: Weekly
Importance Level: Important

Why It's Important: The longer it takes to convert a prospect into a case, the longer the total time it will be in your system.

Ninja Level: Intermediate

Remember that Reaction Time is simply the amount of time it takes between the day a prospect appears on your radar and when that prospect becomes converted into a client (who may have one or more Case Units). Even though this does not figure in to our Throughput Rate calculations, the reality is that every day that passes between meeting prospects and formally representing them slows down your system. It also makes prospects upset to be in limbo. So determine as soon as you can whether you will take a case, and watch your Reaction Times. If they are getting shorter, that's a good thing.

DEADLINE KPI

KPI: Deadline Tracking

Monitoring Frequency: Weekly

Importance Level: Critical

Why It's Important: Keeps you from committing malpractice and losing clients

Ninja Level: Beginner

Here's another KPI that's not necessarily a traditional KPI, but tracking deadlines is no less important for that fact. Lawyers, maybe more than anyone else, know how important deadlines can be. While you might have gotten away with turning in that term paper on Dante's *Inferno* three days late in eleventh grade, try that on an appellate brief to the Fifth Circuit and see what happens.

You have to track deadlines, and carefully. There are many ways to do that, so instead of rehashing those, we'd rather let you choose for yourself how you want to do that, but with two caveats:

1. **Caveat One: No fake deadlines.** The popularity of Outlook and innumerable other calendaring, organizing, and life-changing apps has given us the ability to never miss an appointment or a deadline. We can schedule everything, and it all syncs up beautifully across devices. The great news is this: We have no excuse for ever missing an appointment with a client or a filing deadline. But the horrible news is: We have no excuse for ever missing an appointment with a client or a filing deadline.

In our experience (Dave's as a lawyer and Larry's as a maker of software for lawyers that—among other things—is designed to track deadlines), the availability of these options has led to two phenomena. First, we've become app junkies, thinking each new one is going to change our lives and make everything nice and easy; second, since it takes just a few taps and swipes on these apps to schedule a to-do, we've forgotten what a real deadline is. When you characterize everything as a high-priority task with a deadline, it becomes hard to sort out the "real" deadlines.

2. **Caveat Two: Use a two-week radar.** Although we will discuss this more in Chapter 7, one of the keys to meeting deadlines is to see them coming. You need to be ready for them in time to meet them, but not so soon that you obsess over them and allow the time required to meet them to expand, as work has a way of expanding into the time you give yourself to do it (sorry, Mom, but it's true). Meeting with your staff each week and looking two weeks ahead is an excellent way to make sure deadlines are being met and appointments covered while keeping your focus narrow enough to not drive yourself insane.

Depending on your practice, your radar may need to be longer. But whatever your practice, you need a radar.

OTHER KPIs THAT YOU MAY WANT TO TRACK

Our KPIs for Quantity, Position, and Deadlines represent the minimum of things that you need to be tracking, no matter your resources or firm size. There are, of course, many more things that you could track that may prove helpful. The trick is to find the balance between productive tracking and "paralysis by analysis."

KPI: Net Promoter Score (NPS)
Monitoring Frequency: Semiannually or annually
Importance Level: Nice to know
Why It's Important: Gives you a quantitative feedback score from your clients
Ninja Level: Intermediate

If you've ever answered the question "On a scale of 0 to 10, how likely are you to recommend us to a friend or colleague," you've taken part in a Net Promoter survey.

Here's what's happening on the other side of that question. Something called a Net Promoter Score is calculated, and it works as follows: Respondents who give a score of 9 and 10 are promoters. The 7s and 8s are neutral. Those who score 6 and below are detractors. Subtracting the percentage of promoters from the percentage of detractors gives the NPS.

For example, if 55 percent of respondents give a 9 or 10, and 30 percent give 6 and below, the NPS is 25.

The NPS is a great way to see how your clients view your services as their advocate. They are terrific surveys because they are typically quick to fill out, which facilitates responses, and they give you a solid measurement and methodology. Not only that, but surveying your clients and looking for feedback sends a message that their feedback is important to you.

Often the NPS question is accompanied by one other: a free-form text entry that asks reviewers to explain their score. We have found this question to supply us with some of the best feedback we've ever received.

If you are working with ongoing clients, one of the major strategies is to focus on people who scored you 8 and move them to a 9. In fact, some companies completely revolve around the NPS and make it their major KPI. There are entire businesses run on this method, and if you're interested in exploring more, the classic book on NPS is *The Ultimate Question* by Fred Reichheld.

- ✔ **DO:** Put together inexpensive and highly effective NPS surveys using cost-effective tools like SurveyMonkey or PollDaddy.
- ✘ **DON'T:** Just conduct an NPS once. Make sure you do it regularly and track your score over time.
- ✘ **DON'T:** Ignore feedback! Some of the most important gems for your business you will ever come across will be from an NPS survey.

STAFF-RELATED KPIs

KPIs related to staff productivity, as the politically incorrect expression goes, separate the men from the boys and the women from the girls. While this really only starts to matter to firms with more personnel, the ones that do track them are Numbers Ninjas, and they have an insight into their businesses that their Anti-Numbite peers do not. They have a competitive edge because they are aware of who produces and who does not, and they can use these reports to incentivize work by offering performance bonuses.

Note: These KPIs may seem alien to the solo attorney who does not employ staff, but once you have more than two or three attorneys in a practice, they provide deep insights into who's a superstar and who's just chugging along.

KPI: Utilization Rate
Monitoring Frequency: Monthly
Importance Level: Depending on firm size and fee structure, Important
Why It's Important: Reveals how closely attorneys are tracking against their target billable hours
Ninja Level: Advanced

This one applies mainly to hourly billing firms. The Utilization Rate is a measure of how closely a timekeeper is tracking against target hours. Staff members with a high utilization are more likely to hit their (and consequently, the law firm's) goals than those with a lower Utilization Rate.

Utilization is simply the number of billable hours in a given period (even if something was no-charged as a courtesy) divided by target hours for that period.

For example, let's say your associates, Alice and Bob, are supposed to bill 1,500 hours per year, or 125 per month. In January, Alice performed 125 hours of billable work, and Bob tracked 110 hours. Alice would have a Utilization Rate of 125/125 or 100 percent, whereas Bob's rate would be 110/125 or 88 percent.

By being on top of your numbers, you can have a frank conversation with Bob and find out why he's underperforming.

KPI: Individual Collection Percentage
Monitoring Frequency: Monthly
Importance Level: Important, depending on firm size, especially more than three attorneys
Why It's Important: Reveals which employees are the true revenue generators
Ninja Level: Intermediate

Another metric, mainly useful to hourly billers, is ICP. We examined firm-wide collections previously, but once you have multiple attorneys responsible for bringing in their own clients, you need to know exactly how much revenue they are responsible for. Timekeeping metrics like realization and utilization are important, but ultimately, what we're really interested in is the money coming in.

What's preferable: an associate who works for 100 hours and gets paid for 71 hours, or one who works for 80 hours and gets paid for 72 of them? Lawyers tend to fall into the former group, while it's clearly more beneficial to be in the latter.

A lawyer's ability to collect is affected by many factors: dealing with quality clients, possessing an ability to talk frankly about financial issues, and effectively delegating collection activities to administrative staff. Some staff will be better than others, and you need to know who is weak and who is strong.

If possible, track on an individual basis the amount invoiced for your open matters against the amount collected. For example, let's say Alice sent an invoice of $2,500 to her client and collected $0. Her collection percentage would be 0 percent. Bob, on the other hand, sent an invoice for $8,500 and collected $4,000. His collection percentage is 47 percent. Better, but not eye-popping.

Both Alice and Bob need to be sent to a grueling outdoor wilderness survival training program to get in touch with their collection problems.

- ✗ **DON'T:** Simply evaluate staff based on sheer quantity of billable time. It's how the time is used and, ultimately, what is collected that should tell the story of the individual's contribution.
- ✔ **DO:** Remember the soft skills! KPIs related to individuals have a hard time capturing if someone is a cultural fit for your organization or not.

KPI: Origination by Individual

Monitoring Frequency: Quarterly

Importance Level: Important, depending on firm size, especially more than three attorneys

Why It's Important: Reveals with numerical certainty which individuals are bringing in the most business

Ninja Level: Advanced

In most businesses, you have a marketing team, a sales team, and other differentiated roles separated from the service or product the consumer seeks. Most law firms and professional service firms in general do not function like this; it's typically up to the service providers themselves to "make it rain."

In such a situation, it's critical to have hard data to understand which individuals are originating new business. This is where numbers are great.

They slay egos. The cold, hard facts will reveal if those who have the reputation for rainmaking deserve the title. It's also critical to be able to pull these numbers up quickly to be able to cut bonus checks without spending two full days on calculations.

An origination report should break down the firm person by person, and it should reveal how many dollars have been both invoiced *and* collected for the matters each person brought in.

Let's revisit Alice and Bob, newly back from a remote section of the Rocky Mountains. We should be able to see for each of them:

> Which matters they each originated
> How much total has been invoiced across those matters
> How much has been collected across those same matters

A NON-SCARY LOOK AT FINANCIAL STATEMENTS FOR ANTI-NUMBITES

If you're an Anti-Numbite, you've probably run screaming from your financial reports. Now is the time to face your fears: If you're running a business and not a hobby, you simply have to know this stuff. You or a financial professional can easily generate these statements through your accounting application.

Generally, you should look at these on a monthly, quarterly, and annual basis and compare them to the same time period last year as well as the period immediately previous. For example, when you're looking at your January 2017 numbers, you should compare them to the month directly preceding it (December 2016) and the same month of the previous year (January 2016).

The big three financial statements you need to become familiar with are:
1. The Statement of Cash Flow (SOCF)
2. The Income Statement (a.k.a. Profit and Loss Statement)
3. The Balance Sheet

Statement of Cash Flow
Monitoring Frequency: Monthly, quarterly, annually
Why It's Important: Tells you if you've made or lost cash during a given time period
Ninja Level: Intermediate

This paragraph is very important, so reread it ten times if you have to. Your cash flow is defined as the difference between your cash position at the beginning of a period and the position at the end of the same period. A positive cash flow reflects an *increase* in liquid cash for the business, whereas a negative cash flow indicates a *decrease* in available cash.

There are a lot of line items on the SOCF, but you can go to the most important nuggets:

> Cash at beginning of period
> Cash at end of period
> Net cash change for period

Income Statement (Profit and Loss)
Monitoring Frequency: Monthly, quarterly, annually
Why It's Important: Lets you see if revenue is growing or shrinking and if you're profitable or not
Ninja Level: Intermediate

For Anti-Numbites, this is the easiest statement to read. A grossly oversimplified, yet effective, way to analyze your Income Statement is to look at two line items:

> Total Income
> Net Income

Total Income is also referred to as your top line or revenue. It's the sum total of all money coming in. Net Income is also referred to as your bottom line; it is how much money is left over after you factor out what you spend money on.

It's critical to take a look at your Income Statement every month. Every quarter, you should take a look at it against the previous year and quarter.

There's obviously a lot more to this, but our aim is to get you started. There's a lot of valuable information in the Income Statement that you can use to understand the health of your business. As you become more comfortable, it's worth spending time to understand your cost of goods sold, your gross margin, and your expenses.

Balance Sheet
Monitoring Frequency: Monthly, quarterly, annually

Why It's Important: Helps you keep track of what the company owes and owns

Ninja Level: Intermediate

The Balance Sheet is a snapshot in time that shows you your assets versus your liabilities and shareholder equity. This is where the Anti-Numbites quake in their boots. Liabilities can mean debt, like a bank loan, but they can also refer to balance payments you have to make on large bills or other financial machinations.

This is another super-simplification, but the two most informative things to look for on your Balance Sheet are:

> Total Assets
> Total Liability

Your Total Assets are everything you own of economic value, such as cash or anything owned in the firm's name. Your Total Liability refers to all of your financial obligations. Assets and liabilities are broken down into different types. A detailed discussion is beyond the scope of this book, but it is worth studying more. Not to insinuate anything, but *Small Business for Dummies* is actually a great resource that goes into greater depth, and the corresponding website (http://www.dummies.com/business/accounting/) is terrific.

To get started, the most important thing for you to understand is that you want to look for a healthy relationship between your assets and liabilities. You want to make sure you can meet whatever obligations you have.

TRACKING AND BUILDING DASHBOARDS

For KPIs, the first thing you need to do is accurately generate the data that you need. Financial software and legal practice management programs can help you there. Once you generate the data, we recommend tracking it over time and displaying it.

The easiest way to get started tracking KPIs is with Excel. Spreadsheets are perfect for tracking data like this over time; not only do they store the data in a nice, rectangular format, but you can also calculate ratios easily. For example, in our discussion of leads and new clients, you can create a line item that expresses your conversion percentage, which then can be tracked over time.

To get you started, we've created a sample Excel file that you can use to track your KPIs over time. It's available on our website, leanlawfirmbook.com.

Another tool you might consider is "business intelligence" software specifically designed for KPIs. Not only do these programs track the data, but they build beautiful dashboards that sum up trends nicely. You could even harness your inner software-startup mojo and display them on wall-mounted monitors in your office. We would recommend this for round two, as it may be a little ambitious to set them up at the start.

A very straightforward choice might be SimpleKPI, a basic, low-cost tool. You may also want to consider Geckoboard or Dasheroo.

Law firms may want to seriously consider time and billing and/or accounting software that automatically generates many of these KPIs. Once you're well versed in understanding what it is you want to see, these programs can automate the data gathering.

NEXT STEPS

If you really want to clear the fog and get a handle on your business, start looking at your KPIs. It's easy to be intimidated, especially if you're an Anti-Numbite. We recommend starting small. Get an Excel spreadsheet going, track two or three KPIs to start, and each quarter add two or three more.

CHAPTER SUMMARY

A handle on numbers is critical for running a Lean law firm. Numbers allow you to avoid ego-driven arguments by providing cold, hard facts. They help you to see your business from an objective perspective and direct your attention to what you need to focus on.

Firmwide KPIs

KPI	Monitoring Frequency	Why It's Important
Cash Quantity	Daily	Helps you focus on the number-one resource for your business
Cash Pipeline	At least weekly	Tells you what you have coming in
Firm Collection Percentage	Monthly	Shows you what percent of your invoices you are collecting

Inventory (WIP)	Weekly	Tells you the load on your system and operates as "throttle" for Throughput Rate; one of the elements of Little's Law
Average Case Unit Value (ACUV)	Quarterly	Together with Throughput Rate, determines your Income; shows you what niches to focus on
Average Net Case Unit Value	Quarterly	Shows you which niches, practice areas are most profitable, and what to focus on
New Leads per Month	Monthly	Serves as a leading indicator for future business and keeps marketing accountable
New Clients per Month	Monthly	Indicates ongoing health of business and helps with seasonal and year-over-year trend spotting
Stage/Kanban	Daily	Shows you where every Case Unit is in your system
Throughput Rate	Weekly	Together with Average Case Unit Value, determines your income
Average Cycle Time	Weekly	Determines Throughput Rate; one of the elements of Little's Law
Average Reaction Time	Weekly	Tells you how fast you are converting prospects to clients
Deadlines	Daily	Keeps you from committing malpractice
Net Promoter Score	Semiannually or annually	Gives you a quantitative feedback score from your clients

Individual KPIs

KPI	Monitoring Frequency	Why It's Important
Utilization Rate	Monthly	Reveals how closely attorneys are tracking against their target billable hours
Individual Collection Percentage	Monthly	Reveals which employees are the true revenue generators
Origination by Individual	Quarterly	Reveals with numerical certainty which individuals are bringing in the most business

In addition, it's important to scan your big three financial statements—Statement of Cash Flows, Income Statement, and Balance Sheet—on a monthly, quarterly, and annual basis.

CHAPTER 5

Systems Thinking 2
Bringing Your System to Life

May

Carson stood next to his semi-obsolete racing bike in his cycling clothes on a street at the edge of the park. It was good to get back on the bike. But he wondered why Guy had wanted to meet for their "lesson" way out here.

Although his methods were certainly unorthodox, Guy had given Carson a lot to think about lately. On the positive side, he was finally starting to see the firm as a

system, and a pretty simple one at that: All the Gray Firm (or any firm) really did was take a potential client with a certain kind of problem and, by solving that problem in the best and quickest way possible, earn a fee. It was very simple.

On the negative side, what he saw at the Gray Firm when he looked at it through this system lens wasn't very flattering: They did not have as many prospective clients as they needed for new work, and calls and e-mails from people contacting the firm were not being returned promptly. Frankly, a lot of prospects, even good ones, got tired of waiting and simply went to the next lawyer in their web search. The firm's Reaction Time (and conversion rate) was, frankly, terrible.

Worse still, Carson could see in his position and Cycle Time measurements that, after converting the prospective client to an actual client with a signed fee agreement, the Gray Firm had a tendency to let the new matter languish without any progress or any filing to begin the litigation. Sometimes that was necessary in a personal injury case when the client was still undergoing medical treatment. But many times it was not. At any rate, the habit of letting new cases lie around was entrenched. Carson had never seen the firm miss filing in time to beat the statute of limitations, but he had seen some close calls. He had seen and talked to some clients who were upset about the lack of movement on their cases. He didn't have any great answer for these clients. He couldn't really tell them they were in a "rebuilding year." He hoped that the firm would not be grievanced, but it was a definite possibility. He knew some of these clients were already looking for another lawyer.

The quantity measurements were also not encouraging. When Carson checked Cash Quantity, which he did daily, there was not much. When he looked to the Cash Pipeline, things were not a whole lot better. It was the same with the other Key Performance Indicators (KPIs) that he was able to check just a few months into the year. But at least now he was finally getting a realistic picture of what was going on at the Gray Firm.

Carson had a lot of questions for Guy this morning. But where the heck was he?

Behind him, Carson heard the unmistakably familiar sound of thin tires moving fast on asphalt. Guy and five C^2 Team cyclists, each wearing a different colored jersey, pulled up.

"Carson!" shouted Guy. "Great to see you on a bike again."

"It's been a long time since I've been sitting on anything other than a desk chair on Saturday mornings," admitted Carson. "I'm afraid I'm not in the best of shape. Not good enough to ride with these guys, anyway," Carson said, gesturing to the five thin, fit cyclists flanking Guy.

"No worries, my boy," replied Guy. "They are here for illustrative purposes only. You don't have to race them. Good thing, too," Guy said, looking toward Carson's stomach.

"Hey! Quit that, Guy," said Carson. "So, what's the lesson?"

"A visual demonstration," replied Guy. "OK, gentlemen," he said, gesturing to his team members. "Line up like I told you and put your nametags on."

The five cyclists formed a line from Carson's left to his right and put stick-on nametags on the middle of their jerseys:

P, Q, F, W, D

Guy pedaled over to rider P and, to the rider's left, placed a green start flag. Then he pedaled to the end of the line and placed a black checkered finish flag on the right side of rider D.

"Let's go back to our Income Formula," said Guy. "Remember: Throughput Rate × Average Value per Unit. Like we discussed, we have only some control over Value, and we'll talk about that next month. On the other hand, we have much more control over Throughput Rate—particularly by decreasing Cycle Time—so that's our focus today.

"Now, Carson," continued Guy, "what are the things that slow down Cycle Time? Say you get a new case in the door today. What prevents you from getting that case from start to finish by tomorrow?"

Carson laughed out loud. "You sure don't understand anything about how our legal system works, Guy. The whole system is based on deadlines. Let's say I get a brand new car wreck case in the door today. Even if I filed suit ten seconds after the client signed the fee agreement, I'd still have to serve it on the defendant, who would have 30 days to answer it. So, no way that could ever happen, assuming a case has to be brought."

"Actually, I do understand that, Carson. What you're talking about is an external constraint. Something outside of your control that dictates how fast you can move from start to finish. To continue your car wreck case model, another example of something blocking progress might be that the client would need to complete her medical treatment."

Carson looked nonplussed. "So are you saying that I should settle clients' cases out quick and cheap so we can be more profitable, then? Like I said before, I don't work that way. Ambrose sure as heck doesn't."

"Not at all," said Guy. "Have you ever seen me build a crummy bike on the cheap just to book a sale and get it out the door?"

"No. Never," said Carson.

"I'm not talking about trying to do an end run around the external constraints. In fact, you can actually use some of those external constraints to your advantage through something called 'pull' or As Late as Possible (ASLAP) scheduling. In the meantime, I'd like you to turn your focus to your internal process."

Guy turned to face the five cyclists forming a line from left to right, P, Q, F, W, and D. Guy said, "I've taken the liberty of mapping out your business process for you. This is an obvious oversimplification, so feel free to change this as you want. The important thing is the concept of mapping your process as a left-to-right, start-to-finish system. Here's what the letters stand for:

P—Prospects
Q—Queue
F—Filed
W—Waiting
D—Done

Guy explained, "Prospects. They are your raw material. People with problems who may need a lawyer and may have a case. Somehow they get in touch with you. If you can't help them, you may be able to refer them to someone who can, which has its own value both to the prospect and to the lawyer to whom you've referred them. But, if they have a case you can help them with, they are converted into clients. Either way, you want to decide one way or the other. You don't want to leave them hanging in the 'maybe' category. It's not fair to them. Plus, if you end up taking the case, all those days matter because they increase your Reaction Time. While we don't use Reaction Time in our Throughput Rate formula, anything you can do to decrease the time from when you first meet the client to when you finish his case increases income."

Guy continued, "Now, if your prospect becomes a client, she enters your Queue. The Queue is the place where you begin to track the cases you've taken in but have not yet started. It starts your Cycle Time clock running. It's also one of the places where lawyers get into trouble. Because what is never started or moved past the Queue can never be finished. It's a traditional sticking point for almost any business. New cases, orders, projects pile up here, waiting to be started, but they don't yet seem urgent because you're putting out fires elsewhere. So they sit much too long before getting into the heart of the system."

"The 30-day deadline to answer a complaint—what you called an 'external constraint,'" said Carson, starting to understand. "That clock can't ever be started until a complaint or claim is filed. So when something is not moved out of Queue quickly, what is really happening is that we are adding days to our Cycle Time." More like months or years in some cases, Carson thought to himself.

"Right," said Guy. "However many days it sits there get added to your Cycle Time. And, of course, that slows Throughput Rate, which hurts Income. So the Queue is a place you really want to pay attention to. Although there are certainly times when you may want to intentionally keep something in Queue to limit the amount of Case Units, that is, Inventory, entering your system. Remember, with Inventory—Work in Process, or WIP—you're looking for that sweet spot where Throughput Rate is fastest. But in general, you want to be able to get things out of Queue and into what I've simplistically called Filed as quickly as you possibly can, external constraints like medical treatment aside."

Guy continued, "Next, you have what I call Filed. It's maybe not the best name; I'm not a lawyer. In my factory we call it Production 1. It's where things from my Queue—a signed paper order for bikes—go into actual production. For you, it would be bringing some kind of claim, or taking some affirmative initial action to move the case out of Queue and get things going. And Filed for you would probably include several subprocesses or subsystems, like phases of discovery. But the takeaway for now is: Unless you have too much Inventory in process, move the case out of Queue. Don't let it sit."

Guy concluded, "Next we have W—Waiting. Another oversimplification. But indulge me for a moment. What are the ways that the cases you take can end, Carson?"

"Well," said Carson. "We can take it to trial and win it; we can lose at trial or along the way, or we can settle it."

"Which happens most?" asked Guy.

"Most cases will settle," said Carson.

"And when they do, you've moved them from Filed to Waiting. Why do I call this Waiting? Because you're still not really done, right? The settlement has to be completed. Tax forms exchanged, maybe. A written agreement. Oh yeah, and actually getting the money. That matters, too!" laughed Guy.

Guy continued, "I include this as a category because years ago I noticed in my own business that things had a tendency to bog down here. I would complete an order and mentally check it off the list, thinking I was all done. But three weeks later, I noticed we still hadn't shipped it. Or more typically, 90 days later, I'd notice we still had not gotten paid for it. I finally realized that this waiting was actually part of my production process, and it was part of what was slowing down Throughput Rate by adding days (or weeks) to Cycle Time. Part of the reason we are in business is to make money, after all. So until you actually have the money and the client or customer considers the case or order done, you are never really at the end. I actually began tracking things in this category, to make sure everything I could do was being done to push it toward the finish line."

Carson had never really thought of settlements dragging out like this, but it was certainly true. It was also true that what you were really doing when you settled a case was shortening Cycle Time, although no one really thought of it in those terms. He asked Guy, "What about cases that go to trial?"

Guy replied, "Well, if you win, you'd still want to track the money and make sure you were doing everything possible to get it as promptly as possible. For you, though, I would include in Waiting cases that are 100 percent ready for trial but are simply waiting on being tried. Because (and I know you lawyers love to procrastinate) sometimes you can get that trial scheduled sooner rather than later. Not only would that shorten your Cycle Time, but I would imagine that might give you a tactical advantage over the lawyer opposing you, assuming he's the typical procrastinator. Which might have the collateral positive effect of increasing the value of the case.

"Now Carson," said Guy. "Let's talk about how to optimize Cycle Time. Remember we talked about cyclists riding in a time trial? The goal is simple, to get from point A to point B as fast as humanly possible. How does a time trial team do that? How do they position themselves?"

Carson had ridden on time trial teams many times. "In a line. As close together as possible."

"Like this?" said Guy, signaling to the cyclists, who moved out to ride together down the road circling the park. As they picked up speed, the five riders, P, Q, F, W, and D, packed in tightly, moving in a taut line.

<—P-Q-F-W-D-<

"Let's say one lap of the park represents Throughput. The beginning of the case to the end of the case; we'll use the flags I placed for start and finish markers. What two things determine how fast they can go?"

Carson thought about that for a minute as he watched the riders leave the start line as a pack and watched their speed increase. A time trial team was only as fast as its slowest rider because they had to finish as a team. For that reason—and because a tight line allowed each rider behind the leader to cheat the wind by riding in a slipstream—the riders had to stay close.

Carson answered, "Well, first, there can be no gaps between riders."

"Right," said Guy, signaling to the team as it completed its first lap. At his command the F rider, third from the front, began to slow, allowing a gap to open between F and Q, in front of him. Guy elaborated, "Say this gap represents time. When you allow something to sit in Queue without taking action, you're opening up a gap just like this.

<—P-Q————————F-W-D<

"And what happens then?" Guy queried, as they watched the riders struggle around another lap, much slower than they had the first time.

Carson answered, "The whole thing slows down. Throughput Rate gets slower as Cycle Time increases. And, under your formula, that means Income must go down."

"Correct," said Guy. "And that gap represents WNR, 'Waiting for No Reason,' Time in a system. Any Wait Time will slow our Cycle Time, but the worst kind is like this, where nothing is blocking or slowing the next step, but a unit nevertheless languishes because it doesn't seem urgent. Note that I'm not talking here about our 'W' Waiting stage right before the case is finished. Here I'm talking about the kind of languishing that can happen at any stage of the system. And few things are more urgent than dealing with cases that are not blocked, but just waiting around to be acted upon, no matter what stage they are in."

Guy continued, "So, we know Wait Time is the first thing that dictates Cycle Time. Let's talk about the second thing that determines Cycle Time. Here, this will help you." Guy signaled again and the riders moved back into a tight line, all gaps disappearing. Then, Guy signaled a second time and the lead rider, P, began to slow his pace. While the line stayed nice and tight, the team's speed around the park slowed to almost a crawl.

……..P-Q-F-W-D-<

The answer was obvious to Carson now. "The team can only move as fast as the slowest rider. So, the second thing that determines Cycle Time is the speed of each individual part of the process."

"Yes," said Guy. "That's right. Just like a team is as fast as the slowest rider, a system is only as fast as its slowest part. Systemically, that slow part is a constraint; we can improve that constraint to make it faster. If not, though, or if we overburden it with too much WIP at once, it will still become a sticking point that turns into a bottleneck as the faster-moving units behind it start to pile up.

"So, wrapping it up and making it relevant for your firm: To make more money, you need to increase Throughput Rate. The main way you do that is to decrease Cycle Time. You accept external constraints that you cannot change, but you do not allow gaps—or Wait Time, especially WNR Time—to form between the parts. You relentlessly hunt down and optimize the constraints that cause Wait Time, and you locate languishing-for-no-good-reason cases accumulating WNR Time. Then you make each part move as fast as possible so that, when you are actively working on a case, your work gets done quickly and you can move on to another one. Now, understand you will never get rid of constraints (or Wait Time) entirely—it's an optimizing process. And each time you find a constraint, another will crop up. But this process, repeated over time, will make your Throughput much, much faster, and thus you will become more profitable."

"I get it," said Carson. "So, for example, if we can shorten the gap between Queue and Filing from 30 days to five, we shorten Cycle Time by 25 days. And on a micro level, if we can shorten the time it takes to draft a complaint, say, from three hours to 30 minutes, we've made an individual part faster. We work to find and eliminate sticking points in the system as a whole, and one of the ways we fix those is to improve the speed of each individual part."

"Right," said Guy. "What you're really doing when you improve something like complaint drafting is spending less time working on each part of the case. And, by lowering the time requirement for 'chokepoint' things like drafting and filing the complaint, you've made it that much easier to get something out of the Queue and to the next step. It's all interrelated. Think of the individual parts like riders and their bikes. You can improve the fitness of the rider. You can shave a few ounces off the weight of the pedals. You can improve the aerodynamics of the helmet. There are endless opportunities to improve. Just like a law practice. There are a lot of parts that go into a case. That translates into lots of opportunities to improve. If you can make even incremental reductions in the time you spend actively working on each part of the case, you speed your process as a whole. When you focus on making these improvements in the individual activities that constrain the overall process, you not only improve the speed of that activity, but you also reduce the waiting time for all the other cases waiting for that same activity. You're directing your firepower where it's most needed. With time and repetition, each improvement pays back many times over."

Carson now understood it, theoretically, but he did not quite get how to execute the two goals that had now materialized: reducing Wait Time and making each constraining activity move faster. "How do I do all of this, Guy?"

"Simple," said Guy. "**We find the internal constraints, prioritize our system to address those first, then we optimize each constrained activity through standardization, written processes, and technology.**"

"Simple?" repeated Carson.

"Simple," confirmed Guy. "But not easy. Come on, let's ride over to the coffee shop now and we can talk more."

In Chapter 4, we showed you how to measure Cycle Time, WIP, and Throughput Rate (among other KPIs). You now know the components of the system and how to measure them. But how to put it all together? That's what we'll show you in this chapter. First, we'll talk about the *conceptual layout* of your system. Second, we'll show you how to *visualize* and map your system in real time. Third, we'll talk about how to *operate* your system on a daily basis. Finally, although systems operation is mainly about optimizing Throughput Rate, we'll discuss briefly how to *optimize WIP* (and Average Case Unit Value, too) and point you to the other places in this book that discuss in depth the ways to optimize those components. By the end of this chapter, you'll see how it all fits together.

CONCEPTUALIZING YOUR SYSTEM

Throughout this book, we've asked you to make a fundamental conceptual shift: to stop thinking of your practice as a disparate collection of deadlines, responsibilities, and processes and to start seeing it as the system that it really is. But if your practice is (or should be) a system, what would it actually look like?

The System Runs Left to Right

Our starting point is, again, the idea that what we're really doing is acquiring Raw Material (A) and putting it through a Process (B) from which comes Money (C). In simplest terms, our system looks like this:

A ⟶ B ⟶ C

For whatever reason, we in the Western world tend to think left to right. We read that way. And when we make timelines, the past is on the left, the future on the right. Some researchers even suggest that when we're trying to remember something, our eyes naturally move to our left, and when we are imagining the future they go right. Weird, huh? At any rate, we're hardwired to think left to right. So when we visualize our system, it's going to run left to right, too. We always start on the left and finish on the right.

The System Is Linear

Remember how Guy had his cyclists ride in a line (P-Q-F-W-D) to illustrate Carson's business process? That's because our system is, in fact, linear. Moving the case to the end involves completing a series of steps. Many of these steps involve "dependencies" in that they cannot be started until the step before is complete (e.g., you can't generally engage in discovery until you've commenced the action by filing a complaint). In litigation, these steps and their order are often dictated by ethical and procedural rules. In transactional work, they may be determined by informational steps (e.g., a final deed cannot be drafted until a survey is complete).

While the steps represented by Guy's riders are a bit of an oversimplification, his concept is solid. Our raw material (prospect) enters the system on the left, becomes converted into a client or case, and waits in Queue until some affirmative step is taken to move it out of the Queue (such as filing a complaint). This is true whether you are a small firm lawyer hustling up your own cases or you are an insurance defense lawyer upon whose desk new cases simply appear; at some point, that insurance company was merely a prospective client of your firm.

After being started in some way, the case goes through some kind of "middle" process. Guy, a nonlawyer, called this middle phase Filed because from what he knew of Carson's plaintiff's practice, cases could be moved out of Queue only by the initiation of some kind of claim or suit. Most litigators would recognize that Filed actually involves several subphases (discovery, mediation, etc.) that occur up to and including trial—even though many or most cases will exit the system before trial via settlement. For transactional lawyers, the middle includes everything that must be done to bring the deal to a successful close. While details of the middle differ, there is always a middle. And, as we will soon see, the middle (whatever that means for you) is the phase most affected by all kinds of external constraints outside of our control, including deadlines and waiting periods required by court rules.

After the middle—and much more subject to our control—is what Guy calls Waiting. As Guy recognized, there is a big difference between "almost done" and "really done." Here's a simple rule of thumb: Nothing is done until the case is actually complete and *the money is in the bank*. For lawyers working on a contingency basis, this twilight category can be a Cycle Time killer because we have a tendency to think of cases as done when they are merely settled or otherwise resolved. By letting settled cases drift without pushing to a real conclusion, you add Cycle Time, which decreases Throughput Rate, which, we know from our formula, reduces Income. While the opposition's checkbook may not be in your control, nearly everything necessary to get that check (tax forms, completed settlement agreement, etc.) *is* in your control. When you prioritize the Waiting category to make sure that the other side (or your own client) has everything it needs to issue a check, you are making yourself more profitable.

When the money is in the bank and the case fully concluded, you are finally at the Done stage. Whew. There are more elements to your system than our admittedly oversimplified PQFWD categories, and we'll get to those momentarily. Before adding these details, though, we need to move from concept to a real-time visualization of your system.

VISUALIZING YOUR SYSTEM

Having conceptualized your system as a left-to-right, linear system is only the first step; before you can actually operate and use this system, you have to be able to "see" it. And there's no better way to do that than with a Kanban board.

Enter the Kanban

In Chapter 2, Guy recounted to Carson how he'd first seen Kanban boards on the factory floor when working at Miyoto in the 1970s. Kanban is indeed a Japanese concept and loosely translated means "card you can see." Toyota generally gets the credit for being the first to use a Kanban system in its factories.

The power of the Kanban board comes from its ability to convey to workers vast amounts of information visually. So, rather than spend words describing it here, let's start by looking at a snapshot of one on the next page.

Three things become immediately obvious when we look at this Kanban. First, we see that the system is organized left to right. Second, we see that, as with Guy's riders, each category (or macrostep) gets its own column. Third, we can see that each case is represented by a "card" on the board.

The beauty of this system starts with its simplicity. A worker can tell at a glance exactly which step of the process the case is in. And when that step is

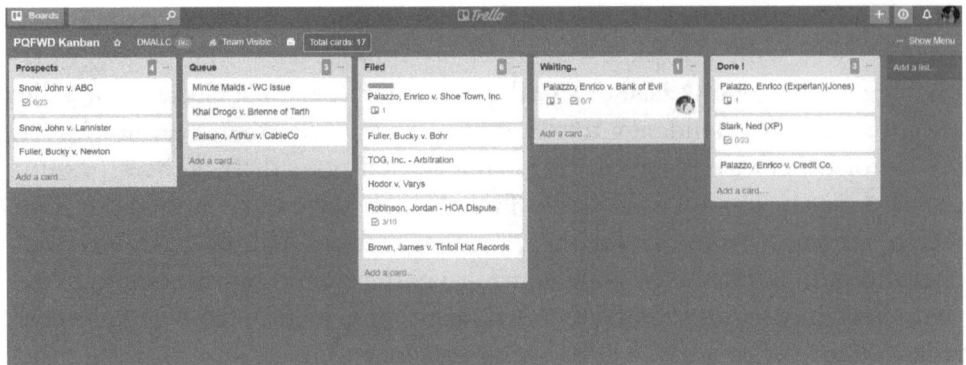

complete, the worker can simply move the card to the next step. The worker can also see how many cases are in process at once (WIP) and can even spot where in the process cases are piling up, indicating a bottleneck is occurring as cards "stack up" behind a particular process. WNR Time shows up as a card "ages" on the board.

These are just the basics, of course. What you can't see in this snapshot is the fact that this board is dynamic. It's continually updated, in real time, and is always accessible to every worker. When Toyota introduced the first Kanban systems, it relied on huge boards on factory walls visible to all the workers on the floor. In the digital age, we don't need to do that. As we will talk about more in Chapter 9, we can put the Kanban right in the office of every firm member with collaborative software, such as Trello. More than that, we can customize it to fit our process and give that worker specific instructions.

For now, realize that this represents just one option (a software one at that) for creating a Kanban board to visualize your system. While you could do this on a whiteboard, we don't recommend that. You'll lose the "real time, available to everyone all the time" advantages that only software can provide. We'll talk more about your tech options for Kanbans in later chapters.

WHAT GOES IN THE MIDDLE? VALUE STREAM MAPPING

In our conceptual model, things move left to right, from Raw Material to finished product for which the money is in the bank. Our real-time visualization, the Kanban board, reflects this, with our example steps (P-Q-F-W-D) appearing left to right. It's easy to see from our example, moreover, how Queue and Waiting can slow down Cycle Time (and consequently decrease

Throughput Rate): If a case can't get out of Queue and into the heart of the system, it can never be finished; likewise, if the case hangs up in Waiting it cannot be finished, either. But that still leaves everything that happens in the middle, which, in our oversimplified example, we've represented as Filed. Clearly, the middle encompasses all the steps needed to move the case forward. But what should those steps be?

First of all, realize that the middle is unique to your practice, so we cannot presume to give you universal process steps that will work for every firm (hence our oversimplified Filed category). What we *can* help you with is how to find them yourself.

One of the core steps of Lean thinking is the idea of a "value stream," that is, the series of events that take a product from beginning to the end customer. In factories like Toyota, managers do something known as "gemba walking," meaning that they walk the factory floor where the real work is done to understand each step of the process. What they are trying to determine in this exercise is which actions add value to the end product and which do not. Actions that do not add value are wasteful, and thus are abandoned. The remaining actions are studied to determine the ideal order in which they should take place.

You can take the same walk through your firm (at least mentally). First, identify every action currently being taken between the start and finish lines for a case. Next, ask yourself whether that action is adding any value to the bottom line. Returning to our Income Formula (Throughput Rate × Average Case Unit Value), value here is anything that enhances either component. You can enhance Unit Value of an individual case by taking a good deposition, for example. Systemically, things that improve Throughput Rate (by enhancing Inventory or decreasing Cycle Time) are also worth spending your limited time on. Conversely, spending two hours a day on listservs is probably not adding much value to your system.

Determining the steps that go in the middle, then, involves examining your firm's unique processes, figuring out which steps add value in terms of our profitability formula, and then discarding the rest. While a full exploration of value stream mapping is beyond the scope of this book, the main principles are to map your process and identify the steps in it that improve Cycle Time, or add to Case Unit Value, versus the steps that do not (or ones that make things take longer without adding any dollars to the Case Unit Value). Keep and optimize the former; get rid of the latter.

Once you've decided which steps add value and are essential to getting your end result, the next step is to think about the order of these steps through the middle. This involves thinking about which of these middle value-added steps depend on the completion of earlier steps (dependencies).

In litigation, the order is also dictated by the rules. That being said, don't be afraid to challenge traditional law firm assumptions; just because you *can* serve interrogatories, and you traditionally have, does not mean that doing so adds any value to your case. Indeed, taking a corporate deposition without having given the other side a preview through detailed interrogatories may create more value by leaving the deponent less prepared. The point is this: Think about what in *your* area of practice makes *your* cases more valuable, and focus on doing more of those things.

OPERATING INSTRUCTIONS—HOW TO WORK YOUR SYSTEM

So now you've conceptualized and visualized your system. How do you "work" the darn thing? We're going to get very specific about that in a moment. But first, let's talk about the seminal unasked question for a lawyer, "What should you be doing right now?"

For most of us, this question lurks in the back of our minds each day at work. We're busy, sure, but are we doing the right things? Are we really moving anything forward or are we just fighting fires? Worse, are we reflexively answering e-mail because it's familiar and easy? Are we creating Wait Time just by the act of having to take time to figure out what to do next?

Most organizational systems are attempts to solve the question of "what to do now." At worst, traditional calendar- and task list–based systems can overwhelm us by making us think everything is high priority; at best, they can make us more efficient processors of tasks (e.g., the Getting Things Done [GTD] methodology). Rarely, however, can they show us where our limited time should be spent in the way that best serves the goal of the system as a whole.

That's why our macro real-time view of the system is so important—it *shows* us our highest and best use in this moment.

MANAGING BY LOOKING AT SCREENS

The beauty of real-time Kanbans is that we can literally see the constraints and Wait Time (including WNR Time) in the system. We can see where cases are starting to pile up when the number of case "cards" starts to increase behind a step in the process (bottlenecks). We can label and identify external and internal blocks. We can even see Wait Time based on the age of the card. *And what we see, we can fix.* Your job as a systems manager (or participant) is to keep the flow moving. You do this by referencing the Kanban board on your screen and directing your attention to the items that are blocking progress or languishing, and thus slowing down Cycle Time.

If you're confused about this, don't worry. We're going to help you out. We'll give you a list of priorities—where to look first—based on where constraints generally appear in a law firm's system. Then we'll return to our example Kanban board and show you where to look after running through these priorities.

KANBAN PRIORITIES: WHERE TO LOOK (AND WHAT TO DO) FIRST

Priority 1: Deadlines. The first Kanban cards we are going to address are the ones flagged with *short-term* deadlines. While this traditional advice violates our rule of prioritizing complaints, it's a practical reality; as lawyers, we have to respect deadlines. Where we part company with tradition is with two corollaries: first, as we discussed in Chapter 4, it's *critical* to distinguish real deadlines from the fake ones. Fake deadlines and "shoulds" will swamp and ultimately sink your system. Avoid them.

Second corollary—start work on deadline items as late as possible (ASLAP). Taking your mom's advice to start work on that term paper two months in advance might feel responsible, but it's actually a bad idea in a law firm. Why? Because unlike that term paper, you may never need to actually write that brief if the case settles, so any work on it is a waste. Also, work has a way of expanding into the time we give it. While only you know how much time something may take, ignore Mom, and don't start any earlier than necessary. Make only real, short-term deadlines a priority. Get them done, then move on to systems priorities.

Priority 2: Waiting. As we've already discussed, this "finish line" is a traditional place where cases get stuck. Address cases stuck here immediately and aggressively, and do everything you can to push them across the finish line.

Priority 3: Queue. The starting line, Queue, is where your Cycle Time clock starts to run. Things not started will never be finished, so get started. Caveat: This category is the gateway into the middle of your system, your inventory/WIP "control valve." When too much inventory gets into the middle of the system, it can overwhelm resources, increasing Cycle Time and thus slowing Throughput Rate. To the extent that this causes mistakes to increase or quality to suffer, it can hurt value, too. We discussed earlier (and will show you later) how you can make a rough calculation for what your WIP should be. But the real number (the one that minimizes Cycle Times while having adequate inventory to maximize Throughput Rate) is arrived at by experimentation. Once you figure out where this number should be, however, a good rule of thumb is to move a case from Queue only after moving one further up the chain into Done, thus keeping the optimal inventory number relatively constant. So, prioritize this category, but understand that there may be times to choke down on Queue.

Priority 4: Prospects. By prospects we mean people (or companies) with problems who have communicated with you about possible work. We don't mean generalized marketing work. As we discussed in Chapter 4, we use the term Reaction Time to describe the amount of time between initial contact with a prospect and taking her in formally as a client. As with Cycle Time, you want this to be as short as possible. So your goal is to determine, as quickly as you can, whether the prospect should become a client. If so, act quickly. If not, let her know that quickly, too.

Priority 5: Patrolling the middle. Later in the book, we will talk about SWOT analysis. SWOT stands for Strengths, Weaknesses, Opportunities, and Threats. The latter two, Opportunities and Threats, are particularly relevant here as you take on your last, but still very important, priority: the middle of your system. From a systems standpoint, the middle is where deadlines reside (since they are mostly imposed after a case is filed). You've already addressed those as Priority 1, though. So what are you looking for now? Two things: Opportunities and Threats.

What do we mean by Opportunities here? We mean a chance to move the case to the end—right now, generally by settlement. In litigation, these opportunities arise all the time, but use your gut. You will know such an opportunity is present in a case by where it is in your process and the conversations and relationships you have developed with opposing counsel. You know it when you see it. From the client's standpoint, if the settlement is beneficial, we are obliged to explore it. And from a systems standpoint, we know that will cut

Cycle Time, increase Throughput Rate, and (systemically) drive income. So when we see such an opportunity, we mark that case card accordingly so that, when we patrol the middle looking for these Opportunities, we can find them.

Second, we are looking for Threats. And we know that the biggest threats to a system are constraints. That means we look for internal blocks, external blocks, and any kind of WNR Time. As we discussed previously, we can often "see" constraints when cards pile up behind a category. So we put our attention on that category.

In our standardization and technology chapters to follow, we'll dive deeper into the individual card level to show you how to use labels and filters on your Kanban board to more easily identify opportunities and threats.

OPTIMIZING ACTIVE WORK

So now you have some idea of how to see your system and in what order to "work" it. Following these instructions will go a long way in helping you improve your Cycle Time (by cutting Wait Time, including especially WNR Time). In other words, thinking systemically, visualizing your system, and following these instructions will ultimately reduce the time each case is in the system and *not* being actively worked. In concluding this chapter, let's very briefly talk about how to optimize the actual work that you do perform on a case. What do we mean by optimizing? We mean simply that in the times when you're actively working on a case, you're doing it better and faster. While the biggest gains in Throughput Rate will come from reducing Cycle Time through a properly running system (thereby reducing Wait Times), incremental gains in Cycle Time can also be achieved by making each part of the active work move faster.

As we will discuss shortly, making active work move faster depends on two things: standardization and technology. We will cover both of these in their own chapters. As you will see, while standardization and technology help our system by shortening active work times, the real payoff will come in the quality of the product we produce and what that means for Average Case Unit Value.

But before we talk about the best and fastest ways to process your raw material, let's talk about how to get more of it through the right kind of marketing.

CHAPTER 6

Lean Marketing

June

Carson walked to the C² building, deep in thought. Guy's lesson with his time trial team had not been lost on Carson. Over the last month, he had taken Guy's advice to heart. He'd started to see the firm not as a collection of disparate activities, but as a linear system that moved raw material into completed cases. After he'd mapped what that process actually looked like, it became much easier to find gaps (WNR Time) and constraints in the Gray Firm's work. Some of what he had discovered had scared him. Litigation cases the firm had taken in—even with no external constraint like medical treatment holding things up—were taking an average of 13 months from the

date the fee agreement was signed with a client for the claim or case even to be filed. Even cases held up because of treatment or administrative appeals were languishing for months after those things were complete. Every day of delay increased Cycle Time. Not good.

Measurements and process mapping were made more difficult by the fact that the Gray Firm handled so many different kinds of cases—Social Security, worker's compensation, personal injury, employment cases, divorce and custody, bankruptcy, small business—and they were billed in various ways (contingent, hourly, flat, mixed). While he could put all of those different types of cases on the same map as part of the same system, they worked so differently that Carson felt like an air traffic controller watching multitudes of planes of various shapes, speeds, and sizes cross his screen. Guy preached standardization. The sheer number of forms all of these practice areas required made standardization difficult and, indeed, none had really existed at the firm, so he was starting from scratch. And what institutional knowledge there was about how to handle each matter was mostly in Ambrose's head. Also not good.

But what was good, Carson thought as he walked through the busy bike factory, was that he was finding the exact kinds of issues that Guy predicted he would find. If he could find them, he could fix them, just like Guy had in his factory. It was a starting point, if nothing else, and he believed the firm's Throughput Rate was improving. If only he could also improve the number of cases in inventory, and the average value of each one.

Carson walked to Guy's office door and tapped lightly.

Carson found Guy crouched in his office chair, lubricating the chain of a pristine, but clearly older model, metallic silver racing bike.

"What's with the antique?" joked Carson.

"It may be old," laughed Guy. "But I'm old, too, and I bet this bike and I could leave you in our dust. You're looking at the first Tsunami. This is the bike my dad built for me in 1974 when I left for Japan. And it's also the bike that changed everything for my company."

Guy continued, "Remember a few months back when we were talking about the 'dark times' when I was trying to keep the company alive?

One of the last and most important things that I came to understand was that we had to stop trying to be everything to everyone. We were making dozens of models of bikes, everything from tandems to unicycles. Our prices were all over the map. We had to keep up with thousands of components.

"I was just starting to understand how important Throughput Rate was to the business, but improving it meaningfully was next to impossible because there were just too many variables, too many processes. One day, with all of those variables spinning through my head, I felt like I was going to blow. I had to get out of the factory for a while. I hadn't ridden in months, and this bike just sat in the corner of my office gathering dust. So I grabbed it, and I just rode it right out of my office, down the factory floor, and right out the front door. And then I just kept pedaling for miles. I had forgotten how good, how simple a thing it was to just ride. To just *go*. The bike felt as tight and fast as it had 16 years before when my dad gave it to me. I thought, 'Why can't everything be like this?'

"It started to rain. I just kept going. I rode over 150 miles that day. By the time I came back, the rain had stopped and everything was clear: Chaplin Cycle was going to become C-Squared—C^2—from Einstein's formula for the speed of light. I had already had the discussions with my managers about what kind of bike to focus on that I mentioned earlier. But that sealed it. We were going to do one thing only: make bikes that felt as good and fast as the original Tsunami. And not only that, we were going to make great racing bikes that people could actually afford. Even back then you would have to have spent $4,000 for a carbon fiber bike that felt as good as the Tsunami. The Tsunami was made of titanium, not cheap, but cheaper than carbon fiber. It was my dad's design work that made it so pure. I knew if I could translate his design and vision into modern components and an all-titanium frame, I could capture a portion of the market that everyone was ignoring: serious riders who wanted to ride with the big boys but did not have the serious money that took. If I could make a bike for those riders and aspiring riders, I could level the playing field. It just felt like the right thing to do.

"I got back to the factory, called everyone to a meeting, and announced a final decision had been made to change focus to just build the racing bikes. And that we were changing our name (to what, I didn't know yet). Huge resistance as you might imagine. People flipped out. But eventually the employees who stuck with me saw how much easier it was to improve Throughput Rate when you were trying to manufacture a discrete number of things, instead of trying to manufacture everything. Doing less had a direct impact on the Throughput part of our formula almost immediately. I thought that would happen.

"But it was what doing less did for the other parts of the formula—the number of bike orders we got, and the value of each bike we made—that really mattered."

Carson was perplexed. "OK, Guy. I don't get it. How would making *fewer* bikes *increase* the number of bikes you could sell? I get how it could decrease Cycle Time and increase the rate at which you could make the bikes. But it sounds like you're saying that making fewer bikes made the demand for your bikes go up! Seems like it would have the opposite effect. People who wanted unicycles couldn't get them from you anymore. You didn't have mountain bikes to sell anymore. You couldn't sell hundreds of kids' bikes to big-box stores.... How is any of that good?"

"It was tough for me to see that too, at first," agreed Guy. "But then I realized: We could never make kids' bikes for big-box stores any better—and certainly not any cheaper—than our foreign competition. It was not a level playing field. We simply could not compete there, and trying to do so was going to kill us eventually. So we had to find those one or two niches where we had all the advantages. We had to be known for something special and unique. Something that was not simply available anywhere. Something we could credibly show we were the best at. That's how you build a brand."

Guy turned the question to Carson. "What kinds of cases does the Gray Firm handle these days?"

Carson replied, "Well, a bit of everything. Social Security, workers' compensation, personal injury, employment cases, divorce and custody, bankruptcy, small business formations, ERISA. Pretty much anything that comes in the door. We can't afford to be turning people away right now."

Guy countered, "What you can't afford is to keep doing what you're doing now. I'm not saying you make the transition all at once. It has to be a process. But you have to find what the Gray Firm is—or can be—great at, not merely OK. And that has to coincide with an existing and underserved market. The ideal overlap lies at the intersection of that underserved market, your reputation or 'brand,' what you love to do, and what you believe can be handled profitably. Underserved market + brand + passion = profit.

"So back to your question: How can finding your niche actually increase the number of cases you have?" Guy explained, "It's because you become the 'go-to' lawyers for people who need the service that you can provide better than anyone. You start to pull in clients from a wider geographic area. Your marketing efforts become focused on that 'one thing' that you do well, and that makes you easier to find for people who need that one thing. Prospects improve, too, because they start filtering themselves. If, for example, you decided to focus only on bankruptcy cases, you wouldn't have to talk to people about child custody cases anymore. You could send those on to a lawyer who practices in that niche, who, in return, would likely send you bankruptcy cases.

"See," said Guy, "making fewer types of things, but making those things very well, improves demand for them. That's because by focusing entirely on your chosen niche, you differentiate yourself in the market. You're not competing against all the other generalists anymore. Demand also improves because, by focusing your efforts on *that* niche, you become the 'authority' within it. That not only increases the demand for your product by attracting *more* prospective clients, but it also improves the average value of each case by attracting clients with good cases who want the best lawyer they can get."

"Why's that?" asked Carson.

"Supply and demand," said Guy. "If people think you're the best, they'll pay more for you. If you owned a classic Ferrari, would you take it to the first mechanic in the Yellow Pages, or would you take it to the one certified Ferrari mechanic in town? You'd take it to the Ferrari mechanic. And not only would you feel more comfortable doing it, you would be glad to pay more for it. So, for lawyers who charge by the hour—and I have some definite thoughts as you know, Carson, which I'll return to later—you can command more per hour. Same with a flat fee. And if you handle cases on a contingent percentage, do you not think an insurance adjuster or opposing counsel might pay more to settle a case against you if they believe you know your stuff? Wouldn't that make you a little scarier?

"So," concluded Guy, "when you find and focus on a niche, you not only increase demand, but you're halfway to increasing value. And the really great news about value is that the other half of it is handled by your efforts to improve your Throughput Rate by optimizing your system. Because the better your process, the better your quality. If my process and materials are great, my bikes will be great, too. But again, only if I stay focused. Ferraris are amazing machines, but if you asked Ferrari to build table lamps, dishwashers, and sewing machines alongside its cars, how do you think that would go? And what would it do to the Ferrari mystique? As long as you're focused narrowly, if you put the right process in place, your cases will be better built. Higher quality and higher value."

"I understand," said Carson. "So I guess all I've got to do now is figure out the one thing Gray Firm is really good at, and talk everyone into just doing that?"

"Yes and no. Think of your one thing as a core concept. With Ambrose's reputation and passion for fighting injustice, there may be a few kinds of practice areas that you should focus on. Probably no more than three or four, though. These things I consider your 'Brand Basket,' all related and fitting neatly together. And they should all tie back to that core concept; that's like the handle for the basket."

Carson said, "I guess there is a reason that lots of small firms focus on personal injury and workers' compensation cases: They are not too different, and they are profitable, and they all have that same handle—some physical injury."

"Right concept," said Guy. "But that market's pretty saturated. That's why within it, you see very successful lawyers who only handle truck accidents or brain injuries, for example. You need to find *your* niche and the Gray Firm's. That's your mission, Carson. Start thinking about that. I want an answer when we meet next month."

After exchanging his goodbyes with Guy, Carson walked out of the factory into an overcast Saturday morning with much on his mind.

A few weeks later.

Carson walked up to Guy, who was decked out in a full C^2 warm-up suit.

"Team looks good, Guy."

"Thanks, Carson," said Guy. "This race is kind of a tune-up for some of our junior guys and girls, as you know. All the big wheels on the A-Team are already over in Europe."

Guy continued, "I'm going to keep our meeting short today, because most of what I wanted you to see is right in front of you. Take a look around and tell me what you see."

Carson looked up and down the racecourse. The C^2 logo was everywhere. And, of course, C^2 Tsunami 6s, 5s, and even some 4s and 3s made up the majority of the bikes. Central City was C^2's home turf, so that was not surprising, but Carson knew that C^2 would be a significant presence in any race anywhere. Not only were they accessible to amateur racers, they were just damn good bikes.

Guy spoke as Carson took it all in. "All that you see, this is not an accident, Carson. Twenty-five years ago, once we decided who and what Chaplin Cycle really was about, what we really could do best, we needed something not only to mark our departure point, but something that really communicated who we were and the one thing we did. As you know, I was inspired by the original Tsunami that my dad built for me. To think about taking his name, Chaplin, our family name, off the company was very hard. But I knew that, other than a once-successful mid-size bike company Chaplin Cycle didn't really communicate anything to our customer. It did not set us apart in the market from Schwinn, Fuji, Raleigh, or anyone else. So we had to come up with something that did.

"We went through dozens of ideas. But what finally clicked was C^2—C Squared. It worked on a lot of levels. It took our old initials, CC for Chaplin Cycle—as well as our home, Central City—and made that into C^2. It was also Einstein-speak for the speed of light. And when it comes to racing cycles, what's more important than speed—except maybe for making bikes that are 'light.' Lightweight! Light on your wallet! And we could take Einstein's formula $E = MC^2$ and play with that. Remember our 'V(ictory) = Me + C^2' campaign? It just worked on so many levels. Most importantly, it communicated what we care about and what we do for the customer. We do one thing: we make light, fast, great racing bikes that are affordable."

Guy was rolling now, passionate. "You know, that's what always bugged me about you lawyers, Carson. No offense, but 'Jones, Snobbly, Wicker, and Smoot' and firm names like that. Unless everyone in the city already knows that Attorney Snobbly is the finest real estate lawyer in town, firm names like that don't tell me one thing about who and what that firm is, or what they do.

"So," resumed Guy, settling down. "We talked last month about how important it is to figure out what your firm really cares about and can do better than its competition. That was your homework last month, Carson. So, did you and the lawyers in your firm figure it out?"

Carson's mind returned to the long, difficult meeting he had had with Ambrose and Briana a few weeks back. At first, they had thought he was insane. Give up family court work and small business incorporations when the firm was already strapped for cash? Why give up any paying work, ever? It had taken a hard sell from Carson to get Ambrose and Briana to realize that this work, which the clients could, truthfully, get from dozens of other lawyers in town (most of whom were better known for it than the Gray Firm), was not something they should try to continue. Carson actually went so far as to get the Yellow Pages and show them page after page of advertisements for lawyers who, like the Gray Firm, advertised that they could do everything.

Some of the family court work (no-fault divorces, for example) was simply a commodity for which there was heavy price competition. Other family court work, like high-asset divorces and child custody cases, was the province of a handful of domestic relations specialists. While Gray Firm's generalized advertising had not attracted the high-asset cases, it had pulled in no-fault divorces and some custody cases. The latter, in addition to being very different than other cases the firm could handle well, were a huge drain on resources. As Briana and even Ambrose finally had to admit, the "dedicated" domestic relations lawyers could handle such cases much more efficiently. These lawyers were in demand, and they often commanded a higher fee than the Gray Firm could charge.

Carson finally sold Ambrose and Briana on the niche concept when he reminded them that de-emphasizing such cases did not mean simply dropping them. They could finish out what they had. But going forward, they would refer those cases out to a select few other lawyers who (hopefully) would be able to return the favor by sending Gray Firm cases it could handle profitably and well. The trouble was figuring out what those "core" cases or practice areas should be. He, Briana, and Ambrose were still hashing that one out.

Carson finally answered, "We've made a lot of progress figuring out what we shouldn't be doing anymore. But we're still figuring out what we should. It's not easy, Guy."

Guy laughed. "It's not. And it shouldn't be. It's a big decision. Let me tell you what I think about your firm, as an outsider, though. And please, promise to take no offense from what I'm about to say."

"No promises," joked Carson.

Guy expounded, "Here's how I see it. The public doesn't really know yet who or what you and Briana are. You were buried in a big firm for the last decade. And Briana is too new. But everyone already knows Ambrose Gray. People remember him from the civil rights era—especially in discrimination cases, and they know he was on the right side of history there. And, of course, for his workplace safety cases. People will always think of Ambrose as a crusader for the little guy. Because that's what he's always been. A lot of firms try to sell that, but Ambrose? He's the real deal.

"So unlike Messrs. Jones, Snobbly, Wicker, and Smoot, Ambrose's name is already kind of a brand. It carries something with it. People know who and what he is. Unlike Snobbly, or Chaplin Cycle, 'Ambrose Gray' is actually quite central to your brand. So even after Ambrose retires (if that ever happens), his name needs to stay.

"The trick, then," Guy continued, "is to figure out what kinds of cases your firm can handle better than your competition, profitably, that are consistent with that 'core brand.' I'm not saying that you can only do one kind of case. But what I am saying, again, is that you need a Brand Basket of a few kinds of cases organized around a core concept."

Carson interrupted, "I understand that. Lots of lawyers put workers' compensation and personal injury together because they can be handled similarly. They both involve dealing with medical providers, involve insurance, involve claims, and can be handled contingently."

"As I've said before, a crowded playing field there," said Guy. "But that's true. There's a reason that works, if you can pull in the business. And to digress for a moment because you mentioned it, let's talk about how lawyers get paid for things. Now, as a business owner, I've had to hire lawyers from time to time. And I have to tell you, as a client, I hated being billed hourly for work. You don't have any idea where it's going to end. It's not predictable. And when you get a bill where you're getting charged $150 for 20 minutes on the phone, I don't know. . . . It just made me feel taken advantage of. Eventually, I started only working with firms who would work on a flat fee for what I needed done. It was more predictable, and it seemed like a much better value to me. I pay them $2,500 or whatever, for a certain result or service, and that's what I get.

"Now, when I put my business owner hat on and thought about it some more, it occurred to me how much better that fee arrangement was for the lawyers, too. In an hourly model, any improvement in efficiency, any shortening of Cycle Time, not only did *not* improve profit, but might actually hurt it. When I plugged that into the Income Formula that I knew from my own business was valid, it undermined the most important variable.

"If you work your way to the top of the big firm food chain with a lot of associates working under you, I guess it could be pretty sweet. But in the end, the only way the lawyers could make more money was to spend more time working. Not so great for their personal lives, I would imagine.

Now, don't get me wrong, hourly lawyers can still gain from improvements in value (because they could charge more per hour) and, to some extent, increase the number of cases they handle—assuming they have the capacity to do the work. But from a pure business standpoint, they cannot reap the benefits of improved Throughput Rate, which I believe is the most important factor in profitability.

"Conversely, lawyers working on a flat fee, and especially on a contingent fee, will make more money with *any* improvement or increase in Throughput Rate. So, in my opinion, the kinds of cases you and your firm should focus on should not ignore this reality. If you are working hourly now, at least consider flat fees. Maybe even a mix of the two. Contingent fee cases are even better, because you get paid back directly for increasing value.

"OK, digression over. We've talked a lot about marketing now, last month and this. So let's try to put it all together. First, back to what kinds of cases Gray Firm should handle. What are your thoughts, Carson?"

"Well," Carson mused, "Ambrose has always loved representing employees in disputes with employers. He was one of the first to file discrimination and sexual harassment suits around here. He's still got most of the big verdicts. To me, he seems happiest when he can take one of those cases and run with it."

"That's a good start," said Guy. "What about Briana?"

"Briana's a thinker," said Carson, "and a phenomenal writer. But she doesn't seem to like going to court; she's fine there, but she would way rather be looking for the smoking gun in a stack of documents. The cases she really seems to enjoy, perverse as it sounds, are what we lawyers call ERISA cases—claims brought for benefits under the Employee Retirement Security Act. These might be cases where someone has disability insurance through their job but, when they get hurt, the insurance company refuses to pay the benefit. Or even disputes over retirement benefits.

"Essentially," said Carson, "if it's a fight that can be had on paper, Briana's all in. She's very tough to beat."

"All right, all right," said Guy. "That's good. What about you, Carson? What were you doing at K&M?"

"What I was told, mostly," joked Carson, blackly. "Actually, when I left, I was pretty much going full time on this big case for a company called General Bearings. It was a products liability case. The bearings that GB made were allegedly defective, causing injuries to people and damage to property when different industrial machines in which the bearings were installed malfunctioned."

"Did you enjoy that?" asked Guy.

"Not really. I did enjoy the litigation part of it, particularly in the personal injury claims. A lot of the people claiming to be hurt—and some of them were actually hurt pretty badly—had filed workers' compensation claims. So I got to learn some things about how that system worked. And even though we were defending the claims, I enjoyed the science behind the scenes, both the mechanical engineering and design aspects, and the medical aspects of the injuries."

"Have you ever thought about doing more of the workers' compensation cases?" asked Guy.

Actually, Carson had been thinking about that. The firm had just a few of them, nothing major, but he had basically taken them over because they interested him. And another thing he had noticed from the General Bearings cases was how the injured workers almost always had a different lawyer representing them in the workers' compensation case than they had in the products case. It seemed to him that if one lawyer could handle both cases, efficiencies might be gained because that single lawyer (or firm) would know the injury, the medicine, and the facts without having to duplicate effort. Also, there was interplay between the workers' comp claim and the products claim involving subrogation, offsets, and the allocation of losses that might be better handled by a single lawyer.

This was technical stuff, which Guy would not understand, though, so Carson simply said, "Yes, I have, actually, even though I don't have a lot of experience. I've also wondered whether my products liability and litigation experience might not be helpful in representing injured workers on other claims they might have. Because lots of times when someone is hurt at work, it might be the fault of a third party, and even though the employee has a right to workers' compensation benefits, that third party—say the manufacturer of a machine—might also be responsible. So I'm thinking of bringing those two areas together."

"That would seem to fit nicely into the basket you're putting together. Seems to me like the Gray Firm could become a one-stop shop for all kinds of employment issues. And there's a need for that, I bet. No one else I know is doing anything like it. I can see it now: 'The Gray Firm: Lawyers Who Help Workers.' What do you think, Carson?"

Carson was already thinking hard. It could actually work....

Marketing! Finally, we get to exercise our right brain and pick out some cool fonts and pictures. Right? Well, not quite.

We've spent a lot of time in the narrative portion of this chapter trying to convince you of something that is simple, but that small firms often fail to grasp: The recipe for starvation is trying to be everything to everyone. Unless you're in a very small market, being a generalist these days fails on several levels. It pits you against all of the other generalists, and you don't stand out in the market. It hides any expertise you have in a particular area. It exponentially increases the degree of complexity in your practice. And it makes standardization virtually impossible. So what are you supposed to do?

Be the real deal. In other words, be authentic and true to who you are. Before we dive into the finer details and metrics of marketing, remember that all marketing has to be grounded on something real. As lawyers, more than almost any other profession, we are selling ourselves. And you can't sell what you wouldn't buy. The practice areas you focus on most should be ones you care about deeply on a real and personal level. Otherwise, your life's work will be only that—work.

Beyond having a passion for your practice area, you also need to "walk the walk." You must become highly skilled in your practice area. While we have to be careful using the words *expert* or *specialist* in the legal field (and we never recommend you do this in your marketing unless you have been certified as one by your bar organization in those words), your goal is to become a real expert. One of the most profound statements ever made about niche marketing was written by Ford Harding in his 1994 book *Rain Making*, and it's this: Experts make themselves. No one starts out as an expert; they make themselves into one.

That involves not only study, but teaching. And, as we will discuss later in our "Content Marketing" section, it means putting information of real value in your area out into the marketplace for the benefit of the public and your fellow practitioners. When you do this, you're not only doing good for others, but you are communicating the depth of your command in your niche area. You won't have to tell anyone you're an expert. They will know.

Beyond personal satisfaction, the benefits of narrowing your focus are considerable. Fewer things to standardize and less complexity lead to shorter Cycle Times, while better "raw material" and your perceived expertise yield higher Average Case Values. Both of which mean more income.

Now, on to the specifics.

BASIC MARKETING CONCEPTS

The Sales Funnel

Do a Google search for "funnel," look at the images, and you're going to see just as many neon sales funnel diagrams as you are going to see actual funnels.

The sales funnel has a long and storied history. The idea is a simple one: At the top of the funnel are prospects that are just beginning to be aware of you. There are lots of those. Out of the bottom are new clients. There are far fewer of those. In between is your marketing and sales effort.

If you've never heard of the funnel, don't feel bad. It's a relatively new idea, at least in a geologic scale of time when we consider the formation of the solar system and the dinosaurs. The funnel was formulated in 1898 by the magnificently named E. St. Elmo Louis, whose AIDA model became the basis of hideously designed business clip art for years to come. Since then, countless sales consultants seeking fame and fortune have riffed on the basic concept, but the AIDA stages, from top to bottom, are:

1. **Awareness**, or becoming aware that a brand or product exists.
   Bob, waking up from a decades-long coma, sees television advertisements for the iPhone.
2. **Interest**, or beginning to express interest in a particular brand.
   Bob, strolling through his shopping mall on an Auntie Anne's pretzel sugar high, stops in to the Apple store and takes the iPhone for a spin.
3. **Desire**, or starting to really want a particular brand or service.
   Bob, tossing and turning during a restless night's sleep, lustily desires getting his hands on an iPhone and firing up The Turtles on Spotify.
4. **Action**, or pulling out the wallet and paying for goods or services.
   Bob shows up when the Apple store opens and shells out a cool grand for a new iPhone and a pair of Beats headphones.

The critical thing with the sales funnel is the concept that there is a *successive series of stages* that brings people closer to your wallet. How you break down those stages may be different depending on the purpose. It is less important that you subscribe to a hard and fixed nomenclature, like AIDA.

For example, when thinking about web marketing, the top of the funnel might be all people who see an advertisement for you. The next stage might be those who get to visit your website. From there, desire might be expressed as someone filling out your contact form or calling you. The final stage would be an engagement letter.

To take this example a step further, we may find that we have:

› 100,000 *impressions* of my Facebook ad
› 1,500 *visits* to my website (a 1.5 percent conversion rate from the previous stage)
› 45 combined *contacts* from form submissions and phone calls (a 3 percent conversion rate from the previous stage)
› 10 *new clients* (a 22 percent conversion rate from the previous stage)

When executives refer to sales as a numbers game, the preceding example illustrates why. If we want three additional clients a month, we can work backwards: By improving our advertisements and ratcheting up the conversion of impressions to visits by 0.5 percent, we can push another 500 people from the Facebook ad to the website. Then, if conversion rates held the same for the remaining stages, we'd end up with 60 combined contacts and 13 new clients. The trick is to continually improve not only the numbers going into the top of the funnel, but the conversion rates from one stage to the next.

- ✔ **DO:** Use the funnel to conceptualize different stages in your marketing and sales process and to think about how people move through those stages.
- ✘ **DON'T:** Use one funnel concept across all of your marketing efforts. Realize that the path will be different depending on the channel.

> **How Lawyers Get Marketing Wrong**
>
> *Larry:* At one point I was helping an attorney, let's call her Jane, with her firm's marketing. Jane runs a decently sized niche law firm with about 15 staff, including a handful of attorneys. It took us a long time to get anything done because of Jane's tremendous focus on typography and colors. They had to be perfect, and we went through a ton of revisions, which required communication cycles with a busy attorney, so we went nowhere fast.
>
> The problem with Jane's approach is that marketing really isn't about color and font. It's about results, and in the marketing world, that means creating leads: new business opportunities that can be closed as new clients. I'm not arguing that font and imagery don't matter—they should reflect your professionalism and uniqueness. But once you get 90 percent on target, achieving the last 10 percent of perfection has very limited returns, and odds are you are not focusing on the issues that drive value.

THE MARKETING NUMBERS GAME

Unfortunately, Anti-Numbites, we have to rain on your parade just when you thought we might break out the crayons. Beyond carefully choosing your niche and "walking the walk," Lean marketing concepts put us smack dab in the middle of a powerful application of Lean ideas and numbers.

Internalize this mantra: If you're not measuring, you're not marketing. Besides effort, marketing involves spending money. If you can't figure out how your marketing spend is driving business, you're doing it incorrectly.

This is a "big data" world we find ourselves in, and we need to take full advantage. Each visit to a website can be analyzed, every click on an ad studied, and trackable phone numbers are cheap. The ability to measure ROI (return on investment) and to experiment has never been greater, finally casting a beacon into the once dark arts of marketing. Indeed, we live in a golden age of technology-driven marketing techniques.

With all of these measuring tools at our disposal, the Lean law firm is in its element. Two partners are arguing about the best slogan or marketing message? No problem. Just design a test, put it on the Internet, and find out who's the winner with actual data. Then take the winning advertisement, tweak it a little, and see if you can improve upon it. You can leave ego at the door and test hypotheses with facts and figures.

Here's what we're *not* going to do in this chapter: We're not going to tell you that there are marketing silver bullets, like Twitter, Avvo, or the latest social media fad. We're going to explore a variety of marketing channels, both offline and on, so that you can diversify your marketing efforts. Most importantly, we seek to instill the mentality that it's critical to understand the fundamentals of how people end up at your front doorstep and how to track which channels are most effective for you.

- ✔ **DO:** Embrace the notion that if you're not measuring, you're not marketing.
- ✔ **DO:** Seek the ultimate goal of determining which marketing channels are most cost-effective and produce the best clients.
- ✘ **DON'T:** Keep doing the same old marketing tricks you've been doing just because you've been doing them. Make sure they work through data.

HOW LEAN LAW FIRMS MANAGE MARKETING

The nature of Lean, with iterative cycles and measurement, could not be a more perfect philosophical complement to modern marketing tools and techniques. It is important that you continue to try out new approaches to your message and refine your existing ones, using data to analyze your success.

Marketing consumes time you'd otherwise be using for legal work, and aside from payroll it can be one of your largest expenses. You can waste huge sums of money by taking a set-and-forget approach. Therefore, we highly recommend that you think seriously about the amount of time you spend on it.

DASHBOARDS

We recommend building a history of your marketing performance so you can see all Key Performance Indicators (KPIs) at a glance. Otherwise, you're going to have to fish through different systems to view your data, making it more difficult to spot trends.

You don't have to get very fancy. A simple spreadsheet will be fine. To get you started, we've created a sample one for you that incorporates the KPIs from this chapter available here: leanlawfirmbook.com

MONTHLY REVIEW AND RETROSPECTIVE

We recommend that you meet monthly to go over your marketing KPIs, paying close attention to the performance of your paid advertising, and to discuss strategy and new ideas. If you don't have support staff, we recommend that you review your marketing KPIs quarterly because corralling your data will take time. Then, at the first available opportunity, hire some help!

Once you go over your metrics, a marketing retrospective meeting, the Start, Stop, Continue Meeting discussed in Chapter 9, is an ideal format for this meeting.

> **WARNING:** If you are spending money on digital ads, especially Google pay-per-click (PPC), waiting a full quarter between reviews of their performance can be costly. PPC is a highly dynamic environment with shifting bid prices, driving up the costs on search keywords based on actions that are completely outside of your control. Moreover, ads have a limited shelf life and need to be revamped; otherwise your PPC effectiveness will naturally diminish over time.

A/B TESTING

In his 2008 campaign, Barack Obama raised $60 million by experimenting with different media and messages on his campaign website. (Obama didn't do this personally; his director of analytics Dan Siroker pulled this off.) The Obama campaign's skill at testing version A of the website versus version B not only changed American history, but it helped revolutionize the way web marketers operate. Siroker took his experience and pain points on the campaign trail and founded Optimizely (optimizely.com), a website A/B testing tool. Now you, too, can raise $60 million!

A/B testing, or the idea of testing a new message or campaign against a control, fits completely within the Lean methodology. You come up with an idea, put it into action, measure the results, and refine. A/B testing helps with the human element as well; marketing often involves creative decisions and ideas, which can lead to staff conflict and bruised egos. A/B testing is a great way to determine, verifiably, which ideas result in better lead generation.

Once we understand our funnel, we can use A/B testing to try to increase our conversion percentages from one stage to the next. You can run two versions of an online ad and see which one gets more traffic to your site. You can run two different versions of your website and see which one results in more visitors filling out your contact form.

A/B testing does not have to rely on fancy technical tools, and it is not the exclusive domain of the web. It is a concept, not a software platform, and it can be exported to your offline activities as well. For example, when someone reaches out to you via phone or your website, you can A/B test your phone scripts. Maybe what you say during an inbound inquiry has the potential to move people toward hiring you or not.

For the personal injury firms out there running bus ads, are you sure your ad copy or placement is as effective as possible? Why not come up with a variant and use a separate call tracking number for each ad and see which one wins?

> **What Is a Call Tracking Number?**
> A call tracking number is a forwarding-only phone number that sends calls to your actual phone number.
> Companies like Plivo (plivo.com) or CallRail (callrail.com) allow you to set up numbers that forward to your regular office phone or cell phone. They also keep tabs on the calls that flow through the tracking number as well as any caller ID information.
> You can set up as many call tracking numbers as you like, making them very potent tools for advertising. You can have a different tracking number for business cards, Yellow Pages ads, your website, or anything you can think of. Just because someone finds you online doesn't mean they're going to e-mail you or fill out a form. They're more likely than not going to call you.
> Armed with call tracking reports, you can see which numbers were dialed the most, indicating which of your marketing sources is generating the most inbound interest.

CONTENT MARKETING

We talked about the value of content marketing earlier. *Content marketing* is really just a recent term for an old concept. You provide valuable information that people actually want and receive brand awareness or potentially contact information in return. By doing so you get a top-of-the-funnel lead. You've probably downloaded an e-book or white paper or attended a webinar where you were required to input your contact information. If so, you've been on the receiving end of content marketing.

Believe it or not, content marketing has been around since the Grover Cleveland administration. John Deere, the agricultural equipment company, started a magazine called *The Furrow* in 1895. It is considered the gold-standard magazine for farmers and other agriculture businesspeople, analogous to *Variety* for the entertainment industry or *Barron's* for financial types. Everyone who is attracted to the wonderful farming content ends up with John Deere's branding in their faces.

Because content marketing provides information to people and is not a direct sales pitch, it is relatively easy to get it into people's hands and raise awareness about your law firm. You might try targeting referral business and create content that is of value to other attorneys. Or you might try to directly target your customer base. Either way, the top of your funnel gets filled by people seeking answers to their questions.

We once worked with a client on a webinar for their referral network. The subject was the ways in which lawyers can identify candidates for our client's labor law practice. Who doesn't love an easy referral fee, right?

A great example on the consumer side is the McIveen Law Firm's free downloadable e-book, *The North Carolina Divorce Guidebook*, directly targeting her geographic prospects. And in South Carolina, one of the best legal content marketers of all, Benjamin Stevens, runs two highly trafficked blogs, *The South Carolina Family Blog* and *The Mac Lawyer*. Ben's blogs build web traffic and personal relationships.

Online video is another ripe source for content marketing. YouTube is the world's second-largest search engine after Google, and consumers flock to it for explanations of complex problems. It's such a perfect mechanism for legal content marketing that a company called TheLaw.TV exists with the sole focus of helping law firms produce question-and-answer videos for YouTube.

- ✗ **DON'T:** Make content marketing an infomercial. If you come off as sales-y or disingenuous, your content will not succeed. It works best by building brand awareness with solid content.
- ✔ **DO:** Cover topics that are directly related to your practice area.
- ✔ **DO:** Disclaim away. Be aware of ethics opinions, and make sure you don't establish any inadvertent attorney-client relationships.

BUYER PERSONAS AND CORE CUSTOMERS

It helps to know who's purchasing your legal services. You probably already know your target demographic, but the Lean law firm approaches its addressable market in a methodical fashion. It helps to conduct a little research. For example, do you know what events trigger your clients to pick up the phone and call you? Do you know who else they called, how they conducted their research, and what were the major deciding factors in choosing you from among your competitors?

Buyer Personas are semi-fictional representations of the people who purchase your services. They help you understand the people you represent and what their buying journey is like, and they steer you toward better marketing decisions. You create Buyer Personas by spending time interviewing the people who chose your service and asking a series of pointed questions. You end up with a playbook, knowing where to spend your marketing dollars, what differentiates you from your competition, and who's really making the purchasing decision.

To learn more, we highly recommend Adele Revella's seminal work on the subject, *Buyer Personas: How to Gain Insight into Your Customer's Expectations, Align Your Marketing Strategies, and Win More Business*. Ms. Revella is a top-tier consultant, so to be able to read her methodology in a book is like having access to the Forbidden City—it used to be only the domain of emperors (and C-level executives).

Related to the notion of a Buyer Persona is the *Core Customer*. The Core Customer differs from the Buyer Persona in that it focuses on your best clients, not necessarily the purchasing process. Your Core Customer is your ideal client: the one that is the most profitable, causes the fewest problems, is loyal, and recommends your services. The two concepts are often used interchangeably, but they are in reality two very different things.

The idea is that you want more Core Customers, not your headache cases that cheap out on you and make life generally miserable. Once you understand your Core Customer, you can work backwards to identify what your special offering is that attracted them to you in the first place. To learn more about developing a Core Customer profile, take a look at Bob Bloom's excellent *The Inside Advantage*.

- ✔ **DO:** Create Buyer Personas by seeking to understand your clients' journeys, from knowing they have legal issues to signing your engagement letter.
- ✔ **DO:** Dig in to your Core Customers and try to define common factors that make them a perfect fit for your law firm.
- ✘ **DON'T:** Confuse Buyer Personas and Core Customers. The former term refers to those that buy your services. The latter refers to the dream clients you seek to attract.

ONLINE MARKETING BASICS

Let's face it: Online marketing could easily be a two-year degree, maybe even a college major. We cannot hope to cover this topic extensively in this chapter. Moreover, the field changes so rapidly that a printed book cannot keep up with the latest information.

Our goal here is to establish some basic principles and measurable guidelines that work for a Lean law firm.

Website

What to Measure: Unique visitors, new visitors, referring sources, conversion rates
Think of your law firm website like a foundation for a house. All of your other online activity should be built upon it. Whatever imagery, colors, logo, and branding you use on your website should be the basis of all imagery across your online persona, presenting a polished, unified front. It should be a goal to have all of your other online activities lead people to your website.

You can employ your website to achieve two primary goals: affirmation and lead generation.

Affirmation is important for your referral network. When your firm is referred to someone, the consumer is going to conduct a little research and look you up online. A polished website is very important. There is no better way to say you're behind the times or second rate than by having a poorly designed website, and unfortunately, the consumer is going to make that assessment in eight seconds or less.

Lead generation is the holy grail of online marketing. The idea here is that you attract people to your website, and you hope they contact you. If this is your goal, you need to pay very close attention to designing a site that not only attracts visitors but compels them to take action to contact you. Having a phone number listed or a Contact Us form is a good start, but it is not enough; you need carefully designed language and buttons to focus the visitor on taking action.

Law firms can build a reasonable, custom, and good-looking site from $1,500 for a simple five-pager to $10,000 for a more data-driven site. If you spend more than this, that's fine, but you will probably see minimally incremental returns. If you spend less than $1,500, you will get what you pay for.

We would not recommend cheaping out on your site unless you are absolutely desperate to retain cash. It's a bad idea, considering that your website is your online foundation.

All websites must have an analytics package running on them. Google Analytics is free and incredibly powerful, so if your website lacks analytics, then your designer either ripped you off or is clueless. Learning Google Analytics can take a while, but here are the basic things to look for:

- **New Visitor**: This refers to the number of people who come to your site who haven't been there before, or at least haven't been to your site in a determined time period.
- **Unique Visits**: This refers to the number of visits from different individuals. If someone visits your website five times from the same browser, it is counted as five total visits but one unique visit.
- **Referring Sources**: Google Analytics can tell you where your traffic comes from. The websites that send visits your way are called referring sources.
- **Conversion Rates**: The percentage of people who visit a webpage who then fill out a form on that page. Many factors can affect form submission, including the call to action language you're using and the number of fields that are in the form (more fields = fewer submissions but more qualified leads).

- ✔ **DO:** Understand that law firm websites can serve the role of confirming competence, generating leads, or both.
- ✔ **DO:** Take the time to understand the basics of web design. Your instincts will likely lead you astray and create friction with your design team. Read *Don't Make Me Think* by Steve Krug and trust your designer's opinion. You know how your clients don't take your advice sometimes? Don't be that guy.
- ✘ **DON'T:** Cheap out on your website. Find the money to build something nice.
- ✘ **DON'T:** Use your kid or cousin to design your logo or your website unless that person is a well established professional.
- ✔ **DO:** A/B test your website. Use a tool like Compete or Optimizely to see what messaging and imagery drive better conversion rates.

Search Engine Optimization (SEO)

What to Measure: Monthly searches, keyword rankings

Let's face it: When we talk about SEO, we're talking about Google (sorry Bing and Yahoo!). YouTube is the number two search engine, and it is owned by Google as well.

Google is only as valuable as the accuracy and quality of the sites it lists, so it is in its interest to serve up real results that people want. It is important to understand this, to keep it in mind at all times, and to let it guide every SEO decision you make. If you are not providing something of value to actual humans, Google will take that into consideration.

> **Things to Look For When Choosing a Website Designer**
>
> If you're not careful, you can end up in a really bad situation when you pick a firm to design your website. We've seen situations where law firms are locked into contracts that cost thousands of dollars a month, draining their ability to invest in other marketing channels. Make sure you follow these guidelines to avoid trouble down the road:
>
> - Make sure you own your domain name. Some companies, as part of their contract, claim ownership of your domain name and will not release it. This gives firms the difficult choice of staying with a subpar service provider or giving up the domain name they've invested time and money in establishing.
> - Make sure you separate ongoing web hosting from initial design. You can find designers who will build your site and deploy it to a hosting company of your choice. If you do choose to get involved with firms that design and host your website, make sure the rates are reasonable and are less than $100 a month.
> - Some companies not only build and host websites, but offer additional marketing support services such as search engine optimization (SEO). Find out if they sell to other people in your geographic location with the same practice area. You're going to be competing with them, and this is not a good thing.
> - If you find yourself stuck in a terrible contract, putting up a big stink and asking to get out of it is often successful. It's worth a try.

SEO is a big subject and an entire industry. It is full of snake oil salesmen, amateurs, and bona fide professionals, and it is a source of stress and headaches for most small businesses. We can't possibly cover the whole topic here, but the following list of advice should cover the basics and point you in the right direction.

1. You cannot outfox Google as it is smarter than us, and if you try to do so, it will come down on you with Samuel L. Jackson–inspired vengeance. In fact, there is no mystery at all about how to succeed at SEO—it is more a question of disciplined execution. Google tells you exactly what and what not to do in its own SEO guide.
2. You need to make sure that the keywords you think you want to place high for are indeed worth investing your time and money in. Tools like Moz and SpyFoo can help you determine which keywords have the most monthly searches and how competitive they are. The ideal keywords are relevant to your business, not highly competitive, and have more monthly search volumes than others.
3. Stick to identifying 25 keywords, knowing which are your top five and ten. Don't go crazy with hundreds of combinations of keywords.
4. A good technique is to come up with an SEO architecture for your site. This is a document that lists what keywords you're going to use for

which pages. The title and description of the page are critical components, so in addition to the keyword, write a good title and description for your pages that incorporate the desired keyword. See an example of an SEO architecture on our website, leanlawfirmbook.com.
5. Don't keyword stuff! Using keywords repetitively and unnaturally in your website copy (known as stuffing) is bad for visitors, and consequently Google will penalize you.
6. Inbound links from reputable sites help your search engine ranking. Work with friendly businesses, charities, and other sites to acquire inbound links in a steady and methodical manner. Don't be tempted to pay money to list your sites in sketchy directories; this can be the quickest way to get punished by Google.
7. Make sure your website looks good on a mobile device. In May 2015, Google announced that for the first time, more web searches took place on mobile devices than on computers. Remember that Google is only valuable to people when it serves up quality sites, so make sure you're not serving up garbage to smartphones.

Numbers to measure:

> **Monthly Searches:** For each keyword you think you should place for, make sure the traffic is worth your while. Understand how many searches take place per month for your top keywords.
> **Keyword Ranking:** What position do you rank for your keywords? And how do these change over time?

✔ **DO:** On a monthly or at least quarterly basis, review your ranking positions for your top 25 keywords.
✔ **DO:** Keep in mind that Google is only valuable when it provides quality results for its visitors, and it does what it can to keep quality up.
✘ **DON'T:** Expect overnight success once you optimize your site. It takes a good six months to start to realize gains.
✘ **DON'T:** Be tempted to pay money to list your site on directories you've never heard of or don't seem reputable. Stick with mainstream ones, such as Capterra, Yelp, Avvo, Yahoo Business, and JD Supra.

Online Advertising

What to Measure: Cost-per-click (CPC), impressions, click-through rate (CTR)
Believe it or not, people do click on online ads, and when used properly, they can be extremely effective in refining your message and reaching your potential audience. The problem with search engine marketing (SEM) is

that there is so much to know about it to do it correctly that it is worthy of a two-year associate's degree. For this reason, we highly recommend you enlist the help of a professional before you invest in advertising; otherwise, you may waste money, not succeed, and forgo a huge opportunity.

Advertising on the web is an amazing resource for Lean law firms. Not only can you produce more visitors to your website, but you can experiment with messaging and imagery. Online ads are the quickest way to A/B test your messaging to see if it is connecting with prospective clients.

Facebook Advertising

Why use it: Inexpensive, very targeted demographic data, great on mobile.
Facebook may not be the hip social network all the kids are on, but it is commonly used by people who can actually afford a professional service. It is a great venue to advertise any content you have and bring brand awareness to your law firm.

Facebook offers you powerful ways to get in front of the demographics you desire. Because Facebook collects oodles of information about its users, you can restrict your ad to people in certain locations who like certain things. Facebook ads have another really great advantage: Ads in the Facebook newsfeed reproduce very well on smartphones. If you're looking for a mobile audience, you can't do much better.

Google Search Advertising

Why use it: Expensive, but connects you with people who are actively seeking a solution to a problem.
Google has multiple ways to get in front of its users, the most famous of which is the text-based pay-per-click (PPC) Search Advertising. For the uninitiated, you can pay Google to surface your ad on the search engine results page when certain keywords are sought. Depending on the keyword, you will pay more or less money each time someone clicks on the ad. Some keywords for the law, like *mesothelioma*, can have a cost per click (CPC) of hundreds of dollars, so be aware of the prices of your desired keywords.

Google Display Advertising

Why use it: Not expensive, allows you to promote your brand and/or content on major websites.
Google also offers Display Advertising, which is a lot less expensive than search-based PPC. Display Advertising is not driven through search; instead,

you get to leverage a network of websites that participate in Google's Display Advertising program. These websites include major sites, such as The New York Times or the Washington Post. Instead of a text ad, you provide graphical banner ads in various shapes and sizes. You will need a graphic designer to create these ads.

Google Remarketing Advertising

Why use it: Keeps your brand in front of interested parties. Gives the impression of massive ad spend.

In addition, Google offers Remarketing Advertising. Have you ever visited a website and all of a sudden you're seeing ads for it everywhere? That's remarketing in action. When a visitor comes to your site, a piece of code called a cookie is placed in his browser. Then, as he surfs the Internet, the Google Display network will look for this cookie and, if present, serve up a remarketing ad.

Remarketing is great because you are supplying more touches to your potential client, reinforcing your brand, and creating the impression that you are everywhere. It makes you look bigger than you are and keeps you in their minds.

Chart your success by measuring:

Cost per Click (CPC): Measures how much it costs you every time someone clicks on your ads. If you use search-based text ads, your CPC will be much higher than it is in display ads.

Impressions: This is the number of times your ad is served up. Each time counts, so if Alice sees an ad three times and Bob sees it five times, there were eight impressions. Ads are often priced on thousands of impressions: If something has a $7 CPM, for example, it means you pay $7 for 1,000 impressions.

Click-Through Rate (CTR): The rate at which people are served your ad and click on it. If you have a CTR of around 2 percent, you're doing all right. If it's 4 percent, you're knocking it out of the park.

- ✘ **DON'T:** Set and forget. Ads need to be changed often, ideally once a month but at least once a quarter.
- ✔ **DO:** A/B test. Online advertising is a great mechanism to see what messaging connects with your Core Customers.
- ✔ **DO:** Make sure you work with someone who understands digital advertising. If you try to wing it yourself, you're going to have a lot of pain.
- ✘ **DON'T:** Ignore mobile. People spend a lot of time on their phones.

> **Landing Pages: Your Advertisement's Best Friend**
>
> When you advertise, a great practice is not to draw the visitor to your main home page. Often you'll have better results with a dedicated page designed to serve the ad, known as a landing page.
>
> Landing pages work because they can easily be A/B tested. You can see quickly if landing page A converts more business than landing page B, especially if you are driving traffic there through advertising.
>
> Dedicated landing pages work really well with Google Search ads because a large component of your ad placement is something called the Quality Score, which in part rates the ad against the page it points to. If there is consistency in experience between the ad and the page, the Quality Score goes up, and the ad placement is better.
>
> Furthermore, a well designed landing page focuses user behavior. For example, there is often little to no navigation to distract the visitor from taking the action you want, which is calling you or filling out a form.
>
> In fact, landing pages are such a crucial element of online marketing that entire products exist just to create them, such as Instapage.

Social Media

What to Measure: Honestly? Nothing

Twitter, LinkedIn, Facebook, JD Supra, and other social networks do offer benefits to lawyers, though the initial hyperbole about their effectiveness is over. Talk to social media junkies back in 2008 or 2009, and they would tell you that Twitter was the key to success. Entrepreneur guru Guy Kawasaki claimed that Twitter was the biggest branding innovation since television.

Lawyers who get sucked into vanity metrics such as numbers of Twitter followers may be wasting their time. Hype aside, the real benefit to social media is its ability to create and strengthen relationships with individuals you don't see every day.

It's important to create an account on the major social networks for the sole reason of protecting your online reputation. Even if you think Twitter's a joke, at the very least grab a handle that's your name so that a bad actor cannot take it and do nasty things.

Make sure your profiles look good. It's worth investing in a professional headshot. A lot of people use friends, coworkers, or family to snap a photo and put it online, but unless they are professionals, that's a mistake. Good lighting and proper lenses are very important to make lawyers look good on camera, and prospective clients pick up on unprofessionalism unconsciously and immediately. So spend $60 and get a headshot professionally taken.

- ✔ **DO:** Get a professional headshot taken.
- ✔ **DO:** Establish profiles on the major social media sites, if for no reason other than to protect your reputation.

It's also a good idea to have a graphic designer adapt your logo and messaging for the different cover images on the varying social networks. Having consistency of branding across your online profile is inexpensive and creates an image of a very sophisticated firm—you will almost certainly look more polished than your peers.

In terms of using social networks, I recommend focusing on the ones you like. View it like joining Kiwanis or Rotary—stick with the environment you feel more comfortable in and build your online social life there. Whether it's Twitter or Facebook or a LinkedIn group or Reddit, pick the place you like and rock it.

✗ **DON'T:** Waste time on social networks you don't enjoy. A lot of people like Twitter, but many more people don't.

For the networks you don't like, dip into them and post status updates when you have something worthy to announce, for example an article you published or some news event for your firm. Another powerful use is the mention. When you call out others on Twitter or LinkedIn in a positive way, it can be remarkably effective relationship building.

Avvo, Yelp, and Google Places

What to Measure: Lead generation
Online rating sites such as Avvo, Yelp, and Google Places can be terrifying for lawyers, since they allow clients to publicly opine on your abilities, anonymously and with no accountability or respect to fairness.

Here's the good news: If you have a bad review or rating, it's not the end of the world. First of all, if the review is unfair, you can try to fight it, and at the very least you can respond to it. Keep in mind that even the greats are subject to trolls in the online world. Do an Amazon search for *The Godfather*, widely considered to be the greatest movie of all time, and read through the one-star reviews. Moreover, most consumers discount one-off bad reviews. If *all* your reviews are bad, then maybe you need to think about your legal skills and bedside manner.

The best strategy with these services is to solicit feedback from genuine clients on an ongoing basis. You're not going to get hurt if you have a lack of reviews, but you can thrive with a lot of good ones. A great thing to accelerate reviews is to conduct an NPS survey, discussed in Chapter 4, and reach out to your 9s and 10s for feedback.

Also, if you haven't already, claim your profile on these sites. Avvo asks you to claim your listing, and you should establish your profile on Google Places and Yelp as well. This is not hard to do yourself, and any

Internet marketing consultant worth their salt should have these on their checklists.

The other important thing to keep in mind here is that just because you're reviewed online doesn't mean your potential clients are going to look at those reviews. The legal business is still primarily referral-based. Newer lawyers, especially those in consumer-facing practice areas, need to pay much closer attention to review sites than established attorneys with a large network.

- ✔ **DO:** Establish your profile on the online review sites. It's good for your marketing, anyhow.
- ✘ **DON'T:** Panic if you get a bad review. Remember, one-off reviews are discarded by most consumers, and even the best movies of all time get bad reviews on occasion.
- ✔ **DO:** Measure the amount of business that online review sites generate.
- ✔ **DO:** Ask clients that you have solid relationships with to give you good reviews. They will likely not do it on their own.

A WORD ABOUT OFFLINE MARKETING

There isn't a lot of mystery to traditional offline marketing efforts. Word of mouth from clients, referrals from other law firms, and in-person networking are pretty well understood by lawyers. The mystery is the effectiveness of these marketing channels. How many leads do you get from referrals? At what rate do they close? Who is sending referrals your way? Are some referring attorneys more productive than others?

What differentiates the Lean Lawyer from his or her peers is the ability to assign a value to a lead source. By continuously experimenting and measuring results, those practicing Lean will be able to know which marketing channels perform better than others and will improve their efforts over time. Every lead goes into your sales funnel, and some of them make it out the bottom. You want to pour in more leads that convert, so whether they come from online or offline sources, you need data to support your decisions.

Many of the same techniques we discussed in online marketing can work in offline marketing as well. For example, if you advertise on billboards or in the Yellow Pages, use a tracking phone number or a dedicated landing page with a unique URL for your campaign. In this way you can track the return on your efforts and take some of the mystery out of marketing.

Ideally you've honed your most receptive messaging with online ads since they are so much cheaper. Before you blanket the tri-state area with a direct mail postcard, for example, hopefully you've optimized your calls to action and messages through inexpensive web experiments. You can also run different versions of your offline ads and A/B test them; you might not get as many results, and they might take longer to get results than online ads. They will certainly be more expensive.

All offline marketing activity should be tracked. It might seem like overhead to track your originating attorneys for referring cases, but there are tools out there that help you do this, which we will explore in Chapter 9.

CHAPTER SUMMARY

If you're not measuring, you're not marketing. Incorporate Lean thinking to reduce waste and improve performance across iterations using hard data and experimentation. Understand your firm's sales funnel and what the different stages are to prepare yourself to measure conversion from stage to stage.

KPI	Pertains to	What It Does
New Visitors	Website	Refers to the number of people that come to your site that haven't been there before, or at least haven't been to your site in a determined time period.
Unique Visits	Website	Refers to the number of visits from different individuals. If someone visits your website five times from the same browser, it is counted as five total visits, but one unique visit.
Conversion Rate	Website	The percentage of people who visit a webpage who then fill out a form on that page.
Referring Sources	Website	Where your traffic comes from. The websites that send visits your way are called referring sources.
Monthly Searches	SEO	The number of monthly Internet searches for a given keyword.
Keyword Ranking	SEO	The position your site ranks in Google's search engine results for a given keyword.
Cost-per-Click (CPC)	Online advertising	Measures how much it costs you every time someone clicks on your ads.
Impressions	Online advertising	The number of times your ad is served to people.
Click-Through Rate (CTR)	Online advertising	The rate at which people are served your ad and click on it.

CHAPTER 7

Locking It Down
Standardization, Written Procedures, and Checklists

July

Carson strode to the entrance of the McSkippy's less troubled than he'd been in months, and anxious to report his preliminary good news to Guy. After his meeting with Guy in June, Carson had shared with Ambrose and Briana his ideas for narrowing and rebranding the practice into a niche, employment-related basket. He had expected the greatest pushback to come from Ambrose, but he didn't get it. Instead, Ambrose agreed that building the practice around employment law "felt right," like a return to his roots. Briana was less sure, but she got on board when she realized that she, too, could do more of what she loved.

Briana even proposed—and the others readily agreed—that she should go after more Social Security disability cases. Social Security claims arose invariably alongside the ERISA disability claims, and they involved much of the same proof. When she saw that she could overlap her own cases in this way, similar to Carson's pairing of workplace product liability claims with workers' compensation, Briana saw the wisdom in the marketing plan.

What none of the lawyers had foreseen fully—and what was a pleasant surprise—was how truly complementary their individual practices were to each other's. That fact was driven home when a new client, Laura Kilbourne, arrived. Laura had been hurt on her job a year ago when a drill press malfunctioned. She could no longer work. Dissatisfied with the progress of her former workers' compensation attorneys, she brought her case to the Gray Firm.

Carson took in the workers' compensation case, and he quickly saw the product liability case against the maker of the drill press. Further questioning revealed that Laura had both a long- and a short-term disability policy through her employer, but she was being denied benefits. Enter Briana, who not only took on the ERISA policy denial but Laura's Social Security disability claim as well. Finally, when Laura said her employer had fired her after she filed the workers' compensation claim, Ambrose came into the picture to investigate a retaliatory termination claim. One client. Five potential cases. Or Case Units as Carson was starting to think of them.

The Laura Kilbourne cases crystallized things and made finding a tagline for their firm easy. Carson, Ambrose, and Briana had shortened Guy's suggestion to simply "The Gray Firm: Lawyers for Workers." The rebrand had given not only the lawyers but everyone at the firm a new optimism and a renewed sense of mission. It might not work, but what they had been doing in the past hadn't, either. At least now there was a clear path toward something new.

But the plan created new challenges, too. It was one thing to develop a central concept to get new cases in. It was another altogether to handle them all effectively. How, exactly, were the lawyers and staff to coordinate and handle these cases effectively? They had the legal know-how, sure, but cooperation between the different lawyers and their (sometimes territorial) staff on cases such as Laura Kilbourne's presented problems. How could they be sure that Laura's case was not only handled correctly, but also moving forward as fast as possible, unencumbered by WNR Time and constraints? Hadn't Laura fired her last lawyers because they weren't moving fast enough? Visualizing the firm's process had helped. But Guy had promised more answers, and Carson needed them now.

Locking It Down

"Well, there you are," said Guy. "Ready for this month's lesson?"

"Absolutely," said Carson. "But I still can't believe you wanted to meet at McSkippy's. Aren't you a vegan, Guy?"

"Most of the time," Guy said, looking momentarily guilty. "But every once in a while I just really need a good burger. Don't tell Kumiko."

"I promise," said Carson. "But before we begin, I want to ask you something. What you said last month about narrowing the practice—we did that. We've done that. And, it's early of course, but things already feel different. The employees at Gray Firm seem, I don't know ... excited. Like they know that something's coming. And I really think so, too. I know our niche marketing efforts won't pay off immediately, of course, but I'm pretty confident they will over time. The only problem with that and what's got me worried is that I want to be sure we can deliver on what we're promising. I want clients to have as good an experience as they possibly can. As I'm learning, a lot of their satisfaction comes from the knowledge that their cases are moving forward. But how can we make sure that's what really happens? I don't want to just make hollow promises. That happens too much in my business already."

Guy walked from the line and sat down with Carson. "Not just your business, Carson. Every business. You just hit on two of the three main points for client satisfaction in any business. If you'll recall, back in February I told you how I envisioned C²'s mission: 'Build something people really want, as perfectly as possible, available when and how they want it.' That's every business's mission, really. Whether you're making bikes or court cases.

Or this delicious, nutritious McSkippy burger." Guy took a big bite of his cheeseburger.

Guy chewed contentedly and said, "Customers or clients choose you because you have something they want or need. That's marketing. But just finding your niche product or service does not fulfill their need by itself. The niche marketing is just the promise. The product itself has to make good on the promise by being 'as perfect as possible.' And the customer has to get that perfect product 'when and how they want it.' Because even if the product delivers on the promise of quality, if the customer's experience is terrible, that's what they will remember.

"So," said Guy, "how do you deliver on the marketing promise by making a great product when and how the customer wants it? By optimizing two things, process and communication."

Guy continued, "We'll talk about communication more next month. Communication is critical not only to the flow of your internal process but also to client satisfaction. For now, I'll just say that your communication needs to be visual and transparent. You will need a way to coordinate visually with members of your firm, and your process will need to become transparent to your clients. For your firm, you've already started working on a Kanban board. But even if you're doing everything right but your clients can't see that, it's as if you're doing nothing at all. But I'm getting ahead of myself. We'll talk a lot more about visual communication with your firm mates and clients next month. Let's get back to process for now.

"As I've hopefully beaten into your head by now," said Guy, "goal number one of your process is to increase Throughput Rate by reducing Cycle Time. Getting from beginning to end as quickly as possible. For you, that means delivering a legal result as quickly as external constraints (like court timelines) allow. Short Cycle Times mean fast Throughput Rate and more profit for you. But this also aligns perfectly with your client's interest: She wants her problem resolved as soon as possible. The biggest thing you can do to shorten Cycle Time is to hunt down constraints and eliminate WNR Time. Because, let's face it, most of the time you're not actively working on a particular case. It's just waiting, either for you to work on it or some other constraint. We talked a lot already about how to make a process move quickly by hunting down constraints and eliminating WNR Time, so no need to revisit that now. Just remember that whatever you do to improve constraints or reduce WNR Time is to the benefit of system Throughput Rate as a whole.

"Let's turn now to the minority of time when active work is actually being done on the case. How do you optimize that active work? From a systems standpoint, we want to do that active work as quickly as possible. Since a lawyer is a limited resource, the faster he can get through his active work on Case A, the less time Case B needs to wait for him to become available. So, one reason for a good process is that it reduces waiting time (and we know that will decrease Cycle Time, and therefore increase Throughput Rate)."

Guy continued, "But your client also wants the best result possible. That's quality, and that's goal two of your process. Maybe it's more accurate to call quality a byproduct of a good process. Good process = good product. And to digress momentarily, when we talk about Value from our Income Formula, that relates to quality. A good case comes in the door with a certain theoretical value. That value gets realized only if you work it properly. Or maybe it's not a great case when it comes in the door, but you can make it great. Either way, the best result possible, quality, depends on the quality of your process. How well you do the actual work on the case.

"So, Carson," queried Guy, "you've begun the ongoing process of reducing constraints and Wait Time in your process. You've thus cut your waiting times. What else can you do to make the process not only move faster, but get the same high level of quality on each case?"

Carson thought about it, stumped.

Guy prompted, "Look around you, Carson. Look at the menu board. Look at the workers making sandwiches behind the counter. Do they make each burger differently, like they've never made one before? No. They make them all the same. They *standardize*. They don't make 100 kinds of burgers. They make five. Just like Ferrari doesn't make sewing machines. Just like I don't make 100 bikes anymore. And how you don't handle every case that comes in the door anymore. Doing only a few things means you can get really good at those few things, because you do them over and over again. That's the power of repetition."

Guy continued, "So when you do a few kinds of things, you get good at them. And you begin to discover better ways to do those things, and these become your standards. You can always tweak and improve those standards; indeed, that never stops. But before you can improve a standard process, you have to identify the process in writing. To harness the power of standardization, you need written procedures, checklists. To make something in a standard way, you have to do it the same way, every time.

"Now, take McSkippy's, for example. If you look behind the counter, you'll see laminated checklists for making each kind of burger. McSkippy's found a great process for making a great burger. They do the same thing, the same way, every time. That prevents errors and ensures quality. It tastes the same in Idaho as it does here. And better still, when they discover some minor improvement that they can make in a standard process, it will be amplified because it's applied across the board. *Kaizen*."

Guy concluded, "I use the phrase, 'Standardize and technologize.' By limiting your practice areas, you are now in a position to standardize their handling, which improves both quality and speed. That's a great start. As for technology, it's true that automation can dramatically improve things, but only after you've defined a standard process. For now, I want you to focus on breaking down each practice area in your new niche areas to their ideal component parts. Your homework is to take these parts and develop checklists for your firm, accessible to everyone, so that each person knows what part of a case they are responsible for and what items on that list have been completed."

"That's a lot of work, Guy," griped Carson.

"It is," agreed Guy. "But you have to be willing to pay the up-front price, Carson. Once you've got your checklists done, it's just a matter of tweaking and improving them over time. And once you have these lists in place for each standard practice area, you'll have the keys for much greater quality and shorter Cycle Times. Don't underestimate the power of checklists.

"Whew," exhaled Guy. "Long lesson. Let's get out of this dive and go for a ride, Carson. You been riding much? You're almost starting to look fit again. You better watch it with the McSkippy's."

Carson, head swimming, tossed his burger into the trash and grabbed his bike, only too happy to agree to any physical activity that did not involve more thinking.

Fire. The wheel. The plow. Add the humble checklist to that list of humanity's most powerful inventions, especially for those of us in mission-critical knowledge industries.

It may seem boring to follow standard operating procedures all the time, but in reality, you'll end up with less busywork if you do a good job with your process. Standardizing the routine is like stomping down the garbage: You reduce the quotidian down to a smaller size. As a result, you leave more room for creative problem solving and the real fun stuff.

Moreover, consistency saves lives. Checklists and standardized repeatable processes keep mayhem at bay by forcing people to stick to a script when environments become complex and stress invades the office.

To understand the power of the checklist, consider the crash of a prototype of the B-17 bomber. The pilot of the aircraft, Major Peter Hill, was supremely experienced but missed one teeny tiny detail in flight prep, which cost him his life. As a reaction to the tragedy, U.S. Army aviators were inspired to create preflight checklists, which would have prevented the disaster from occurring. Since then, the aviation industry has gone checklist wild, making sure that every situation conceivable can be handled by a series of steps.

When there's no room for error involving life and limb, as it is with the great altitudes and speeds of airplanes, the checklist is employed.

Atul Gawande wrote an entire book about checklists called *The Checklist Manifesto*. He discussed what happened when a doctor at Johns Hopkins, Peter Pronovost, used the ideas from aviation and injected them into hospital protocol to make sure simple things didn't get missed.

The results were remarkable. Fewer mistakes were made, and infection rates lowered dramatically, leading to better health care for the patient and lower expenses for the hospital. To be honest, 200 pages about checklists and their history was rather dry reading, even for a process nerd like me, but the takeaways are critical:

1. Checklists provide guiderails for the experienced so that they don't overlook small items when situations go sideways.
2. Checklists provide step-by-step instructions for neophytes.
3. Checklists ensure consistency of a service or product and reduce errors.

It's safe to say that mistakes made by lawyers can be very bad, including damaging a client's case and possible disbarment for the attorney (mistakes in aviation or in medicine are far worse, however). But to go beyond merely "avoiding bad things" benefits, look what else you get with checklists:

1. By reducing errors, checklists create a higher-quality finished product, which increases Average Case Unit Value.
2. By making things repetitive, checklists increase the speed of work, which reduces Cycle Time and increases Throughput Rate.

Standardized processes are perfect for Lean law firms because first of all, you can ensure that things are done right the first time, ensuring value for the client. Much time gets wasted having to go back and do things over again. Furthermore, the Lean law firm can constantly improve written procedures to get rid of *muda*, or waste.

CATALOG PROCESSES THAT SHOULD BE STANDARDIZED

Step one: Rid yourself of the erroneous notion that every matter is different, therefore standardized procedures do not apply to your firm. Malarkey. Many attorneys share this mistaken belief to their detriment. Even the most unpredictable cases follow rules of civil procedure. They involve different phases, the accessing of information, and storage of files, all of which can and should follow specific protocols.

Client Intake

Let's take a look at client intake, which usually is the closest thing most law firms have to an existing standardized process. Typically, intake starts with a paper form that clients fill out when they arrive for their first appointment. Usually something like this happens: A receptionist greets the new client and hands over a clipboard and a pen. The client fills out the form and hands it back to the receptionist. Someone on staff, receptionist or other, updates the firm's billing system and management system with the client's data. An engagement letter is generated by hand.

There's no reason why the intake process should not be scripted into a standardized process. Let's look at what happens when a firm takes a step in this direction and writes up an intake checklist. It would look something like this:

> Assemble intake packet, consisting of client intake form and credit card authorization.
> Hand client clipboard and pen with intake packet.
> Collect intake packet and scan original documents.
> Run conflict check (may require its own independent checklist).
> Enter intake information in practice management software.
> Create matter in practice management software.
> File intake documents with new matter.
> Generate engagement letter and hand to attorney.
> Collect signed engagement letter from attorney and scan engagement letter.
> File engagement letter with matter in practice management software.

It's a simple checklist. But making sure it gets followed can prevent even the most disciplined and veteran of employees from making a mistake when the inevitable work crises arise. And when you have a high-turnover position like a receptionist, the new ones can get up and running with minimal chance for error and miscommunication.

Taking a closer look, you can already see room for more standardization. "Create matter in practice management software" leaves a lot of room for interpretation. Opening a matter should be closely controlled via its own separate checklist to ensure that folder structures are created properly, the correct tasks are assigned, and the right billing structures are set up.

In addition, once you've codified the manual steps required for a process, room for improvement is immediately visible. Can you reduce the number of steps? Is there waste going on? Room for human error? For instance, in our intake example, the paper forms are problematic. They have to be printed and assembled. Once the client fills them out, they need to be entered into the case management system, which is both inefficient and subject to a data entry error.

Once you have your process nailed down, perhaps at a quarterly Retrospective meeting (see Chapter 8), you might discuss intake and decide to invest in an intake product that integrates with case management, which can then generate an engagement letter—things that web-based legal practice management products like Clio, Rocket Matter, and MyCase provide. Your process could now be as follows:

> Hand client iPad with electronic intake form loaded in browser.
> Generate engagement letter in practice management software and hand to attorney.
> Collect signed engagement letter from attorney and scan engagement letter.
> File engagement letter with matter in practice management software.

Billing

From what we've seen working with thousands of law firms, billing processes in law firms are full of holes. This observation is backed by data: According to a Georgetown Law study, lawyers only collect on 71 percent of the work they perform.[1] This is a shame, since, unlike product companies, a law firm's revenue is limited by the amount of hours its professionals can work.

Law firms already have the challenge of reducing administrative work to free more time for legal work. To squander those precious hours is reminiscent of an uncapped oil well, spewing uncollected money. While one approach that we counsel is to examine contingent or flat fee arrangements, if you're going to bill hourly, you must standardize it.

---

1. Thomson Reuters and Georgetown Law, *2015 Report on the State of the Legal Market*, available at http://www.law.georgetown.edu/academics/centers-institutes/legal-profession/upload/FINAL-Report-1-7-15.pdf.

Billing can be broken down into two main components, invoicing and collections. Hourly billing firms also have time capture as a third major component, which we explore in the box that follows. As we discussed in Chapter 4, cash is the oxygen for your business, so of all standardized processes, one might argue that these are the most important things to focus on. A sample checklist for the firm might be:

> On the first of every month, run pre-bills for all active matters on an attorney-by-attorney basis.
> Institute a billing lockdown period, when no additional billable activities can be added to the system.
> Deliver to each attorney pre-bills for approval.
> Once all approvals are in, lift the lockdown period.
> Generate invoices.
> Fold invoices.
> Address envelopes.
> Stuff envelopes and apply postage.

If your firm moves to an electronic billing system, where invoices are e-mailed, you can eliminate the last three steps from the preceding list. Any time you can remove steps, that is a good thing.

The collection process needs to be looked at as well. You need to be able to understand, for example, the average collection time. How much money is typically collected at 30 days, 60 days, 90 days, and longer? What are the protocols for following up with delayed payments? Do you have mechanisms like keeping a credit card or banking information on file for automatic withdrawals?

We highly recommend you write out all steps of your billing and collections process as an exercise. If anything needs to run smoothly without missing a beat, it's your invoicing, and analyzing your process can lay bare the inefficiencies.

You will likely find parts of the process that are jury-rigged together with duct tape. This exercise is especially important if one key employee owns the billing process and knows the ins and outs of how you bill. Should something happen to that person, your firm will have a crisis on its hands.

Matter Setup

Whether you are working with the most routine and straightforward file such as trademark application, or you're working on a complex piece of litigation, matter creation should be standardized. You typically deal with the same tasks, deadlines, roles, billing rates, and documents in similar matter types within the same jurisdiction, which cries out for doing things the same way each time.

> **Tracking Billable Time**
>
> The third leg of the billing stool, after invoicing and collections, is time capture. Even for firms that do not bill by the hour, tracking time should be a strong consideration. Since a firm's productivity is limited by the number of hours its professionals can work, it makes sense to understand the return on investment of a contingency or flat fee matter. In addition, should the court request time records on a matter, the lawyer does not need to frantically produce an inaccurate timesheet.
>
> Tracking time is a small activity that's not quite a process. However, it should be standardized: How and when people track their time and what information they record should be spelled out. We've found that the best policy is to track time while you're doing an activity (as opposed to afterwards) and to use more descriptive language than not.
>
> For lawyers who dread time tracking, it is worth noting that many legal practice management systems help you out by converting routine activities to time entries. Calendar events, tasks, even routines like tracking phone calls or uploading documents can be funneled easily onto invoices.

It's critical that you have a formalized, written protocol for setting up a matter. When coming up with your standardized steps, we recommend the following:

1. Describe your naming convention. At the risk of floating a master-of-the-obvious notion, you need a consistent, firmwide taxonomy for your matters. Their names should be unique and intuitive so that there's minimal risk of creating duplicates. If you have multiple people creating matters in your firm, and you're finding that people are mistakenly adding time to different matters in your system, the likely culprit is your naming process.
2. You're going to want to ensure that each matter has a file directory structure that's consistent across your practice. Nothing is more frustrating than not being able to locate a file. Everyone needs to be on the same page when it comes to how files are named and how they are stored. See the next section on document naming and filing for an example.
3. Consider investing in a practice management system that allows you to define custom matter templates. These allow you to define your own tasks, calendar events, and deadlines—even billing types, rates, and data fields to go along with your file. A good matter template is as close as you can get to programmatically defining a standard way of setting up a matter. Some programs even allow you to layer in partial templates, for different phases of a matter.
4. Another way to help standardize matter creation is the use of a rules-based calendaring program. Programs such as LawToolBox

automatically calculate all of your deadlines based on the matter type and location.
5. Your firm may greatly benefit from Kanban boards to visualize matters as they travel through different phases. In our discussion of Kanban in Chapter 9, as you see matters progress from one swim lane to the next, you will start to see where your process is efficient and where you have slowdowns.

Document Naming and Filing

For firms looking to reduce waste (*muda*), going paperless is not a maybe, it's a must. The amount of *muda* involved in printing, filing, and locating paper files is too great when the digital alternative is so much better. The tools and technologies involved in digitizing files are powerful, mature, and inexpensive.

With scanning, it's critical to come up with a rock-solid plan to maintain digital organization. Keeping all of your documents in consistent shape over the years is a tall order unless you're vigilant about your filing and naming practices. For naming, it's often good practice to encode the following into your file names:

1. Date—in YYYY-mm-dd order, for example, 1776-07-04. When the year comes first, files will always be sortable in chronological order. If you put the month or day first, you lose this inherent feature.
2. Description—briefly, what the file contains.
3. Author/Recipient—using the initials of the person.
4. Regarding—usually a matter indicator.
5. Suffix—possibly a version or indicator to know if something is a final, encrypted, or executed copy.

Following are two example file names based on these guidelines:

2017-01-04 Motion for Partial Summ Judgment LP M123 v1.docx
2018-02-15 5301 N. Federal Hwy Lease DM M345 EXECUTED.pdf

Likewise, the way your files are organized in folders needs to be contemplated and made consistent globally. Each matter resides in its own folder and contains, every single time, a specific directory structure that maintains corresponding documents. A simple example is the following structure:

1. Admin
2. Attorney Notes and Research

3. Client Documents
4. Correspondence
5. Costs
6. Discovery
7. Drafts
8. Pleadings
9. Trial Prep

The illustration shows this folder structure executed on a PC. This structure can be implemented whether you're on a PC or a Mac, using Dropbox, Box, OneDrive, Google Drive, or a legal software package.

Document management systems (DMSs) are an option law firms might want to consider if they are looking to unify document access firmwide. Many legal practice management systems have a DMS built in, but standalone systems are also available.

Document Creation through Templates

In terms of standardization, another thing you might want to consider is leveraging document templates to generate your files. Templates are fill-in-the-blank documents that allow you to merge data into them, allowing for instant file generation. You have to invest time up front (or have a specialist help you) to set up the templates, but once that's done, you can say goodbye to searching for similar files and using copy and paste to create a new document.

Rocket Matter, itself a consumer of legal services, has had at least three occasions since its beginning when attorneys counseling the company have included old company names or other terms that were clearly vestigial clauses from copied documents. It's unprofessional and embarrassing. You do not want to be that guy, and document templates help you to avoid this situation.

Document templates can be created with dedicated software packages like HotDocs and Doxsera, and they are a common feature in practice management programs like Rocket Matter, Clio, and MyCase.

ADDITIONAL PROCESSES TO NAIL DOWN

The more you can document standard procedures, the less your firm will generate errors, the easier it will be to train new people, and the better your efficiency will be over time. Take a look at your processes for dealing with the following:

1. E-mail—What's in your signatures and disclaimers? How do you organize and file your e-mails? Are staffers expected to constantly have e-mail open, or should they only respond at certain designated times throughout the day? What's the threshold at which something is too sensitive (or too large) for e-mail and needs to be transmitted another way?
2. Computers—How and when are you applying updates and security patches? What is your password policy? How often do you replace machines, and what happens if someone's machine is unusable for whatever reason? How and when do you back up your data?
3. Physical Security—What do you do to lock sensitive data at night? Who is allowed access to what resources? What are individual employees obligated to do to ensure that their desks and physical artifacts are secure?
4. Business Continuity—This is near and dear to those of us living in hurricane territory. Where does everyone go in the event of a disaster? How are files backed up? Are you going to send someone to another destination and keep the lights on, or are you going to shut down?

TIPS AND TOOLS FOR CREATING STANDARDIZED PROCESSES

1. The good news about creating standardized, repeatable processes is that you do not have to invest in an expensive tool. A simple Word document will do the trick.
2. Not all checklists are created equal. According to Gawande, well-designed checklists are short, between five and nine steps. Once checklists become lengthier, the thinking goes, people start to skip steps.
3. Another important tool to help keep your team in synch is the flowchart. Flowcharts are helpful process documents that are especially useful when activities might take different directions based on the situation. They can easily be created using presentation software like Keynote or PowerPoint.
4. Consider printing critical processes out and distributing them to your staff in binders. For more common processes that happen all the time, laminating and handing out sheets that are in constant view is a great idea.

CHAPTER SUMMARY

Standardization doesn't just get your team on the same page; it helps veterans to avoid errors and gets rookies up to speed quickly. Simple tools like the checklist are much more powerful than they seem, allowing you to put on paper what you have in your head and to spot opportunities to streamline processes. We recommend taking a look at the mission-critical processes in your firm and putting them in writing. Take a look at your processes over time to continue reducing the risk of error and maximizing your profitability.

CHAPTER 8

Visual Communication, Meetings, and Rhythm

August

Rain was starting to fall just as Carson parked his car near the door of the C² factory. He was riding his bike more and more these days and feeling great, but he never enjoyed riding in pouring rain. Thankfully, those days were over. There was something to be said for a desk job.

Since their McSkippy's meeting, Carson had invested nearly all of his time into breaking down each of the practice areas that the firm had selected for its ultimate Brand Basket into its component parts, then writing checklists covering each area from intake through file closing. He had then coded the checklists so that each team member knew, theoretically, which items on the list were his or her responsibility.

But while things were finally becoming standardized, Carson was still having trouble communicating that standardization firmwide. While the checklists provided great clarity and ensured that nothing would be missed, they had created friction as well, particularly at the point where one staff member finished an assigned task and handed the case off to the next. It was hard to tell who had the ball sometimes.

Carson was also troubled by the fact that when someone else was working on one of his cases, he did not really have a sense of what progress was being made or if any was being made at all. It was as if the case disappeared into a black hole and re-emerged later. He didn't like that feeling of not knowing exactly what was going on—not only with his own cases, but with the firm's as a whole. How could he see constraints and Wait Time when he couldn't even see where the case was in the overall process? He had called a meeting with all the staff to try to fix this, but that had only devolved into a two-hour finger-pointing session. A complete waste of time.

He hoped that Guy had some answers today.

"Carson!" shouted Guy. "Are you here? Come into my office. I want to show you something."

Carson walked into Guy's office to find Guy holding an old framed picture. In the picture was an older Japanese man standing next to a much younger Guy on a factory floor.

"That looks ancient. When was that taken, Guy?" asked Carson.

Guy replied, "That's me with Mr. Aoki in 1979. On the floor of the Miyoto microwave oven factory. Mr. Aoki was the manager. One of the smartest guys I ever met."

Guy continued, "But that's not what's important in the picture. Look closer, Carson. Can you see what's up on the factory wall behind us?"

Carson squinted at the yellowing photo in the frame. Barely in focus, but on the wall behind Guy and Aoki, were large black screens with red light-up letters, like old scoreboards in the pre-Jumbotron era.

Guy explained, "Those are Kanban boards. You see them in factories all over the world now. We implemented them at C^2 years ago, just about the time you went off to school. Having a big screen on the factory floor that every worker can see lets us optimize the flow of our work here. Everyone knows, at a glance, the status of every order in our process. Everyone knows what they are working on, who is responsible for what, and, most importantly, if any undone task is blocking the flow of the process. See those red Xs? They symbolize a block that needs to be addressed immediately. We can also find WNR Time—where things are just sitting there for no reason—because, after a certain time, the order starts to turn gray on the board. We can also see bottlenecks develop when units begin to pile up at some point in the process. The Kanban board is what ties everything together and allows us to communicate visually without even having to talk."

"I like that," said Carson. "I'm fresh out of a two-hour meeting at Gray Firm that went absolutely nowhere. I was trying to just get some idea of where each case stood, and what was blocking progress. I now have this great mental picture of the firm as a system, but communicating it was a nightmare, and it wasted not only my two hours, but everyone else's in the whole firm."

Guy considered that, and replied, "Sit-down meetings have their place. We have a short 30-minute one every Monday morning. But it's a terrible way to try to communicate status, progress, and issues company- (or firm-) wide. Factories understand that better than service businesses. Especially lawyers—you all sure like to talk! But like I keep saying, a business is a business. For visualizing the overall flow of work and optimizing it, Kanban boards communicate that far better than meetings.

"And one more thing I should say about communication while we're on the subject, that I promised last month to address," said Guy. "Communication with your customer."

Guy elaborated, "Remember last month at McSkippy's when we talked about building 'something people really want, as perfectly as possible, available when and how they want it' as the keys to customer satisfaction? I left out something important: You have to *tell* customers what is going on. Better still, they have to be able to see progress.

"There's a reason, Carson, that car washes have windows so you can see your car going through the process of getting clean. If you'll notice, lots of times, the car wash even has the windows separated by each part of the process, like undercarriage wash or wax. Psychologically, people love to see the positive progression. To the customer, the visualization of progress might be even more important than speed itself. So you have to communicate that. At C^2, we have not only a 'Track My Order' feature on our website, but integrated webcams on the floor so customers can actually see their orders being made. Now, you can't do that in a law firm, of course, but you need to find some way to make your process transparent to your client."

Carson considered this. He wondered if Laura Kilbourne would have fired her last lawyers if they had been better at communicating to her what was going on. After all, didn't lawyers have an ethical obligation to keep clients informed about the progress of their cases? And wouldn't more transparency make that obligation easier to meet?

Guy took Carson by the arm out to the factory floor, where Kanban boards glowed above the frame assembly line. "C'mon out to the factory floor, Carson, and let's look at all of this up close and personal."

If you're becoming a Lean law firm, you're building an efficient engine. Engines are complex machines that require distinct parts to fire together in a coordinated effort (you and the people in your law firm are the "distinct parts" in this analogy, by the way).

At first, your newly fired-up Lean law firm might be a sputtering, slow engine, reminiscent of something that might blow black soot all over someone in an old movie. Eventually, however, with enough cycles and dedication, your firm will hum like a Maserati V8.

The trick is the steady, rhythmic building of *alignment*. Alignment sounds like one of those awful business words, like *synergy*, but it is very important to the long-term success of your organization.

Alignment is created by getting everyone on the same page. Up, down, and across your organization, your goals and priorities need to be crystal clear. And there is no better way to pull this off than through face-to-face meetings and powerful visual artifacts. In this chapter we will be discussing best-of-breed meetings and returning to our beloved visual process driver, the Kanban board.

Let it be known that we are against meeting for the sake of meeting. A law firm cannot afford non-billable-hour meetings that absorb everyone's time. Lean is as much about eliminating waste as anything, so we are not going to recommend anything that's a waste of time. We are advocating quick, efficient meetings that are powerful, painless, and get the job done.

Before we get into the meetings, we suggest that if you're going to pick one meeting from this list to implement, make it a monthly Retrospective meeting, which we describe in this chapter. That's the one meeting that will spur the adoption of better business methods for your firm. Think of it like first gear: It gets you going. With that one meeting, you can start introducing the other techniques listed in this chapter.

Additionally, we are not preaching orthodoxy here. These meetings aren't out of a Lean playbook per se; they come from related fields, including Agile project management and general business management techniques.

But they support the overall goal of eliminating waste and working in iterative cycles.

> **I Don't Have Time for Strategic Meetings**
>
> Yes, you do. If you are running a business, not just a law firm, and you can set aside disconnected time for hearings or CLE, then you also have time to get aligned with your team!
>   Make sure phones are silenced and laptops are closed. If you're going to take people out of revenue mode (i.e., providing legal services), make sure the time counts.

MEETING RHYTHMS

Daily Standup Meeting
Importance Level: Critical

Law firms that adopt the daily standup love it. This meeting comes from Scrum, another project management discipline, and it is one of those techniques that, when we present it at conferences or webinars, people report back that they love it. The daily standup meeting happens early in the day, after everyone arrives to work and gets initially organized. Our team's daily standup happens at 9:30 am sharp and has been going on since Rocket Matter's inception in 2007.

The meeting is called the daily standup meeting because you have it every day, and because you do it standing up. No one enjoys standing for extended periods of time, so the act of standing keeps it short. It should really be no more than ten minutes.

Each person comes to the daily standup prepared to state three things:

1. What they worked on **Yesterday**
2. What they're doing **Today**
3. What's **In Their Way**

Here's an example from our old friend Alice:

Yesterday: I drafted a pleading for the Hobbs complaint. I researched case law for the Sky Brothers trademark issue. I went to Rotary and networked at lunch.
Today: I have to reach out to the other side for the Delta mediation and get a date set. I need to respond to opposing counsel about the Hobbs hearing. I also have to continue some investigation into the trademark issue.
In my way: Bob. Bob is in my way. He still hasn't finished his initial draft of the Yosemite motion.

Such a simple meeting held while standing up seems like a hipster way of doing things worthy of mockery on the show *Silicon Valley*. In reality, the daily standup needs to be strictly regimented. These three items are very important. You want to know what happened **yesterday** to see if your team moved the ball forward as they said they would. You want to know what's about to happen **today** so that you can see if momentum is being continued or if you, as a leader, feel that priorities need to be reshuffled.

Finding out what's in someone's way reveals *dependencies*. Dependencies are deadly in an organization because they prevent work from being done, and often they chain together in invisible threads that trip your law firm up. When people say what's in their way, they reveal what obstacles lie in their paths that prevent them from achieving their objectives. The leader's job is to find a way to remove the dependencies so that work may proceed.

A couple of other considerations/rules for hosting a long-enduring daily standup:

> No one can be late; the daily standup has to be crisp and efficient. Some teams enforce a strict start time by having a dollar jar that you must contribute a dollar to for every minute you are late.
> If people start having dialogues about their work with more than just status updates (and this will inevitably happen), your standup will spin out of control quickly. The group leader needs to enforce this. A gentle "take it offline" or "let's discuss after standup" from the leader keeps the quick meeting on track and gets it over with.
> There should be no more than eight people in a standup meeting; otherwise the meeting will take too long. If you have more than eight people, consider having several separate standup meetings, with key individuals attending multiple standups so they can make cross-team reports.

If you follow these simple rules, the daily standup introduces a tremendous amount of accountability into your organization. People cannot hide behind excuses. Our friend Bob may be in serious trouble. You will see who moves quickly and who lags behind. When an employee keeps reporting in about the same things every day, leadership needs to take a look at this. Is the employee procrastinating? Ineffective? Not reporting dependencies?

My experience is that when you heighten accountability through visibility of action, things change. Not everyone in your organization may like or even survive the transition to Lean. Be aware that the productive thrive, and the laggards may very well end up leaving either by choice or by force.

To see a standup meeting in action, check out a YouTube video we made here: leanlawfirmbook.com/standup.

- ✘ **DON'T:** Skip the "in my way" part. You need to see what's blocking people.
- ✘ **DON'T:** Allow the standup to devolve into a conversation about particular issues. As a leader, direct such talk to take place after the meeting. Keep everyone on task.
- ✔ **DO:** Religiously hold a daily standup every day.
- ✔ **DO:** Consider using software like GoToMeeting, Appear.In, or Skype to videoconference with remote or traveling participants.

Monthly Retrospective Meeting
Importance Level: Critical

If there is one meeting you need to introduce right away to transform your law firm into a Lean machine, it is the Retrospective meeting. As we have mentioned, the Retrospective is like first gear in that it gets you started. With this mechanism, you can inject new processes and perspectives into your firm.

In the monthly Retrospective, as in the daily standup, you discuss three questions as they pertain to your operational processes:

1. What should we **Start** doing?
2. What should we **Stop** doing?
3. What should we **Continue** doing?

Here's an example:

> *Alice:* We need to STOP having people fill out intake forms and then have Sheila enter the information into the system. We're introducing too many errors.
> *Bob:* We need to START holding daily standup meetings!
> *Charlene:* I think we should CONTINUE tracking our website KPIs through Google Analytics. We're getting a lot of solid information from our site visitors!
> *Alice:* Bob needs to STOP leaving his filthy dishes in the sink.
> *Meeting Leader:* Alice, may I remind you we are here to talk about process.

The meeting leader or facilitator needs to write the commentary down. That way it can be reviewed and referenced later. It's important to see if you actually did what you said you were going to do so that the output of the meeting is actionable; otherwise, you're going to continue making the same mistakes.

In a small law firm, it's important to have all players at the firm involved. You need to have direct feedback from whomever is actually performing the work. For example, you cannot improve your billing process without your back-office people, nor can you improve your intake without your receptionist or other personnel who are in charge. Go directly to the source, and make no assumptions.

It is critical to note that the Retrospective is about process improvement. It is not a forum for people to air personal grievances. If you have a lot of interpersonal conflict in your organization, either keep out the bad eggs or be prepared to aggressively mediate the situation. In the preceding example, the facilitator should gently remind Alice that the purpose of the Retrospective is not to personally criticize Bob.

Once you get above eight people attending a Retrospective, staff is often too hesitant to speak up because the size of the group affects participation. In this case, we recommend breaking into smaller teams or having your existing teams conduct Retrospectives and report their findings up the chain.

It isn't uncommon for small and medium-size law firms to employ people who are very set in their ways and territorially guard their workflows. As a leader or change agent in your organization, you must be aware that such employees may be threatened by any change to process or the status quo. Analysis might reveal comfortable but inefficient practices relied upon for years. In some cases, it may be revealed that someone's job is no longer needed.

If there's anyone on staff whose knowledge of a process is proprietary and strictly guarded, you have a problem on your hands. I'm not talking about a complicated process that is tough to learn; I'm referring to people who relish their situation of exclusive knowledge. First of all, you are at risk for a lack of business continuity should something happen to your resource. But moreover, recognize that you are being held hostage by this person.

- ✗ **DON'T:** Restrict attendance at the Retrospective to managing partners. Make sure anyone who participates in your processes attends.
- ✓ **DO:** Make sure the Retrospective is focused on process, not individuals.
- ✗ **DON'T:** Let the Retrospective devolve into a whine session about your business or people there.

> **Give Your Monthly Meeting a Little More Power**
>
> Once a month is a good interval to review your Key Performance Indicator (KPI) spreadsheet or dashboards described in Chapter 4. As we mentioned, some of these measurements are important to look at on a monthly basis.
>
> Before you commence with the Retrospective, we suggest you begin with a review of your monthly KPIs. This will invariably spur conversation. If numbers are down, you will want to know what you should do to correct them, if anything. If numbers are up or the same, you will likely want to know what contributed to their movement or lack thereof.
>
> Once the overall snapshot of the business has been established through your KPIs, the Retrospective will likely be richer because all parties are more informed of the state of things.

Annual Planning and Goal-Setting Meeting
Importance Level: Critical

Just to be clear, there is nothing particularly Lean about holding an annual planning meeting. Businesses of all stripes do this. However, the annual planning meeting gives you the opportunity to reinforce the Lean nature of your business and give a strong shock to the system. Viewing the annual planning meeting as an opportunity to iteratively improve and eliminate waste, in addition to charting out your strategic goals, is a critical accelerator to helping you become a much stronger organization.

Annual planning meetings should ideally be held offsite. If you can treat your leadership team to a weekend away from the firm, whether at a resort or at a swanky AirBnB rental in Key Largo, it will help you keep the day-to-day slog at arm's length. You gain new perspective this way. There are no interruptions. Your team can bond in a more relaxed atmosphere. If this is too ambitious, contact a local Regus or executive suite center and rent a conference room for a couple of days. The most important thing is that you get out of your office.

The complete particulars of holding an offsite annual planning meeting are beyond the scope of this book. For our purposes here we want to recommend some exercises that specifically help with Lean techniques. To learn more about hosting a quality annual offsite, you will be well served by Verne Harnish's techniques described in *Scaling Up*. Verne's techniques, known as The Rockefeller Habits, ask businesses to consider ideas posed by some of the great business thinkers of our day, in particular Jim Collins. Furthermore, we suggest investing in a business coach to help facilitate this meeting.

- ✔ **DO:** Conduct an offsite annual meeting to address the strategic direction and performance of your firm.
- ✔ **DO:** Make sure the rest of your staff is aware they must not interrupt you unless absolutely necessary.
- ✔ **DO:** Consider hiring a business coach to help you with your yearly planning.

Exercise 1: Review All KPIs and Set New Targets

We'll talk more specifically about goal setting in Chapter 10, and we will dive deeper into how to set goals for your most important Income Formula KPIs, including Annual Income, and the components that determine it such as Cycle Time. In general, though, looking at KPIs over the last 12 months is a great way to start any annual planning session (if you skipped or forgot Chapter 4, now might be a good time to get a little intimate with it). Each member of the leadership team should be accountable for and report on specific KPIs. Assigning responsibilities for tracking and improving KPIs helps ensure that they move in the right direction. We will talk about this in significantly more detail in Chapter 10, and we'll also introduce you to the concept of the **October Surprise**, an annual event where the focus of the firm shifts temporarily to system improvements.

The annual planning meeting is also a good time to start incorporating more tracking by absorbing more KPIs to track. It's never a good idea to start tracking everything at once, as it can become burdensome and doomed to failure. Instead, Lean businesses are best served when they evolve over iterations. Along those lines, it makes sense at your first annual planning meeting to track a small number of carefully selected KPIs, then continue to add more over time as you become more comfortable in your operations.

The other thing to think about is setting goals for each KPI. Harnish recommends that each KPI should have a "green" number, or the number that you would be happy with, and a "red" number, or one that you would not be happy with. That way, when the next year rolls around, you can tell objectively if you've been successful or not.

- ✔ **DO:** Establish both high and low KPI targets to guide and measure performance.
- ✘ **DON'T:** Bite off more than you can chew. Build momentum by only bringing in a few KPIs to track at a time.
- ✔ **DO:** Assign accountability for KPIs to individual team members.

Exercise 2: SWOT Analysis

SWOT stands for Strengths, Weaknesses, Opportunities, and Threats. A SWOT analysis is a widely used business tool, so much so that it was lampooned in the show *Silicon Valley* on HBO.

In a SWOT analysis, each participant in the meeting writes down the strengths, weaknesses, opportunities, and threats to your organization. This is done in isolation for ten minutes or so. A good way to do this is to provide everyone with a stack of index cards and a marker. They write down one idea per card.

The ideas or observations should be something that's very solid and defensible and not likely to change. Allow me to share some inside information of my own company by way of example.

> ❯ A strength of my organization is that we are very good at branding and design. This starts at the top and is a characteristic of the people we hire.

> A weakness for my organization is that we have large, billion-dollar competitors.
> An opportunity for us is that as of this writing, many older PC-based legal software is not modern.
> A threat for us is the constant innovation in technology—we are only one brilliant competitor away from obsolescence.

Once everyone writes down their SWOT cards, the meeting leader or facilitator arranges them into SWOT quadrants. All feedback requires attention, but when you start seeing duplicate information across multiple people (remember, this was done in isolation), you know you have an item that needs particular TLC.

Shown here is a visual representation of a SWOT board.

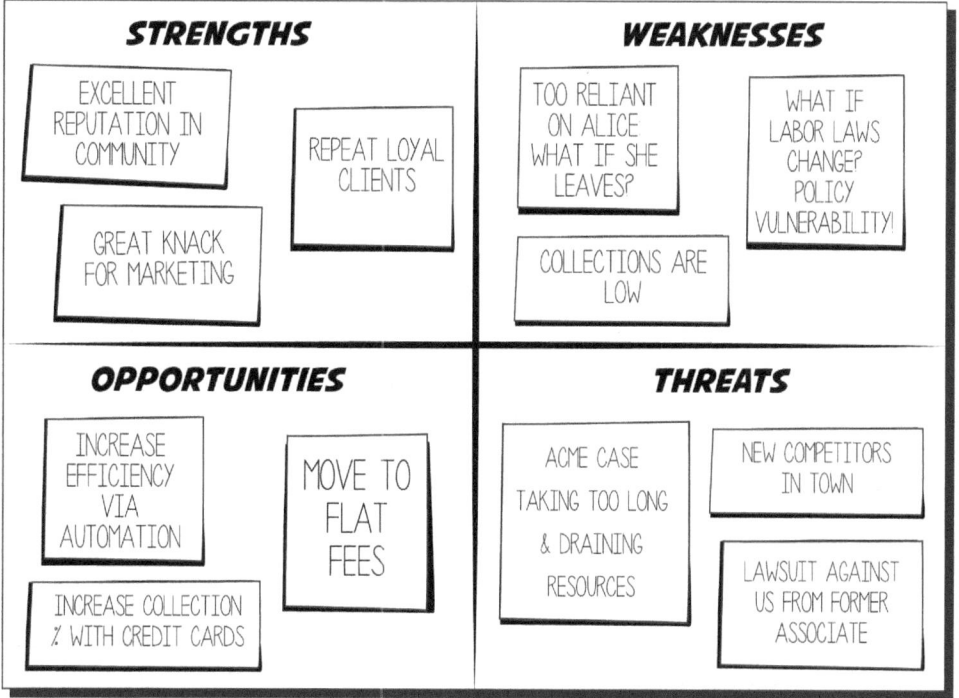

✔ **DO:** Have everyone work independently for approximately ten minutes or so.
✔ **DO:** Write one idea per index card.
✔ **DO:** Take a picture of the quadrants or transcribe your SWOT analysis once the exercise is complete.

✗ **DON'T:** Confuse threats and weaknesses. Threats are something external that can kill you. Weaknesses are internal problems that you must fortify.

Exercise 3: Retrospective

What better time to conduct the Retrospective than at the annual review? This is the 50-thousand-foot view of the business, whereas you're a lot closer to the action when you hold a monthly review. You're with your leadership team at an annual offsite, not the rank and file, so the issues you see will not be so detail oriented. They may be more strategic than process oriented.

Like the SWOT, the Retrospective is a great way to involve everyone's thoughts in the process and look for commonalities and agreements. It's also a very easy session to conduct.

> **The Almighty One-Pager**
>
> One-page summaries about strategy or problems are incredibly helpful. They force you to think through important issues and to write your thoughts out succinctly.
>
> Toyota's A3 Problem Solving technique is named for the size of paper it is written on: A3. The idea is that you describe a problem, analysis, and steps for corrective action on one piece of paper. A template is available here: http://www.lean.org/downloads/a3_word_template.doc.

Even though it's not directly out of Lean orthodoxy, you might find the Gazelle organization's One-Page Strategic Plan (https://gazelles.com/static/resources/tools/en/OPSP.pdf) to be invaluable to walk you through your annual planning. It forces you to evaluate who you are and where you want to go. If you fill the entire thing out, you will know the following about yourself:

› Your core purpose and core values, as discussed by Jim Collins in his seminal paper Building Your Company's Vision (available for purchase at https://hbr.org/1996/09/building-your-companys-vision).
› Your three- to five-year goals and what initiatives you will embark on to get you there.
› Your one-year goals and critical numbers for measuring success.
› Who your critical people are and how to measure their success.
› Your BHAG®, or Big Hairy Audacious Goal, another Jim Collins inspirational invention (https://en.wikipedia.org/wiki/Big_Hairy_Audacious_Goal)

Last but Not Least: Quarterly and Weekly Meetings
Importance Level: Critical

If you meet daily, monthly, and annually, you're well on your way to creating alignment in your organization. However, you may also want to consider meeting on a weekly and quarterly basis to go over business strategy.

It might seem like overkill, and it could be for your organization, but here's the idea: If you come up with a coherent annual strategy, organizing your tactics on a quarterly basis serves to keep you on track. The annual initiatives you come up with need to be reinforced with quarterly priorities.

Quarterly meetings, since they serve as a boost for the annual goals, happen every 13 weeks and should also be conducted offsite. You might want to consider doing some of the things you do at an annual meeting, such as a SWOT analysis or Retrospective. However, the output of the meeting should be your priorities for the next three months that will get you toward your annual goals. For more direction on quarterly meetings, Harnish's *Scaling Up* is a great resource.

Weekly meetings are great touch points to survey the battlefield. Many law firms do this to go over the status of their cases. This is where the visual assistance of a Kanban board can be of great help. In addition to case status, weekly meetings are a great time to briefly go over key performance indicators affecting the firm and to bring up any odd issues that arose during the week.

> **On Weekly Meetings**
>
> *Dave:* I'm actually a fan of the weekly meeting. We do it every Monday morning. On one big screen, we project our Kanban board. Then we go through the calendar, looking at what's coming up in the next two weeks, and we assign responsibilities on the Kanban to team members. Next we check our deadlines, which we keep in the Task feature of our case management system. Again we assign responsibilities and mark deadlines on the Kanban. Finally, we look only at the Kanban itself, touching on each Case Unit "card" on the board and briefly discussing what needs to be done to move it to the next stage (or even better, to Done). Again, we assign Kanban responsibilities. Afterward, the vast majority of our "meetings" simply involve back and forth messaging over the Kanban board. The whole thing takes an hour, and after it is done, everyone is crystal clear on their responsibilities for the coming week.

KANBAN BOARDS, PART DEUX

While Carson is only now discovering Kanban boards, we introduced them earlier in the book to you because they are transformational. We hope we've convinced you already how great Kanban boards are at helping a team "see" their system and process flow. Now let's dive deeper into the parts of Kanban. The basic elements are swim lanes and cards. The stages of a process are laid out in order from left to right. The card is an item that goes through the process, from one stage to the next. It is physically moved from one swim lane to the next.

Here is a simple example of a Kanban board:

As we've mentioned previously, we are mapping a left-to-right flow. Usually, the leftmost swim lane is an "up next" type of staging area, and the rightmost lane is a "done" one. In the middle of the board are our work-in-progress lanes, also known as WIP. A Kanban board could be physical, with index cards moving across lanes marked with tape, or virtual, using a tool such as JIRA, Leankit, or Trello (we used Trello in Chapter 5). We will discuss tech tools more in Chapter 9.

Kanban boards used to be unheard of in law firms, but their use is starting to rise. Typically, one index card represents one case, and it is tracked through the various stages of the case, whether it is litigation-based or transactional. (As we've discussed before, we recommend that a card represent a Case Unit in your system.)

CASE STUDY

How Paul Saunders, attorney in the large firm Stewart McKelvey in Halifax, Nova Scotia, uses Kanban boards and daily standup meetings

One of the teams where we had the most success with Kanban was our team of insurance defense lawyers. We had a number of associates and partners, paralegals, and legal assistants servicing one of our major clients, who had a portfolio of about 70 or 80 active litigation matters that were in various stages.

We put a Kanban board up on a wall and identified all the different key stages that every one of these insurance defense files would go through, from client intake all the way to closing the file, including distribution of the file to collection of information, pleadings, pretrial, trial, appeal, and every phase in discovery.

Every card represented an active matter, which would have on it who the plaintiff was, who the defendant was, proposed trial date, or any other relevant information. Then we moved the cards from left to right and indicated on each card who's responsible for moving that along between now and the next meeting.

We followed the daily standup, and we time-restricted everybody to two minutes to answer those three basic questions. What did I do since the last meeting? What am I going to do before the next one? And what's blocking me?

Kanban makes nonvisual work visual. Unlike a bike moving through a factory, it can be hard to "see" the progression of a legal case. The Kanban board makes the case and its movement through the system visual and lets the team see where all of its cases are in the overall system, in one central place.

THE LAST WORD ON KANBAN BOARDS (NOT REALLY)

The (almost) last thing we want to emphasize about Kanban boards is how customizable they are. Every firm is different and has different processes. But Kanban boards can represent them all. Web-based versions can also do some things that paper boards can never do: help you identify your blocks, threats, and opportunities through the magic of technology.

We talked earlier about how most computerized Kanban boards will allow you to label or otherwise mark a case card as "blocked." That means everyone looking at the board can see it and, as we said earlier, what you can see you can fix. The block (if internal) can be addressed immediately. Most web-based products (Trello, for example) also allow you to create custom labels. We suggest you create a label to identify a case as one that is currently a prospect for settlement. Why? Because when you're "patrolling your board," after you've gone through the priorities we discussed in Chapter 5 (Deadlines, Waiting Cases, Queue, etc.) you want to be able to identify these opportunities so you can act on them. Remember: The chance to move a case from an earlier stage to Done (if favorable to your client) allows you to leapfrog intervening phases in the process—and shortcut Cycle Time. That's highly favorable for your income.

Web-based software (like Trello) is great because it lets you filter your cases in many ways, one of which is by label. In this way, you can immediately focus not only on blocks in the process, but opportunities.

CHAPTER SUMMARY

To continually improve, Lean law firms need to be in constant alignment. The best way to create alignment is via meetings and visual artifacts. Since we don't want "death by meetings," it is important to avoid waste and employ well-understood, efficient meetings. The daily standup, the monthly Retrospective, and annual planning can all be used to employ Lean methodologies. Kanban boards are helpful to visualize the progress of cases, eliminate the meetings that many firms have reflexively, and make the ones you do have more brief and effective.

CHAPTER 9

Getting Control of Technology

September

As Carson pedaled his bike to meet Guy in the park, his mind was on the problem of Briana Reyes.

Briana had been the most highly prized law school recruit from the class of 2014. Following an unspectacular high school performance, she squeaked into State University with scant financial aid and modest expectations. She had to put herself through school by waiting tables. But midway through her freshman year, she had been talked by her roommate into joining State U's Robotics Team. There, something finally clicked. She loved the cool, binary logic that operated the machines and became, even as a freshman, the team's MVP. And she finally started to see her own potential. Her beliefs were validated when she was the only student to ace her first-year engineering finals.

She graduated from State U with a near-perfect GPA and a double major in electrical engineering and computer science. Despite multiple scholarship offers to hard science graduate programs, she turned them all down to attend law school, enthralled by logic of a different sort. Again she excelled, becoming editor of the law review, graduating number one in her class, and still finding time to volunteer for the pro bono disability law project and to embrace the latest technology. She seemed able to do the work of three people.

K&M's recruiters fell all over themselves trying to land her but, true to form, Briana shocked everyone by showing up on Ambrose's doorstep to beg for a job. Ambrose could not pay nearly as much as the big firms, but he was never a fool, so he scratched something together and hired her immediately. Ambrose was hoping Briana's raw talent and tech expertise could turn things around for the firm. And for Briana—who grew up in town and was familiar with the legend of Ambrose—it was a dream come true. She saw herself taking on the kinds of cases she wanted, ones that made a difference. It should have been a win-win.

Unfortunately, it had not worked out as either of them had hoped. The problem was not their working relationship, as they clearly liked each other very much. It was the clash between Ambrose's methodical, old-school, pen-and-paper way of doing things and Briana's boundless energy and enthusiasm for all things technological. Ever eager to please and show that she could turn things around, Briana had talked Ambrose into one technology initiative after another. First, a new and improved network; then new case management software. Then document automation software. Dual monitors. Yet another case management software when the first had not worked as hoped. Ambrose's suspicion of technology had only deepened as a result.

Briana's youthful enthusiasm got her into trouble in other ways, too. She had marketed herself and the firm on every social network for every conceivable practice area, and she had made herself available to her clients 24/7 via various technologies. Her office sounded like NASA Mission Control, with beeps, pings, and pop-ups emitting from her computer screens, cell phone, and tablet. While her attempt to be constantly available was admirable, it (and Briana's natural tendency to multitask) denied her the focus that she needed for her caseload, which required a significant amount of legal writing. This she could only seem to find time to do at night, after everyone had gone home. It seemed, finally, that even her boundless energy had limits.

Carson had been struggling with this problem since starting with the Gray Firm 11 months earlier. He still did not know how to address it tactfully. Many of Briana's technology ideas were great ones, even if adopted without a coherent plan. Carson knew one thing for sure: The Gray Firm needed Briana to focus. She was, by far, the biggest brain in the firm and was key to its future.

With all this playing through his helmet-covered head, Carson pedaled his bike to a stop before Guy, who was people-watching from a park bench.

"Look at this, Carson. The leaves are turning, the air is crisp. One of the most gorgeous days of the year. And all these people walking around, looking into little screens. Maybe I'm just too old, Carson, but I don't get it."

Carson nodded. But then he remembered the time months before that Guy had monitored his junior women's team remotely on his cell phone from a park bench. "You use technology all the time, Guy. You're no Luddite."

"True," admitted Guy. "But you have to learn to use it. These folks are letting technology use them. They are getting run by technology. To the point where they'll interrupt a nice conversation that they are already having with a friend in the park to reply to a text message from some other friend. People just don't know how to focus anymore. They just can't resist those little pings."

"Aren't we here to talk about technology, Guy?" Carson asked.

"We are," Guy confirmed. "But before we can get into specifics, we have to talk about behavior, Carson. There's a reason that I brought you here. I wanted you to see all of these people 'multitasking' their day away. No focus."

"What's wrong with multitasking?" asked Carson, recalling how he had managed to fix the kids breakfast that morning while answering his e-mails and eating an English muffin simultaneously.

"To start with, it's a myth," said Guy. "We see computers do it and we think we can, too. But while computers look like they are doing lots of things at once, really they are just doing things in a series, one after the other, very, very quickly. People are the same. We can really only do one thing at a time. But not as fast as a computer. And the problem is that every time we have to shift focus from one thing to another, a little bit of time gets lost in between. Remember how I told you about when C² was still building hundreds of different bikes, and we'd have to stop the line to change out the tools? Multitasking for people creates the same kind of Wait Time. It's just not so obvious because it isn't as long. But make no mistake, it's there."

Guy asked, "Case in point: How often do you check your e-mail each day?"

Carson laughed. "Just once—all day! C'mon, Guy, I'm a lawyer. I have to be available."

Guy furrowed his brow and said, "You're not doing it once, Carson, you're doing it a hundred little times. Every time you do it, you're changing over and losing focus. You're creating mini–Wait Times. These add up. And they generally also hurt the quality of whatever else you should be doing by distracting your focus. Back when you were racing, if you pulled over every five minutes to check your tire pressure, how much do you think that would have hurt your times? Same here: Focus on your race. Do the real work. I promise you, it's a competitive advantage because almost no one else will. It's much easier to answer e-mails all day because you feel little bits of accomplishment each time you answer. You give yourself a little mental cookie. But for the most part, at the end of the day you'll find that you won't have really done anything."

Carson thought about some of the e-mail listservs he was on and how certain lawyers seemed to haunt them every day, commenting on everything. He'd often wondered how those lawyers had time to do anything substantive.

"So," said Guy, "that's technology lesson one: It's as much about how you *don't* use technology as how you do. Now, on to lesson two: the right way to use technology. This is far from simple. But, in general, a new technology is valuable only if it gives me either a Production Advantage or an Information Advantage."

"What do you mean?" asked Carson.

Guy explained, "A Production Advantage is exactly as it sounds. Something that decreases Cycle Time by optimizing a constraint or reducing Wait Time. It can also be something that, if you think back to our Income Formula, improves the quality of the finished product, thus impacting Average Value. An example from C²: A few years ago we realized that forging the crankset components of our bikes was slowing down the line as a whole because the frames were being built faster than the cranks could be made. Thus, frames sat around without cranks, waiting for that part of the process to catch up. We invested in new machinery that could 'crank out the cranks' better and faster, optimizing that constraint, to allow the entire process to move faster. Frames stopped piling up behind crank assembly. And, voila. Production Advantage."

Guy continued, "Technology that confers an Information Advantage is also valuable. You've already seen at C² how our Kanban boards allow us to identify constraints and Wait Time in our system in real time. Technology that gives you that kind of system oversight is essential, whether you're manufacturing bikes or cases."

Guy said, "And in your business, where information is truly power, knowing your case better than the opposition may be the biggest advantage you can have. So, software or other technology that allows you to know your case better, I would imagine, would be most important of all."

Concluding, Guy said, "None of this is easy, I know. But at least now you hopefully have a way of evaluating and choosing technology: Does it give a Production Advantage? Does it provide an Information Advantage? And most of all, does it help or hurt focus, if used properly?"

Once again, Guy had Carson's head spinning. He mounted his bike. "I've got a lot to think about, Guy. I think I'll sort this out on a good, long training ride."

"That's my boy," said Guy. "Go get 'em. See you next month."

Once upon a time, books were a new technology. Using a scroll? Passé, like using a fax machine. Before that, the alphabet was the hot innovation, though it was likely not heralded on stage by a man in a black turtleneck. We don't think of these things as tech because for many of us, technology is synonymous with computers, smartphones, and all things digital. In truth, what we're talking about is the application of new ideas for practical purposes. Or—as this book hopefully illustrates—the application of existing ideas in a new way.

Historically, tech can be both a friend and an enemy, as anyone in Chicago during 1871 could attest about the harnessing of fire. Facebook is great at reconnecting people with old friends, but when abused it can spread misinformation and bust up marriages. Smartphones give us the collective knowledge of civilization at our fingertips, but they are so entrancing that many cannot put them down even when speeding down highways.

For these reasons, we approach technology with this simple, overriding question in mind: What tools can you use to build a better business?

We are not going to explore the entire spectrum of legal technology in this chapter. Rather, we will examine which tools we can use to implement Lean principles.

If we are running a Lean law firm, we're going to want to embrace any tool we can get our hands on to streamline operations, gain insight into our business, and track our progress. We're not interested in tinkering for the sake of tinkering; this is about the practical application of technology to the task at hand.

One note: Keeping up with technology is a tall order since it advances so rapidly. The companies that deliver our new wonder-tools are one step away from irrelevance if they do not continue to innovate, so competition drives ever faster and more sophisticated developments. This chapter is therefore a snapshot in time, and it will no doubt appear quaint to future readers. To the lawyers of the future, we know we look like cavemen with our 2018 tech from your vantage point, but give us a break. We're trying our hardest here.

- ✔ **DO:** View technology as a tool that can help you build a better business.
- ✘ **DON'T:** Get caught up in tech because you're simply supposed to, or because things are simply new and exciting. In other words, resist the urge to tinker.
- ✘ **DON'T:** Text while driving.

WASTE REDUCTION AND EFFICIENCY

In Lean, waste is bad and must be eliminated whenever possible, which is where technology can really shine. Waste is referred to as *muda* and is broken into two types:

> *Muda* **Type 1**: Non-value-added activity *necessary* for the end customer. This *muda* should be reduced as much as possible until, if possible, it can be eliminated. An example of this in a law firm would be anything in the law firm that could be automated but isn't, such as document assembly.
>
> *Muda* **Type 2**: Non-value-added activities for the end customer that are not necessary. You want to eliminate this type of waste altogether. An example of this in a law firm would be any process that does not improve the quality of the product you're providing, such as delays caused by work pileup.

Beyond dividing *muda* into two broad categories, Taiichi Ohno, godfather of Lean, identifies seven forms of waste, depicted as follows:

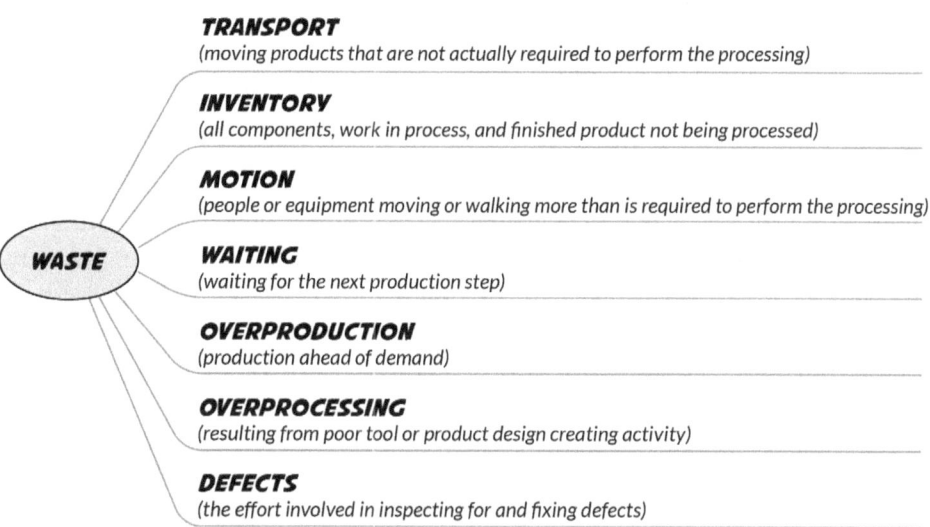

In particular, law firms are at risk of Motion, Waiting, and Defect waste. The other forms of waste are manufacturing-related and not as applicable to knowledge industries, but they are worth meditating on to draw parallels to legal work.

✔ **DO:** Take some time to identify wasteful practices in your business.

✔ **DO:** Identify what actions you take that are wasteful and not adding value, versus wasteful aspects of something you're delivering to a client.

Going Paperless: Scanning and Document Storage

If you're not running a paperless office, you're neck-deep in *muda*. Paper-related activity is the aspect of your business that is probably most wasteful right now. The difference between a lawyer's desk heaped with stacks of accordion files, like a poor fellow in a stock photograph, versus a clean one with a laptop speaks volumes about efficiency. We've seen a lot of both.

From the law firms we've dealt with, our data suggests that finding a paper file in a multi-lawyer office can take from 2 minutes to 15 minutes. This time includes the trip to the filing system, tracking the file down when it's not where it's supposed to be, and getting distracted along the way. Furthermore, this presumes that you're talking about "the file"—a physical file—meaning that only one person can view it at once.

When you consider that files can be located on a computer filing system or via search in a matter of seconds, and that multiple people can view them at once, you're staring some *muda* straight in the face.

Scanners

A personal scanner is one of the best investments you can make as a lawyer. If you're in a group of multiple attorneys, you might have a large industrial scanner in a common area. It is still worth having a personal one. You have your own waste bin and laptop, as one practice management adviser told me, so why not your own scanner?

For your needs as a document professional, we recommend against multifunction devices (the ones that copy and print as well). Get a device that does one thing and does it well.

Recommendations

> - The Fujitsu line of ScanSnap scanners is, at this writing, widely considered to be a best-of-breed device, especially the workhorse ix500 (or whatever the modern equivalent is to future readers).
> - Fujitsu also sells a less expensive mobile version as well—ix100—for half the price (we highly recommend investing in the faster, larger scanner unless you truly need a mobile solution).
> - Jeff Bennion, technology columnist for *Above the Law*, recommends the Epson WorkForce DS-510.

✔ **DO:** Invest in a personal desktop scanner.

✘ **DON'T:** Get a multifunction device for your scanner. You are a document professional. Use best-of-breed tools whenever possible.

Document Storage

Once you scan, you need to store. From a storage perspective, there is no reason why you can't digitize your entire office.

We live in a golden age for digital storage: Moore's Law and commoditization have continually pushed hard drive prices lower. If we assume, generously, that the average size of a Microsoft Office document is 300 KB, you can buy a hard drive that stores over 1.3 million of them for $100. And for readers in the future, we're pretty confident you'll be able to store a bajillion documents for $50. That is our prediction. Call us Nostradamus.

This is all good news because having global, instant, and simultaneous access to your legal files eliminates one of the biggest forms of *muda* in your law firm: storing and retrieving paper files.

There's also no need to set up your own file server if you're not inclined to. You might be better off using cloud document storage (security concerns will be discussed later in this chapter). When you use a cloud storage service, you can check your documents from anywhere, on any device. You also don't have to buy and maintain a machine for your documents, and maintenance is critical because in today's age, security patches must be applied immediately. Last but not least, most cloud document software allows you to share your documents with others.

For some firms, cloud storage might not be the best option. Compatibility with existing systems might come into play. On-premise solutions are worth pricing out if the number of users in a large firm makes a cloud option economically difficult. If you do wish to set up your own file server, make sure you do so with the initial and ongoing help of an IT professional or consultant. Security is a big deal, and you don't want to get anything wrong.

A question is: How much functionality do you need with your document storage? All cloud storage services allow you to upload documents and organize them into folders. From there, they diverge. Some provide automatic versioning, allow workflow functionality, enable you to associate folders with matters (or sync with software that does), or add billable time to your document.

Recommendations

> If you want a simple, general-purpose document storage solution, Dropbox and Box work really well.
> If you're tied into the Outlook or Google ecosystem, Microsoft's OneDrive and Google Drive are natural options, respectively.
> If you're using a practice management solution, odds are it provides document storage or integrates with market leaders.
> NetDocuments and Worldox provide more sophisticated document solutions (with a more sophisticated price), including full-text search, workflow, document retention policies, and more.

✘ **DON'T:** Pay a lot of money for document storage. It is arguably the most commoditized resource in the computing industry.

✗ **DON'T:** Overcomplicate. Don't make your storage process burdensome. Encourage use by making life easy and reducing friction.
✔ **DO:** Spend some time defining folder structures and file naming conventions.

Document Assembly

Document assembly is the automatic creation of a document by merging a template with data. Some practice areas are obvious candidates for this type of automation, such as immigration, estate planning, or trademark law. But even heavily customized law specializations have engagement letters, standard motions, and court filings that are paint-by-numbers and thus candidates for automation.

We commonly observe the wrong way to do things: Law firms produce documents by taking an existing document, copying it, and making changes. This is an error-prone, *muda*-rific process that leads to copy-and-paste mistakes. This method is tedious and slow. In addition, attorneys waste time searching for documents to serve as examples. The copy-and-change technique is suboptimal.

Instead, we recommend investing in automating your document creation process. You or a consultant will need to create template documents, which are the legal forms themselves with placeholders where your variable data will be merged. These templates can be Word documents or in a proprietary format, depending on the technology you choose. Some software, such as Doxsera, HotDocs, or INSZoom, have libraries of templates ready for you to use out of the box.

The first thing you need to do is choose a tool (recommendations follow). The next step is to prioritize the creation of your document templates: Identify which are your most commonly used and time-consuming documents and automate those first.

Recommendations

› One of the most powerful document assembly tools on the market is HotDocs. Because of its power, it is a complex product and may or may not be the right fit for you.
› Another extremely powerful platform is a Microsoft Word add-in called Doxsera/The Form Tool. The Form Tool is a free (yet powerful) version by the makers of Doxsera; the higher-end product, Doxsera, is extremely powerful and can, for example, create multiple different documents (e.g., complaint, interrogatories, certificates of service) from the same data set.
› Contract Express is another stand-alone option.

> More general practice management software such as MyCase, Clio, and Rocket Matter allow you to upload Word templates with merge fields, which can be configured for "if-then-else" scenarios.
> Heavy document creation practice areas such as trust and estates, immigration, and intellectual property have software and templates specific to them.

✗ **DON'T:** Create documents by the copy-and-change method. You're going to make mistakes and embarrass yourself in front of your client.
✔ **DO:** Realize that getting started with document assembly requires an investment in either your time or your money that will pay huge dividends later.
✔ **DO:** Start by automating your most frequently used documents.
✔ **DO:** Seriously consider hiring someone to create the document templates for you. It can be laborious, so it might be the kind of thing you want to leave to someone who's done it hundreds of times.

Invoicing and Collections

Invoicing and collections is a huge form of waste for law firms and needs to be tackled aggressively. Most law firms have terrible billing practices and, on average, collect on only 71 percent of the work they perform, according to a Georgetown Law study.[1] The smaller and less standardized a law firm is, the worse performance tends to be.

There are many reasons for law firms leaving money on the table, ranging from poor billing practices and the unpalatable nature of asking clients for money to a lack of investment in good technology.

The good news is that we can improve the payment process by breaking it down into discrete steps: tracking time (especially for billable time practices but also important for others as a form of measurement), generating invoices, and collecting payment. The less friction introduced into each of these steps, the better.

For billable-hour professionals (and those who are seeking to track their time on cases), selecting a tool that reduces the burden of time tracking is fundamental; otherwise you'll find yourself sorting through legal pads, e-mails, and calendar events trying to reconstitute your month. You'll procrastinate on finishing this horrible exercise, leading to delayed invoices,

---

1. Thomson Reuters and Georgetown Law, *2015 Report on the State of the Legal Market*, available at http://www.law.georgetown.edu/academics/centers-institutes/legal-profession/upload/FINAL-Report-1-7-15.pdf.

which in turn leads to reduced payments. When you finally get around to it, you'll likely underbill for services. *Muda*-city.

Generating and sending invoices is the next step in the process. Most firms still rely on the following steps: creating invoices, printing them, folding them, stuffing them into stamped envelopes, and mailing them.

Going back to Lean principles and our definition of *muda*, is there anything in those steps that adds value to the client? Many clients are perfectly fine with and would even prefer an electronic invoice. Selecting a program that can send electronic invoices and can batch-bill (send out all bills at once) greatly reduces time spent and resources required for this critical piece of your business.

The final step is the collections process, possibly the weakest link in a law firm's revenue production chain. Calling the people you're assisting and asking for money is a tall order, and it gets in the way of legal work. In my experience working with thousands of law firms, the highest percentage of invoices collected I've ever seen is 92 percent, pulled off by a husband-and-wife team where the husband performed the legal work and the wife was a regimented bookkeeper.

For collections, your first order of business is finding a tool that can help you discern what percentage of billable work you're collecting (see Chapter 4 on KPIs for more information about financial reports).

The next step is to move toward client payment automation. This is accomplished by signing up with a payment processor who can help you safely keep credit card information (or bank account information) on file. This arrangement, which can be specified in an engagement letter, allows you to automatically collect from clients when legal work is performed. In this way, you can also set up payment plans and recurring payments, which automate collections and provide a predictable stream of revenue.

Payment processing is not limited to credit cards. Clients, especially large enterprise ones or general counsel, may wish to pay with bank account information. In that case, ask your payment processor if it offers ACH (Automated Clearing House) or e-check processing.

If fully automated payment processing is not an option for your practice, at least giving clients the ability to pay their bills online will reduce your cash collection cycle. Online payments are faster and more convenient for many people than it is to cut a check. Additionally, many people want to build rewards points by paying all bills with credit cards.

Recommendations

> Some of the most powerful tools on the market for time and billing are the cloud-based legal practice management platforms, including Rocket Matter, Clio, and MyCase.

- ❭ Of the traditional, noncloud platforms, market leaders include PC Law and Tabs 3. We suggest hiring a knowledgeable consultant to assist with the installation and maintenance of such systems.
- ❭ Find a payment processor such as LawPay or LexCharge that specializes in the legal profession, understands the ins and outs of trust and operating accounts, and can help you set up payment plans and recurring billing.

✔ **DO:** Understand that your process and workflow for getting paid for your work are as important as the systems you invest in. Spend time thinking through and standardizing a solid, repeatable process.

✔ **DO:** Make sure you track your collection percentage.

✔ **DO:** Reduce friction in all three aspects of getting paid: (1) time tracking (if applicable), (2) invoicing, and (3) collections.

✔ **DO:** Make your collections more predictable and streamlined with credit cards, ACH, e-checks, payment plans, and recurring billing.

✘ **DON'T:** Embrace technology that will in any way delay sending out invoices. The single most important factor in collecting what you're owed is timely billing.

Practice Management Software

Law firms can survive without legal practice management software. Almost all larger law firms choose not to, but many small firms forgo this critical tool. However, when law firms duct-tape together their own systems from Word, Excel, and QuickBooks, they are very inefficient and create *muchísima muda*.

The advantage law firms gain over competitors when they embrace practice management software is that their businesses run better. All case information is in one place and easy to retrieve. When clients call in, you can easily let them know all the particulars of a case and where they stand in their invoicing.

Calendar events, tasks, documents, and notes are all associated with matters, available quickly to anyone (with permission to see them). They have client relationship managers (CRMs) so that you can keep track of client and lead information and maintain notes about them. Deadlines and to-do items can be quickly calculated and scheduled with matter templates or calendar software.

Most practice management software providers offer solutions for document assembly, as we described earlier. Cloud-based programs often feature portals or other online sharing features so that clients can exchange documents, review and pay invoices, and keep up to speed with their cases.

Some practice management systems come with integrated accounting features, including tracking and balancing trust accounts. Many programs track time and contain an integrated invoicing program. Others do not; they instead have a separate program that handles the back-office functionality.

If you choose not to use practice management software, observe that the disorganization that comes with stitching together different systems can negatively affect relationships with clients. Susan Cartier Libel, creator of Solo Practice University, blogged about an episode with a lawyer in which a client relationship was destroyed because of bad organizational practices due to a lack of practice management software.

> "Law practice management software is often touted as the holy grail for lawyers, a way to be extremely efficient and effective when organizing your back office," she writes on her blog. "It's mobile, it's time saving, it does everything if you will learn how to use it and let it perform its magic."

A note of caution: As someone who has seen thousands of law firms adopt practice management software, some more successfully than others, I urge you to take the time to train and learn the system. Invest time and money in training. Don't rush your law firm's implementation. Otherwise, you will likely fail and never get organized.

Recommendations

> - There are many cloud-based practice management solutions. The largest three and the ones that have stood the test of time are Rocket Matter, Clio, and MyCase.
> - Likewise, there are many on-premise practice management tools to consider. These include Time Matters, Practice Master, and ProLaw.
> - A full list of practice management software is maintained by the ABA's Law Technology Resource Center (LTRC). You can access it at http://www.leanlawfirmbook.com/pm-software. See also http://www.leanlawfirmbook.com/aba-practice-management-software.

✔ **DO:** Seek out a practice management system to run your practice and keep you organized.

✘ **DON'T:** Assemble a duct-taped case management system consisting of Word, Excel, QuickBooks, and other disparate standard office systems.

✔ **DO:** Spend time training in your new practice management system. Strongly consider bringing in a paid consultant to help you and your staff know the system.

✔ **DO:** Consider whether you want to maintain the software and hardware for your system in your own office or whether you would like to use a cloud-based system.

✔ **DO:** If you want desktop-based software but don't want the headache of installing and maintaining your own server, ask a consultant about a hybrid approach of using cloud-based desktops to host your software.

BUSINESS ACCELERATION

The second broad function of technology for the Lean law firm involves building your business. Eliminating *muda* is one thing, but if we are to continually improve in our quest for *kaizen*, we need measurement tools, dashboards, Kanban visualizations, and technology to fuel growth. We need ways to gather and display the Key Performance Indicators (KPIs) we discussed in Chapter 4. We need to keep the team aligned as discussed in Chapter 8.

KPI-Tracking Software

If you're going to do the work of collecting the KPIs we discussed in Chapter 4, you're going to want to visualize them quickly, like this:

How awesome would it be if you could have this level of business intelligence at your fingertips? It's not impossible.

It is likely that your KPIs are going to come from a variety of sources. If I had to predict, your cash position will come from QuickBooks, your cash collection percentage will come from your practice management software, and your Net Promoter Score will come from PollDaddy or SurveyMonkey.

For this reason, a software category exists for tracking KPIs and providing dashboard views of them. Dashboards can be configured so that you have public-facing ones, which many companies display in monitors in their common work areas, and private ones, such as those intended for the eyes of management or financial employees.

More expensive software options will integrate with popular programs; less expensive ones will require manual data entry.

You will need to spend some time fiddling with your dashboard view options, such as what kinds of charts you wish to view and over what time periods. For ongoing tracking, I am a big fan of either a moving six-month window or year-to-date (YTD) information. The moving six-month window tracks the most recent six months, so a new month is always being added and an old one is dropped off. YTD is great because it is simple and expresses your progress over the year.

> **A Word on Reporting to Generate Your KPIs**
>
> If you're duct-taping a system together with Word, Excel, and QuickBooks, you're going to be in a world of pain trying to build the reports we discussed in Chapter 4. Calculating your firm collection percentage, origination, and utilization this way will take a lot of time and spreadsheet wrangling every time you go into KPI mode. Odds are, you and your team will end up not investing the time required to do so.
>
> This is another reason why it's a good idea to take a hard look at legal-specific software for practice management and time and billing with powerful analytics packages.
>
> That said, it really depends on how deep you want to go with your analytics. Tracking cash and financial reports can be done easily with QuickBooks. Deadlines, Average Case Value, and Work in Process (WIP) can be tracked with a basic practice management program like MyCase. Supplementing practice management software with Kanban software is, of course, a must in running a Lean firm, and web-based software such as Trello, Jira, or Leankit can fulfill this need.

Recommendations

› A good, simple option is the aptly named SimpleKPI. It's inexpensive, which is rare in this category, and fairly intuitive.
› Geckoboard may also be a good choice, but it can be expensive once you add more than one dashboard.
› Alternatively, use a spreadsheet and get good at charting. Keeping KPIs in a locally stored Excel document is not a good idea, since

sharing it is cumbersome. Online tools like Google Sheets may be a better choice.

- ✔ **DO:** Visualize your KPIs with dashboards.
- ✔ **DO:** Consider radiating the data in your KPIs firmwide by displaying them on TVs in communal office locations.
- ✘ **DON'T:** Try to display and visualize all KPIs at once. Start slow, with the most important ones, and add more over time.

Kanban Boards

Have we mentioned Kanban boards enough yet? Sorry to beat you over the head with this, but they really are that great. As we discussed in Chapter 8, Kanban boards are great systems for keeping the team aligned. A lot of teams use index cards on a wall with physical swim lanes, but this practice has some very bad drawbacks:

› Unless you have a webcam trained 24/7 on your physical Kanban board, you have no way of viewing it if you're not in the office.
› If you're a remote worker or want to get work done at night, you're out of luck.
› Additionally, often you want to keep documents or data associated with a Kanban card or see its history. Index cards are small and cannot accommodate that need.

Web-based Kanban software solves these problems. You can check your board from anywhere. You can define and redefine your swim lanes. You can add documents and notes to your cards and track them through the system. And because everything is tracked in a database, you can run reports on your swim lanes and calculate how long it takes a card to get through your system. Voilà: instant metrics for WIP, Cycle Time, and Throughput Rate. (Many web-based products actually track these metrics automatically, as do numerous add-ins for web products like Trello.)

The reality is that the popular Kanban systems are project management tools in disguise. If you start using them as we recommend in this book, you will end up with a whole lot of knowledge about your work process, inefficiencies, and choke points. Your practice, and possibly your whole life, will change.

Recommendations

› Trello is a very simple-to-use and inexpensive product. The base product is free, but it has certain limitations, although there is a paid version that offers more options. One of the benefits of Trello is that there are hundreds of add-ins you can use to customize it.

› Jira and Leankit are a bit more sophisticated, but for more involved projects, they might be a better fit for your team.
› If you are using Kanban software, KPIs may be baked in as part of the package. If you're using Trello, however, there are numerous add-ins (such as Screenful and Corello) that will keep track of your Lean metrics, including Cycle Time, WIP levels, and Throughput Rate, automatically.

✔ **DO:** Opt for a virtual, as opposed to a physical, Kanban board. This is really a no-brainer.

✔ **DO:** Maintain your Kanban board on a regular basis. Not updating the status of your projects regularly makes it completely useless.

Final Deep Dive into Kanban: Kanban Cards

We've talked throughout this book about the benefits of Kanban in terms of visualizing process flow and improving communication. But we have not really discussed what things should look like at the individual "card" level. Remember that, for our purposes, each card represents a Case Unit flowing through your system.

The beauty of software-based Kanban systems is that we can customize them to model our process. At the macro level, we do this by showing our "stages" in left-to-right order on the board, from Prospect to Done (and whatever comes in between for you). At the micro, or card, level, we can tell the team member assigned to the case exactly what needs to be done, and we can put labels on the cards that we can filter. Let's return to our Kanban board from Chapter 5 and add a few things:

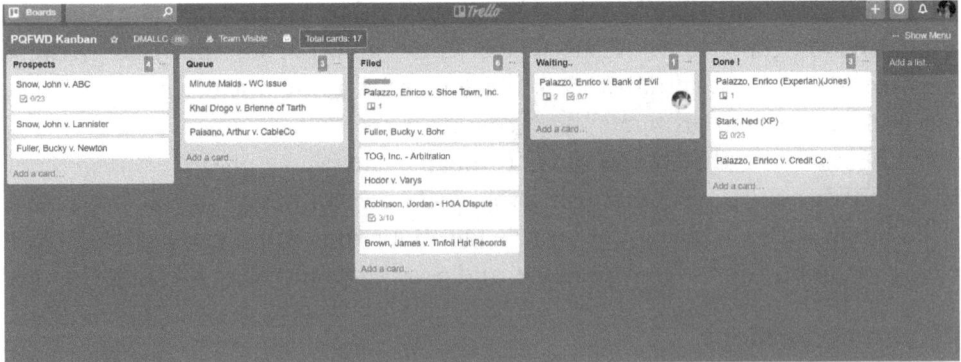

Now the real power of the board starts to emerge. For example, while this Kanban board (made with the cloud app Trello) is visible to every firm member, each team member has an icon. They can thus see at a glance which cases they are responsible for working on right now. We can also put labels and markers on each card to further indicate a problem or status (e.g., external constraint, upcoming deadline). These will help us greatly as we "operate" the system.

Now, let's look into a Case Unit card on this board. Remember our discussion about the power of checklists? We can create these for our board and apply them to any card with a few clicks, like this.

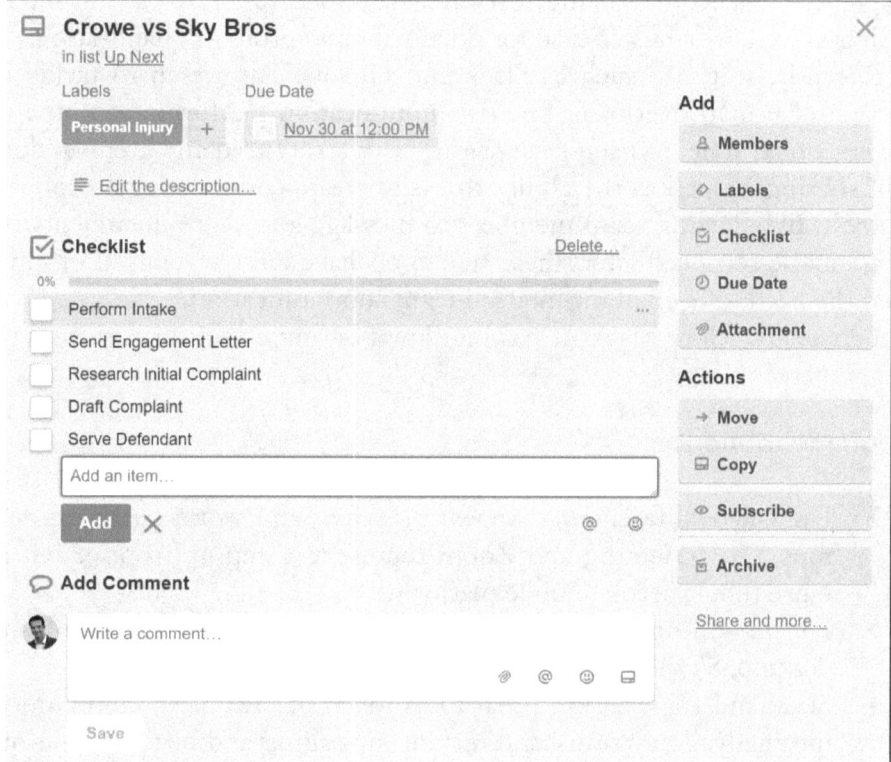

Checklists that indicate what standard items have been completed (or that give instructions for a specific task), a log of past conversations related to the card, and attached documents are all included. But it's the checklists that—together with automation—are the backbone of standardization. Standardization, in turn, is what drives both speed and quality.

Remote Communication Software

A tightly aligned team communicates. For a law firm with a couple of people, this is easy enough: You're ready to go with cell phones.

Once the team grows, however, keeping track of what's going on can be a little more complicated. The nature of the legal business doesn't help, either. Lawyers are often all over the place to begin with, hustling to and from court, depositions, or meetings with clients. Combine this frenetic activity with satellite offices, trends toward telecommuting, and hiring remote contract workers and you have a full-fledged need for remote communication tools.

When you're not working in the same space, it's important to maintain face-to-face communication. The good news is that lawyers face no lack of inexpensive videoconferencing software. Any such software can do screen-sharing as well, which is critical for document and project collaboration.

Recently, software such as Slack and Hipchat has arisen to tackle the problem of e-mail overload. Their communication platforms combine the conversational style of instant messaging with structured and archival document sharing, as well as the ability to easily create conversational groups or channels. By allowing team members to message and share documents that can easily be retrieved later, these new tools have largely reduced or eliminated the need for e-mail for internal team communication.

Personally, I love Slack. It has cut down on my e-mail processing by at least 50 percent.

Recommendations

- For videoconferencing, Appear.in is free and works great on desktops. GoToMeeting and Zoom represent a step up in price but are more robust across mobile platforms.
- For one-on-one communication and to make outbound calls from a desktop, Skype is still a great option.
- Slack and Hipchat are great tools for entire teams to communicate internally. They transcend instant messaging and become an e-mail replacement.

✗ **DON'T:** Spend too much here. Most of this software is very commoditized, and good-quality options are plentiful.

✔ **DO:** Test out messaging tools like Slack with one or two people in the firm before you roll it out firmwide.

Marketing Software

Marketing is one area where you can constantly strive for improvements in true Lean style. Now that we've left the days of the Yellow Pages (you're not still buying expensive Yellow Pages ads, right?), marketing has become eminently measurable.

Remember this mantra: *If you're not measuring, you're not marketing.* You're going to want to approach all of your marketing efforts from a numbers perspective. Otherwise, you have no idea if your marketing spend is having any effect at all, and you'll find yourself standing in two feet of thick, nasty *muda*.

At a minimum, you're going to want analytics software on your website, which will inform you about how people arrive at your site, meaning from what organic keyword searches and from which referring websites. You'll be able to tell how much time people spend on each of your pages and what country and city they are from. The KPIs we discussed in Chapter 4, unique and new visitors, and a whole host of other information are at your fingertips.

The next basic thing to pursue is software for your e-mail newsletters, which you should definitely be sending. Newsletters allow you to stay present in front of your potential clients, existing clients, and referral network. The type of company you use to send e-mail blasts is called an e-mail service provider, or ESP. This is an inexpensive but highly valuable cog in the marketing machine. You can see who opened what, who clicked on what, and which of the links in your e-mail were the most popular.

A slightly more advanced item you might want to think about is call tracking software. The day of the same 1-800 number you plaster everywhere is over. Instead, you can spin up telephone numbers whose sole purpose is to forward to your permanent office number. This technique enables you to create different numbers for your website, local advertisements, TV spots, or whatever your imagination allows, then see where the inbound calls are coming from.

If you start getting really sophisticated, you can start exploring a category of software called marketing automation software. This stuff does not come cheap, but it really helps you understand where your leads are coming from and how effective your campaigns are. Marketing automation software also helps nurture leads, meaning that once someone contacts you, it can add them to an automated e-mail list.

Recommendations

> For web analytics software, look no further than Google Analytics. It's free, and every Internet marketer worth his or her salt is fluent in it.
> MadMimi is a very easy-to-use e-mail service provider. Constant Contact is the market leader, so many readers might be familiar with it. Both have great deliverability (meaning their e-mails don't get caught in spam filters).

- › For call tracking software, CallRail is one of the less expensive options and most straightforward to set up.
- › Once you're ready to start exploring marketing automation software, Hubspot, Marketo, and Pardot are the category leaders. Be prepared to invest a lot of time training on these powerful systems—and tens of thousands of dollars.

✔ **DO:** Honor the mantra "if you're not measuring you're not marketing."
✘ **DON'T:** Advertise in the Yellow Pages anymore, unless it is free.
✘ **DON'T:** Use your own e-mail program to send your newsletter. Your deliverability will degrade over time, and you run the risk of being blacklisted by spam servers. Find a good ESP and let them fight those battles for you.
✔ **DO:** Consider investing in call tracking numbers if you are going to run any type of display, direct mail, or print advertising.

TECHNOLOGY CONCERNS AND CONSIDERATIONS

I've laid out thousands of dollars' worth of possible tech expenditures in this chapter, and the amount of information is overwhelming. I'm sorry. The point is not to overhaul your practice overnight but in the spirit of *kaizen* to gradually improve over time. Identify the top priorities for your firm and move forward deliberately and at a sustainable pace.

Let's be 100 percent clear: Tech does not come without risks. We don't need a conspiratorial science fiction movie to lecture us about engineering gone awry to know this. The most obvious concern is data security and client confidentiality. However, another sinister and often overlooked risk has to do with how technology changes our workflow and our habits. Before you jump into a complete overhaul of your systems, make sure you're familiar with the following issues.

Personnel Problems

When you adopt new software, you're going to adopt a new workflow. One thing you have to recognize immediately is that you're not going to be able to jam your new technology into your current process and down your team's throats—you will need to keep an open mind and adapt accordingly. Perform a mental scan of the personalities on your staff, and recognize that for some more than others, software migration and workflow changes may not be easy.

Unless you have your team on board, a new software rollout can be disruptive. There may be individuals who stonewall, resistant to change. You might have people using software incorrectly, which in the case of financial ledgers can cause significant potential problems down the road. The best way around these issues is to recognize ahead of time that they exist and need to be dealt with.

Recommendations

> - Before you decide on a particular technology, envision how it will affect your processes. Involve your staff in this discussion, especially the cranky ones.
> - Once you make a software purchase decision, make it clear that there will be negative implications for stonewallers or anyone undermining the deployment.
> - Invest in training, whether that is from a financial or time perspective. It is worth it to make sure you are getting the most out of your software and that everyone is using it properly. Otherwise, your project has a good chance of failing.

✔ **DO:** Recognize that a technology change is a workflow change, and as a consequence some employees may not make it through the transition with their jobs.

✔ **DO:** Strongly consider investing in training when you have a major new software rollout. Don't be penny-wise and pound-foolish.

Multitasking and Focus

We talked about this earlier, but it bears repeating: Don't multitask. In his excellent 2011 book *The Shallows: What the Internet Is Doing to Our Brains*, Nicholas Carr explored a wealth of research pointing to a sobering conclusion: The use of the Internet is changing the way our brains work, and not always for the better. Let's put it this way: If you have a nagging suspicion that your ability to focus is not what it used to be, you're on to something.

Carr cites multiple experiments from Stanford and Cal Berkeley that demonstrated a lack of ability to focus among heavy web users. The haunting part is that these experiments tested causality, not correlation.

In terms of multitasking, we're fooling ourselves. We aren't doing multiple things at once. Instead, we are doing something called "rapid toggling between tasks," which results in gross inefficiencies and the inability to filter out nonsalient information. Multitaskers are "suckers for irrelevancy," according to sociologist Clifford Nass at Stanford, who studies the subject.

In general, the research shows that the tools society is embracing are moving away from our abilities to concentrate deeply on one sustained subject. Odds are, if you've gotten this far through our book, you're not having an issue with focus. But be warned: This phenomenon is real, and we're all best served by making sure both we and our staff are aware of these issues.

The good news is that regular practice of focused, nonelectronic activity such as reading, offline hobbies, exercising, and meditation can restore the cognitive abilities we lose when we multitask, surf the web, and get interrupted constantly by texts, tweets, and messages.

- ✔ **DO:** Recognize that there is a cognitive price to pay for deep engagement with web usage and technologies that interrupt you, such as messaging applications.
- ✘ **DON'T:** Multitask, and if you do, realize you're kidding yourself.
- ✔ **DO:** Counteract the effects of heavy digital tech usage with sustained concentration activities, such as reading or playing chess.

Security

Not a week goes by without our hearing about some sort of data breach. With the U.S. government accusing the Russian government of hacking during the 2016 U.S. presidential election, the specter of cyberwar is upon us. The dark web, the deep underbelly of the Internet, is host to "a wretched hive of scum and villainy," as Obi-Wan Kenobi described Mos Eisley in *Star Wars*.

All of us must do our part to be as careful as we can with our data. We live in a world dependent on electronic data, but we also live in a world teeming with cyber threats, which means we need to take all reasonable precautions. For law firms, you have an ethical responsibility to secure client confidential information as well as you possibly can.

Whether or not you store information exclusively on your local laptop or in the cloud, you're at risk. The truth is, most data breaches are remarkably uninteresting, physical in nature, and unsophisticated from a technology perspective. They rely on the human element. Edward Snowden did not hack into the Pentagon, he copied information and snuck it out. The naked celebrity photo fiasco involving Jennifer Lawrence and others was enabled by bad user password policies. John Podesta and Colin Powell's e-mails were stolen via a phishing attack, described in the next section.

(Highly) Recommended Personal Security Practices

The following suggestions are critical for things you have direct control over. I originally published them on the Legal Productivity blog post, "Seven Rules to Stay Safe Online in a Scary Digital Age," and they are reprinted with permission here.

1. **Use strong passwords that cannot be found in the dictionary.**
   So-called "dictionary attacks" brute force their way into systems by trying known words. Best practice is to use a combination of punctuation and numbers.

   TIP: Try catchy phrases with numbers, and use punctuation that looks like letters, such as Tofu2E@t (tofu to eat) or Dog8Hom3work (dog ate homework).

2. **Use different passwords.**
   Usernames are bought and sold on the black market. So if access to one of your sites is compromised, all of your logins are vulnerable if you use the same password.

   TIP: Use a tool like 1Password or LastPass to manage your different passwords, or invent a password that has a variation in it.

3. **Change default passwords.**
   Default passwords for routers or other Internet of Things devices (such as baby monitors and thermostats) are easily found online. Access to such devices can be used to launch attacks.

4. **Never, ever click on a link in an e-mail to log in to an account.**
   So-called "phishing attacks" are what got John Podesta (and Colin Powell) into e-mail trouble. The perpetrator sends you an e-mail that looks to be legit, telling you there's something wrong with your account. You click a link, go to an imposter site, and hand over your username and password to a bad actor.

   TIP: Make it a rule to never click on links in e-mails for account information. Always type the Internet address directly into the browser.

5. **Always lock computers, handheld devices, or anything else with sensitive data.**
   People lose devices all the time. Tens of thousands of them in a single month. When someone has access to a device, you're giving them keys to the kingdom. Make sure they can't log in.

6. **Make sure ALL devices you own are up to date with the latest security patches!**
   New vulnerabilities are discovered all the time in the cat-and-mouse game that is cyberwar. The vulnerabilities, once found, are sold for money on the black market. There is no excuse for falling victim to an attack that leverages a known vulnerability.

   TIP: Turn automatic updates on for all of your devices' operating systems.

Cloud-Based Software

As of this writing, twenty-plus state bar associations have weighed in on the ethics of cloud computing. They have opined that attorneys can use cloud computing as long as they take reasonable care to understand the security practices of the company. The LTRC maintains an ongoing list of which states have an ethics opinion, which you can access here: www.leanlawfirmbook.com/cloud-ethics. Perhaps the Pennsylvania Bar sums it up best when they ask:

> May an attorney ethically store confidential client material in "the cloud"?

and answer:

> Yes. An attorney may ethically allow client confidential material to be stored in "the cloud" provided the attorney takes reasonable care to assure that (1) all such materials remain confidential, and (2) reasonable safeguards are employed to ensure that the data is protected from breaches, data loss and other risks.

Practically speaking, "reasonable care" shifts the burden to the attorney to learn about the providers and who they are getting in bed with. There's an exhaustive list of things to consider, but to cover your "reasonable care" behind, focus on the most critical items.

1. Any client confidential information sent over the net needs to be encrypted over 128-bit encryption or greater. Encrypting information is like blending a bunch of fruit for a smoothie, with the difference that once the data is received by your cloud provider, they have a reverse blender. If you're using HTTPS in a browser, you are safe to use the web resource even over a public wifi network.

2. Make sure you understand the data policies of your provider. As silly as this seems, you need to own your data and be able to download a human-readable version of it whenever you want, ideally without the need of a consultant. These practices need to be spelled out in the provider's terms of service or subscriber agreement.
3. Understand your cloud provider's backup policy. Ideally, they should back up data to multiple geographic locations. You're also going to want to know if your provider destroys your data in case you leave (it's a bad idea to leave stuff lingering in cyberspace).
4. Know who has access to your data and in what circumstances. No one should be able to access your account without your permission.

These concerns are the core concerns, but you can go a lot deeper. An industry trade organization called the Legal Cloud Computing Association (LCCA) has developed a set of standards in conjunction with legal technology security experts. These standards mandate what member companies must adhere to and also serve as a guide for bar associations about cloud safety. For more information, you can access the LCCA standards at www.leanlawfirmbook.com/lcca.

CHAPTER SUMMARY

We live in a time of amazing gadgets and computing wizardry, but when you get down to it, technology is really just a tool to get stuff done. For the Lean law firm, it's important not to get caught up in the hype and glitz, but to select software that helps you eliminate waste and build your business. However, as Uncle Ben told Peter Parker (Spiderman for the unenlightened), "with great power comes great responsibility." Know how to use technology responsibly, stay focused on security, and maintain your ethical requirement to keep up to speed.

CHAPTER 10

Goal Setting and the October Surprise

October

It was nice to be able to relax, thought Carson, as his eyes ran along the shelves of business books. He remembered leisurely Saturday mornings with Pam before the kids, when they could wake up late, get a coffee, and just browse books. They were both avid readers. But life had not allowed much time for that lately.

Carson had to admit, however, that things seemed to be getting a lot better. After nine monthly meetings with Guy, this was the first Saturday that Carson didn't feel the need to rush back to work right afterward. He and Pam had a sitter coming, and they were actually going to go out to the movies. He'd almost forgotten what that was like.

The Kanban board had been a struggle to implement in the beginning for several reasons. Most practically, unlike C², the Gray Firm was not a big, open space. Operating from a large old house, the firm was a warren of hallways, offices, and a few conference rooms, with no central or open area. But that problem had been overcome when Briana had located Kanban software—accessible to every employee in real time—that performed the same function as the huge screen at C^2: constantly updated visual communication showing the position of each case, who was working it, blocks, bottlenecks, opportunities, and Wait Time. It had taken some getting used to, but after just a few weeks even the firm's hardcore Luddites were getting the hang of it.

A harder nut to crack was the firm's tradition of meetings. Weekly meetings with all employees, daily meetings for teams, and countless impromptu meetings when someone would just drop into Carson's office. Having sometimes felt isolated at K&M despite its size, Carson liked the interaction. But all the talking about doing things made it hard to actually get anything done! He knew that this created Wait Time and slowed progress. It certainly stole focus time—that most valuable of commodities—from everyone.

Ironically, it was only after yet another contentious, drawn-out meeting that Carson finally persuaded everyone to stop meeting so often. The firm finally resolved that they would have one single meeting a week, on Monday mornings, when they would look at the upcoming two-week "radar" to see what court appearances, appointments, and deadlines needed to be addressed in the short term. They would then quickly, and as a group, review the online Kanban to identify cases that were blocked or sitting idle so that the forward flow of progress could continue.

After just three weekly meetings, it was clear that things were vastly improved, and more was getting done. Carson felt great about that. But the meetings just covered the short term. What about long-term planning? Shouldn't the firm be meeting about that? He didn't see where that fit into the big picture. And what was the "surprise" that Guy said he had? And why did Guy want to meet at the bookstore?

Carson's reverie was interrupted by Guy's stage whispering Carson's name and his sudden appearance on the other side of the bookshelf.

"Hey, Guy," said Carson, looking up. "So what's the surprise? And why are we meeting at the bookstore? Is there some book you wanted to show me here?"

"Yes and no," replied Guy cryptically. "You see all these books on this shelf, Carson? They are all about goal setting and motivation. Some of them are great. But a lot of them, I think, get it wrong. So forget about them for a moment, and come over to this table. I've got something I want to show you instead."

Guy walked Carson over to a large library table and, from the messenger satchel over his shoulder, dumped out a jumble of yellowed, spiral-bound notebooks. "Remember these?" Guy asked.

Carson hadn't seen the notebooks for years, but he recognized them instantly. "My old yearly training journals! I can't believe you kept these, Guy!"

"I never throw these away. Too many good memories in here."

Carson thumbed through the journals, recalling in vivid detail the gut-wrenching workouts that looked so benign when merely written on a page. "I remember puking my guts out after a few of these," said Carson. "Good memories for you maybe, Guy."

"Most definitely," said Guy. "It's good to be the coach. But flip to the front of the notebook and tell me what you see."

Carson did as instructed, turning to the first page of the spiral notebook marked "2001 Training Journal." There he found, all on a single page, his goals for that year. Under the heading "Outcomes" were the four races that were his focus for that year, together with the times he hoped to ride in each race. Underneath each race, in abbreviated form, were the training "goals" that Guy and he had decided he would need to achieve in order to ride those times. Below all of that were bullet points about specific aspects of his riding that he wanted to improve and, under that, a wish list of equipment upgrades that he dreamed of, and some places he wanted to ride just for the experience. All on one page.

After taking it all in, Carson said, "I see the whole year on this page. I must have looked at this page 100 times in 2001. I could almost see it in my sleep. I won three of those races, Guy, remember?"

"How could I forget?" said Guy. "But remember how you won them. By riding the time or better that we decided beforehand you needed to ride to win them. We didn't write down 'win' the race. Because that's not in your control. The best you can do is put yourself in a position to win. So, instead, we focused on what you had at least some control over: time. We set an optimistic but achievable time for you that, if you rode it, would put you in a position to win. The time was our 'Outcome Goal.' The training objectives we set underneath the Outcome Goal for each race—for example, 'Complete 15 hill workouts with at least 5,000 feet in altitude gain'—those were our real goals. And whether you met them or not was 100 percent within your control. We call those Task Goals. We knew that if you completed your Task Goals, the Outcome Goals were likely to be met. And if the Outcome Goals were met, then . . ."

Carson completed Guy's thought. "Then the Results would likely follow."

"Right," said Guy. "We *dreamed* of Results, like wins, for example. But we focused on Outcomes that you had some control over, like racing times. Then we underpinned those Outcome Goals with Task Goals that were fully in your control as to whether or not they were met. Finally, underneath all that, we put things you would like to do or achieve that would contribute to the Outcomes and Goals, or that were simply fun. All on a single page you could refer to often. Worked pretty good, didn't it?"

It had, Carson thought.

"Now flip through the rest of the book, Carson. What are the other 300 or so pages all about?"

Carson again did as asked. After the first page, the remainder of the notebook read like a diary; it was a record of Carson's daily training work, with notes depicting changes or corrections. If Carson was meeting his training Task Goals, there were notes about what went right; if not, the notes were about adjustments or improvements. Carson had forgotten how Guy would observe the training and make tiny tweaks along the way according to how things were going. All those little course corrections had apparently added up, as Carson had met or beat his hoped-for time in all four races and had won 75 percent of them. Not bad.

Carson finally answered, "The other pages are all about the work. What was going right. What wasn't. And all your little tweaks, Guy."

"Exactly," Guy proclaimed. "What you call little tweaks you should now recognize as *kaizen* in practice. Glad you noticed that. But the other thing I wanted you to notice was that, after we established our goals, all of the rest of the book is about the work. It's not much about *thinking*. It's about *doing*. That's the problem with the way businesses set their so-called goals these days. Tons of planning. Tons of assessment. Too many goals, some of which are totally unrealistic. Followed by all of these monthly reviews. Paralysis by analysis."

Guy continued, "My point is this: Spend time thinking about your wished-for Results. Dream about them. It's OK to dream big. Visualize them. Whatever works for you. But don't be too attached to them because, remember, they are not necessarily within your control. Underpin those with Outcome Goals that you have some degree of control over. And build those upon Task Goals—things you CAN totally control—which are likely to get you to your desired Outcome Goals. Feel free to list some other things you want to achieve, too. But keep it all very simple. Make it fit on one page that you can look at whenever you want. Look at it every day if you want. But after you do that, focus on the process. Do the work. Keep notes on how you're doing, and make little tweaks along the way."

Carson thought back to all those years of training. It had all been so much simpler than the lengthy and complex annual goal setting, frequent overhauls of those goals, and performance review process at K&M. And much more effective.

Then Carson remembered Guy said he had a "surprise." "I get it, Guy. And I believe you on this because I've done it. So, what's this 'surprise' you mentioned?"

"Oh, that," said Guy. "You mean the October Surprise."

"Really?" said Carson sardonically. "And what's that exactly?"

Guy replied, "You know, in politics we usually have elections in November. So candidates sometimes unleash or 'create' a news event just at the right time to influence the outcome of an election. Any earlier and it wouldn't have the same impact. Any later and it would be too late.

"I kept hearing that phrase around election time, and it got me thinking about how October is the perfect time of the year to make meaningful improvements in your process. It's like a sprint where all of your efforts are concentrated. And why October? It's because you have lots of good intelligence by then. Most of the hay is in the barn already. You can look back over the last nine months and really see what worked and what didn't. You're also starting by then to think about the coming year. We have a tendency in our annual planning meeting to look ahead, but we forget to look back into the just-finished year. In October, though, you haven't mentally flushed all that insight away yet, like we tend to do once we close the books on a year. And, since you start all this at the beginning of October, you still have enough time—about three months—to influence your Outcome Goals for the year that you're still in.

"So at C^2, every October we take what we've learned and focus the majority of our efforts for that one month on fixing and improving our process. Anything we've seen that we can use to our advantage we use. If we see a way to do something with fewer steps, we do it. If we discover technology that can cut our Cycle Time by 2 percent, October is the month we implement. We don't forget about production entirely, but for that one month we focus less on what we are making, and as much as possible on how we are making it. Every employee has a voice, and everyone's ideas get considered. We're not afraid to experiment. And just like with race training, it all adds up. We get better and faster every year. Sometimes we have to take a step backward to take two forward. But over time, there's an upward spiral of improvement. And the employees look forward to it all year."

Carson was more than a little skeptical. "Turning away from the cases and focusing only on improving the process seems like kind of a dangerous luxury."

Guy pointed to the bookshelf, where several copies of *The 7 Habits of Highly Effective People* by the late Stephen Covey were grouped. "Remember what Covey said about 'sharpening the saw'? He told the story of the woodcutter who never took the time to sharpen his saw because he had too much wood to cut. And he worked twice as hard and long as a result. Don't be that dude, Carson." Guy concluded, "I promise you the earth will not come crashing down around you if you give priority to improving your process. Give it a try, Carson. Have I steered you wrong yet?"

There's always a first time, thought Carson. But he resolved to nevertheless give it a try.

A couple of caveats before we dive into how to set annual goals and hatch your own October Surprise. First, whenever we start talking about goals, we begin heading into the fuzzy realms of human psychology. We're all different and, consequently, we're motivated by different things. And when we imagine the future (which is where all goals take place), we do it in unique ways. Some of us need to visualize it like a movie; some of us like to hear it spoken aloud. Others need to write it down and read about it.

Whatever your preference, the point is that goals are emotional and highly individual. That means you are going to need to find a goal-setting process that works for you (and your firm). But make no mistake: If you are to move forward, you need *some* kind of goal-setting process. The nature of that process is up to you.

The method we present next is only one way to do it. As with all things in this book, use what is helpful, but don't be afraid to experiment to find something better. (And if you do, let us know, because we may want to "borrow" it from you!)

The Dangers of Goal Setting

The second caveat about goal setting is this: While it is absolutely necessary to go through a process of goal setting, there are some inherent dangers in it as well. One danger is becoming a slave to your own ambitions and losing perspective on how a goal relates to your life as a whole.

Achieving any goal necessarily involves sacrificing other things. The life of an Olympic swimmer, for example, is focused entirely on her sport. There's little room for anything else. That's fine, and necessary. But it's also temporary. As lawyers, though, we are in it (hopefully) for a much longer haul. We want the satisfaction of achieving, improving, and building—but not at the cost of our families, free time, or health. Being single-mindedly focused on work goals for extended periods of time is not healthy. Especially when failure to meet such goals feels like a soul-crushing defeat. That's why in our system we will distinguish Results (which you can't control) from Outcome and Task Goals (which you mostly can). We use these visualized Results to motivate us, but our focus is on simply completing the Outcome and Task Goals without being too attached to the Result.

Our system is also intended to make the process of setting goals simple. There are literally tens of thousands of books on how to set goals, many of them excellent and the vast majority well intended. But lurking in all goal-setting advice, apps, systems, and books is the danger of hopping on the gerbil wheel of that goal-setting system—especially ones that emphasize constant measurement of progress—and forgetting the main point that the goals are simply a tool for improvement. While setting and achieving goals is one of life's great satisfactions, the real satisfaction comes from the journey and from improvement itself. Goals are a means to that end, not the end. So, if a system requires time-consuming daily interaction and daily measurement, it's probably too complicated. Our time and mental energy are limited, and we need to spend what little of it we have on action. Constantly measuring = never doing. If, on the path to achieving your goals, you're dragging out the topographic map to replot your progress every 50 yards, you're not going to make much actual progress. A quick glance at the compass to make sure you're headed in the right direction is all you need. So here, we'll keep it simple and, like Guy, we'll put it all (Results, Outcome Goals, and Task Goals) on a single page—your firm's ROT sheet.

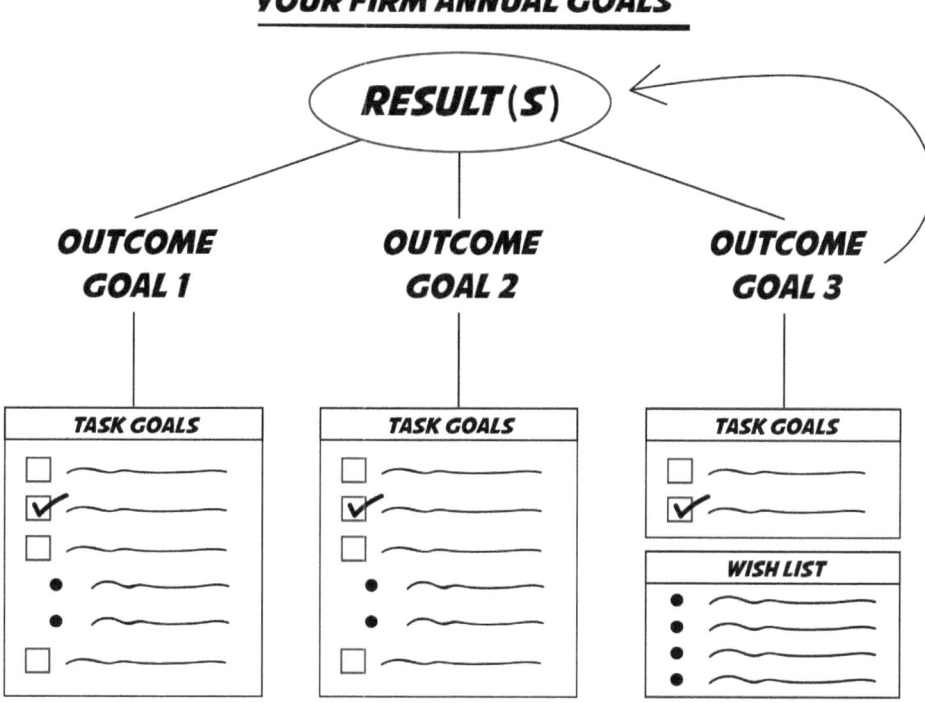

Goals versus Results

Before we get started, we need to distinguish what we call Goals from what we define as **Results**. The popular definition of goal is some kind of end or outcome, such as "My goal is to win an Olympic gold medal" or "Make a million dollars." The problem with this definition (especially where it involves competition for a single prize where there can be only one winner) is that whether you achieve such a goal or not is outside of your control. Lots of people are competing for that single gold medal. Both sides want to win the trial. While Vince Lombardi might say it's just a question of who "wants it the most," in reality, the best you can ever do is create conditions where winning Results are likely to occur by taking ownership of that which you *can* heavily influence or fully control. *It's the completion of the things that we can totally or mostly control that are our real goals.* For Carson and Guy, Results were about winning races. For you and your firm, Results equate to annual income (more on that later).

Supporting the envisioned Result are **Outcome Goals.** Outcome Goals are optimistic, but achievable, consequences that logically follow the accumulation of completed Task Goals. Outcome Goals are mostly—but not fully—in your control, as they tend to flow naturally from consistently completed Task Goals and effort. For Carson, Outcome Goals were the times that Carson hoped to ride in races that he and Guy had chosen at the beginning of their training year. For you and your firm, annual Outcome Goals will correspond directly to the elements of our Income Formula (Income = Throughput Rate × Average Case Unit Value).

Finally, supporting the Outcome Goals and at the lowest, rubber-meets-the-road level, are the goals that are fully within our control. We call these **Task Goals**. They are exceedingly simple because they are pass/fail. You either complete them or you don't, and whether or not you do is 100 percent up to you. For Carson, Task Goals were his daily workouts. He either completed them as prescribed by Guy, or he did not. Pass/fail. For you, a simple example of a Task Goal would be to "draft and file three complaints this week" (but since you're hopefully now thinking systemically and in terms of Cycle Time and Throughput Rate, a better example would be to "advance three cases from Queue to Filed" [or whatever you've decided to call stages in your process]).

So, there you have it: the nuts and bolts of goal setting (Results, Outcome Goals, and Task Goals). But before we show you how to assemble them, there's one paramount thing we need to discuss that governs the entire process: Vision.

Vision: Your Firm Constitution

As we have said, Result equates to annual income. Surely there must be something higher and more altruistic than that, right? Well, of course there is. While even Ambrose Gray recognized that you can't help people if you can't keep the doors open, we never want to forget who we are, what we aspire to be, and what we are trying to build. That's why, even as we stress that your Result should be an annual income number, we never forget that our **Vision** is paramount and permeates everything.

What do we mean by Vision, and how does it fit into your annual goal-setting process? Vision is simply the picture you have in your mind (or the collective, brainstorming mind of you and your firmmates) of what you want to be and what you want your firm to become. It's about what you value and care about, and the purpose behind your work as a lawyer. It's what gets you up in the morning, and the injustices you want to correct that keep you up at night. For Gray Firm, the phrase "Lawyers for Workers" was more than just a tagline. It was a statement of who the firm was, what it did, and what it stood for that permeated everything the firm did (marketing, niche selection, systems, etc.).

So how do you define your Vision? Like much else in this chapter, that's highly individualized. But here is a suggestion. In Sam Carpenter's outstanding book, *Work the System: The Simple Mechanics of Making More and Working Less*, the author describes his early struggles to manage Centratel, his Oregon-based telephone answering service. An engineer by training, it was only after Sam began to see his business as a system that it started to make sense. Besides establishing and documenting standard working procedures for his business, Sam created a document he called Centratel's "Strategic Objective." The **Strategic Objective** was the "what" of his company, and the basis for all of its decision making. Much more than a simple mission statement, the Strategic Objective described what the company aspired to be, what it valued, its competitive advantages, and how it intended to achieve its aspirations. You can see an example of Centratel's Strategic Objective at www.leanlawfirmbook.com/strategic-objective.

Getting back to your own Vision, there is no better way to define it than to go through the process of putting together a Strategic Objective. Think of it as your firm constitution, not only a statement of what you believe but a living document capable of evolving as your focus and beliefs evolve over time. And that's what makes it better than five- or ten-year "plans," which are generally just future wishes not hitched to who you are or your current reality. The great news is this: Once you've done it, in subsequent years you have only to review and refine it as things evolve. But do revisit it each year. Remembering who you are, what you believe, and where you want to go is the unifying power behind the nuts and bolts of the annual goal-setting process.

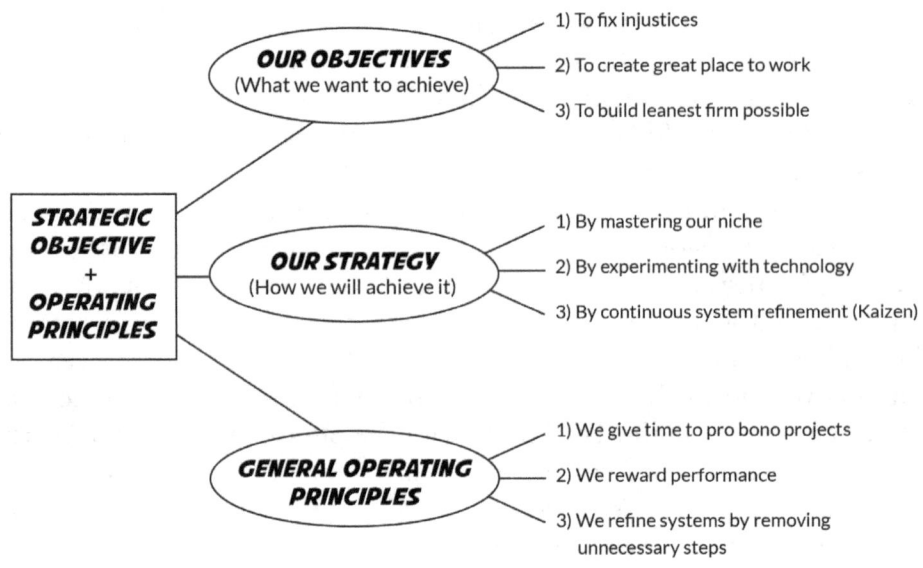

ANNUAL GOAL SETTING

With your Vision now defined, you are ready to narrow your focus down to the coming year. Here's the entire process:

Step 1: Reexamine the Vision (Strategic Objective).
Step 2: Set the annual Result in terms of gross income for the coming year. This number should be realistic, optimistic, and (obviously) one that results in a net profit.
Step 3: Set Outcome Goals that yield the preceding result. Going back to our number crunching in Chapter 3, we know that Income = Throughput Rate × Average Case Unit Value. We can now set Outcome Goals for both of these Key Performance Indicators (KPIs). Remember, however, that Average Case Unit Value (ACUV) is far less in your control than Cycle Time. When we get into the mechanics, we'll show you how, by starting with a realistic-optimistic Average Case Unit Value based on past performance, you can find the Throughput Rate that you need in order to reach your desired Result Income through simple math. With a little more math, we can then set Outcome Goals for that Throughput Rate's components, Average Cycle Time and WIP (Work in Process, or Inventory).
Step 4: Define the Task Goals that will support the Outcome Goals.
Step 5: Add fun/motivation to the Wish List.

Now let's get into the details of this process. We already talked about Vision, so let's now talk more about Results. You may wonder why in this book we continually talk in terms of gross income instead of gross annual profit. Three reasons. First, while it's important to control costs (excessive costs are a form of *muda*, or waste, after all), *cost cutting can never make you profitable if there is not enough income*. On the other hand, enough income can overcome any cost issue. As Ambrose said, if you rub enough of the "green salve" on a problem, you can usually make it go away. Focusing on costs instead of income takes our energy away from what really matters.

Second, focusing on costs introduces an unhelpful additional variable into our Income Formula. Since our Outcome Goals require us to do some math, we want to keep it simple.

Third, you are already going to take your costs into account as you set your Results number. Your ultimate aim is to be profitable, right? So, in setting your Result, you first consider how much income, over and above expected costs, will make you that way. Beyond this break-even point, the number you set is up to you. Your number should be *realistic* in that it is based on what you've earned in the last year and what you have in the pipeline for the next. But it should also be optimistic and aspirational.

How much profit is enough? It's tempting to say that more is always better, but that's not necessarily true if that "more" comes at the expense of your free time, your family, and your health. One of the highest decisions you can make about your life is how much of your time you're willing to trade for money. And as a now-famous Princeton University study (https://www.princeton.edu/~deaton/downloads/deaton_kahneman_high_income_improves_evaluation_August2010.pdf) by Angus Deaton and Daniel Kahneman showed, beyond a certain income (found to be $75,000 in 2010), people report no increases in happiness. So choose wisely.

One last thing: As we start plugging in numbers for the three-lawyer Gray Firm, remember that the Result we've chosen for them is just to illustrate the process. Your Result number should be whatever works for you (provided it makes you profitable). This number obviously varies by firm size, practice area, geography, and a host of other factors. Equally variable are WIP and Cycle Time numbers; some practices are high volume with modest per-case values (e.g., consumer bankruptcy), while others are low volume–high value (e.g., truck accident). Your mileage therefore may vary. Lastly, remember that Cycle Time may be affected by the type and complexity of cases you bring, as well as the efficiency of your local court system. The Cycle Times we use here are therefore just for illustrative purposes. That being said, a significant amount of the Cycle Time will always be due to your own inefficiency, particularly with respect to how long cases spend waiting for you to act. In any jurisdiction, there is much you can do to improve this.

The Process

Let's say that the Gray Firm, having considered its expenses and the other factors we have described, sets an income Result for the upcoming year at $1,700,000. It's enough to make the firm profitable taking into account expenses, and, while it represents a substantial increase from the prior year, it is not simply wishful thinking. It's a realistic-optimistic extension of what happened the year before.

Gray Firm's next step is to take what they already know about their Average Case Unit Value and find the Throughput Rate number that will yield that Result. How do they do that? Let's sit in on the Gray Firm's annual planning meeting.

The firm knows, from looking at the last few years of deposits, that its Average Case Unit Value, that is, the amount the firm makes from each unit, is right around $10,000. Since this is the least (easily) changeable component, it's a good place to start. Assuming ACUV stays the same at $10,000, in order for the firm to make $1,700,000 it will need a Throughput Rate of 170 Case Units per year [$1,700,000/$10,000 ACUV = 170 Case Units per year Throughput Rate (R)].

But how is the firm going to achieve that Throughput Rate? Let's go back to Little's Law:

Average Inventory (WIP) = Throughput Rate (R) × Average Cycle Time (CT)

Moving things around:

$$\frac{\text{Average Inventory (WIP)}}{\text{Average Cycle Time (CT)}} = \text{Throughput Rate (R)}$$

Going back to the firm's desired Throughput Rate of 170 cases per year, things would be very simple if the firm had 170 Case Units in inventory and its average Cycle Time was one year. The problem, of course, is that it does not. Not even close, really. The Gray Firm's current WIP is 150 cases, and its Cycle Time is 18 months (1.5 years).

What Throughput Rate does its current actual WIP and CT yield? Using Little's Law:

$$\frac{150 \text{ Case Units (WIP)}}{1.5 \text{ year (CT)}} = \text{Throughput Rate (R)}$$

$$\frac{150 \text{ (WIP)}}{1.5 \text{ year (CT)}} \ 100 \text{ Case Units/year} = 100 \text{ (R)}$$

We see that the Gray Firm's current Throughput Rate is 100 cases per year.

Per our Income Formula, a Throughput Rate of 100 × ACUV of $10,000 is only going to yield $1,000,000 in income. Not enough. So, what should the firm do?

Let's look at Cycle Time. Currently, an average Case Unit will spend one and a half years—18 months—between the start and finish lines of the firm's process. But thanks to Carson's (and Guy's) efforts over the past year, the members of the firm know that they can do much to improve this. If they can get Cycle Time down to one year, at their current WIP level of 150, things look like this:

$$\frac{150 \text{ Case Units (WIP)}}{1 \text{ year (CT)}} = 150 \text{ (R);}$$

150 Case Units/year = (R).

Throughput Rate (R) becomes 150 Case Units per year. Multiplying that by an ACUV of $10,000 would give the firm a projected yearly income of $1.5 million.

Things are starting to look good now. As we've already discussed, decreasing Cycle Time is one of those things that the firm can really get both hands on by making "active work" move faster (through standardization and technology) and even more by decreasing Wait Times by optimizing constraints (clearing blocks, reducing WNR Time, etc.).

Theoretically, it's also possible that the firm could increase its WIP to raise Throughput Rate. But the current WIP is already 50 Case Units per lawyer. While some firms might have hundreds of units per lawyer (and some only a handful), given the type and complexity of the Gray Firm's cases, that's quite a load on each lawyer. Moreover, in the real world, introducing more WIP into the system usually slows Cycle Time. So, more WIP may not be the answer here. In fact, the opposite approach may work far better.

Remember that another thing that can be done to reduce Cycle Time is to take the counterintuitive step of intentionally *reducing* WIP, that is, reducing the inventory of cases between the start and finish lines of the system. Might this work? If so, how?

With their current WIP of 150, Carson, Briana, and Ambrose are each responsible for around 50 Case Units. But if they dropped firm WIP to 130, each lawyer would then only be responsible for about 43 Case Units. This cut in active WIP would mean a decrease in the number of things each lawyer (who are themselves a type of resource constraint) must handle. Reducing the number of cases allows each lawyer to put more time into each one and spend less time moving between them. And the Gray Firm figures that if it drops WIP from 150 to 130 (a reduction of 13 percent), this will allow the firm to decrease Cycle Time by 25 percent, cutting it from one year to just nine months (0.75 of a year, or 274 days).

If we do the math with these numbers (new WIP of 130 and new CT of 0.75 year) we get this:

$$\frac{130 \text{ Case Units (WIP)}}{0.75 \text{ year (CT)}} = 173 \text{ (R)}$$

173 Case Units/year = (R)

If this works as planned, the firm's new Throughput Rate is 173 Case Units per year. Assuming its ACUV remains stable at $10,000, that would mean $1.73 million in income. Result met!

Determining Your "Ideal" WIP Level

While the real-world effect of reducing WIP is that Cycle Time shortens, there is, of course, a point where drops in WIP will do more harm than good. There is a practical minimum Cycle Time in the practice of law (i.e., very few cases are resolved within their first 30 days or so). There is also a point at which reduction in WIP no longer benefits Cycle Time (or more accurately when the benefits of further CT reduction are outweighed by the harm caused by reduction in WIP). So, how do you find your "ideal" WIP level?

While it's more an art than a science, if you have no idea what your WIP should look like, you can find it using Little's Law. If (like the Gray Firm) you have figured out your desired Throughput Rate and Cycle Time, you can calculate the resulting WIP simply by multiplying those two things together:

WIP = Throughput Rate (R) × Cycle Time (CT)

Plugging in the Gray Firm's numbers:

$$\text{WIP} = \frac{173 \text{ Case Units}}{1 \text{ year}} \times 0.75 \text{ year} = 129.75 \text{ Case Units (effectively 130)}$$

This tells us that with a Throughput Rate of 173 Case Units per year, and a Cycle Time of 0.75 of a year, a snapshot of our current WIP at any given time (the number of cases between start and finish) should be around 130. If we are measuring Cycle Time in days (which is sometimes easier than converting to a decimal), we can do the same math like this:

$$\text{WIP} = \frac{173 \text{ Case Units}}{365 \text{ days}} \times 274 \text{ days} = 129.97 \text{ Case Units (130)}$$

But remember, this WIP number is only a starting point. The Gray Firm might find that even with 130 Case Units in inventory at any one time, they're still getting bogged down and that Cycle Time is being slowed by too much WIP. If so, they can easily regulate WIP by briefly holding new cases longer in a backlog and not initiating them until WIP capacity opens up. While this hold adds time to the overall process (i.e., increases Lead Time), it suspends deadlines and other work on the new cases briefly, allowing more focus to be placed on pushing older ones across the finish line. The firm members watch their Cycle Time KPI to see, week to week, what effect the drop in WIP has upon it.

Once you've found a WIP level that feels ideal, regulating the flow of WIP into the system might mean not starting a new case in your system until another one finishes, thus opening capacity. After all, your goal, in the end, is not to have lots of WIP; it's to have your Case Units flowing past the finish line as quickly as possible.

Representing this backlog on a Kanban board is easy. Add a column such as Backlog to your Kanban board to the left of your Queue column (yes, we know they kind of mean the same thing). Backlog would include cases formally taken in but not yet introduced into the system. You will still measure WIP as the number of cases in and after Queue, all the way up until they hit Done. And your Cycle Time KPI will still be measured starting at Queue and ending at the last column before Done. However, Reaction Time will now include your new Backlog category, where cases have been formally taken in, but no active work has started.

Recap of Result and Outcome Goal Setting

1. Determine your realistic-optimistic income Result.
2. Find your ACUV (based on past data).
3. Determine the Throughput Rate Outcome Goal needed for the income Result (income divided by ACUV).
4. Set a realistic-optimistic Cycle Time Outcome Goal.
5. Use Little's Law to calculate a WIP level Outcome Goal.
6. Tinker and adjust as necessary.

Well? How Do You Get There? Defining the Task Goals That Support Outcome Goals

Having defined the KPI for WIP level and Cycle Time as Outcome Goals, the Gray Firm's one-page Annual Goal document now looked like this:

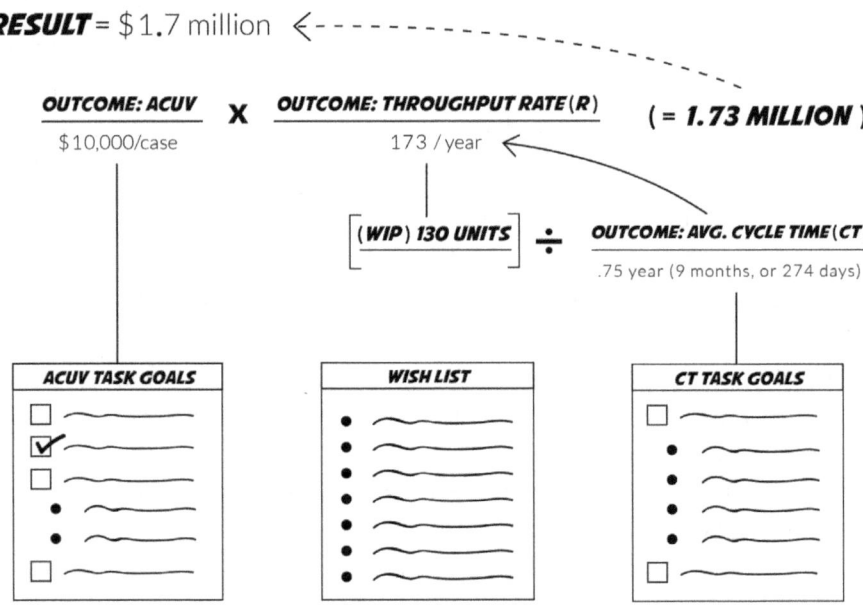

Stated as a sentence, the firm hoped to achieve the result of $1.7 million in income or better over the next year by throughputting 170 Case Units in one year with an ACUV of $10,000. This was to be accomplished by reducing average Cycle Time to nine months and holding an average WIP of 130.

How is the firm going to do that? Well, if you've been paying attention while reading this book, you should already know what drives each of these Outcome Goal KPIs. If not, here's a summary:

Outcome Goal KPI	See Chapters:	Explanation
WIP	3, 5, 6, 9	Having sufficient WIP depends on niche marketing (Chapter 6); beyond getting enough cases, it's all about finding the right level of WIP.
ACUV	6, 7	Having valuable cases depends first on niche marketing, and afterward on quality of process, which depends on standardization and written procedures to ensure quality and (interestingly) lower WIP for greater focus on each case; in litigation, an opponent's perception of both "focus" and its relative "speed" can drive settlement.
Cycle Time	2, 3, 5, 7, 8, 9	Depends on systems, particularly optimization of constraints and communication between team members so that there is awareness of the constraints and reduced waiting; depends to a lesser extent on speed of active work, which is driven by standardization and technology.

One last thing: It's fine to set a goal for ACUV; being driven by outside forces, it's a hard KPI to influence directly, but as we've said, good processes over time drive this number up, as does the influx of better cases that comes as a by-product of that.

The brainstorming process of identifying your Task Goals might take several days. At the end, you may have ten or more Task Goals supporting each Outcome Goal. More or less is fine. The distribution of these among your WIP, ACUV, and Cycle Time columns is also highly individual. You may have far more in your Throughput column than in your ACUV column. That's fine, too. But take your time, and choose carefully, because whatever Task Goals you write down you must ultimately check off as complete.

SUMMARY OF ANNUAL GOAL SETTING (AND THREE BONUSES)

Your mission is simple: Define (or refine) your Vision through your Strategic Objective. Then set a realistic-optimistic Result. Determine the Cycle Time, ACUV, WIP, and Throughput Rate Outcome Goals that will get you that Result. Then, finally, use what you've learned in this book, what you know from experience, and whatever else you can concoct to set concrete Task Goals whose completion will support your Outcome Goals.

At the end of the annual goal-setting process you will have two pieces of paper, your Strategic Objective or Vision sheet and your ROT sheet. Together, these two documents will be your firm's compass and map for the coming year, and the years after that build upon it.

But wait, there's more.

Bonus 1: The Wish List. Remember how Guy and Carson put a Wish List section at the end of their Goals page? You should, too. This can be whatever you want. Artwork for your firm? Espresso machine? Or even better, traveling to a conference for your niche practice area in an exotic locale. Anything that makes your practice better or more enjoyable.

Bonus 2: The Journal. Remember how Guy and Carson used a yearly training journal? The first page was the ROT sheet. But the rest of their spiral notebook was just a journal where Guy jotted down notes about what was working (or not) and made little tweaks here and there. You can (and should) do the same thing. Whether you capture it on paper or digitally, have a space just for notes about how things are going and, most importantly, ideas for improvement. By the time you roll around to October, chances are you will have jotted down numerous ways you can make things just a little bit better, particularly with respect to Throughput Rate.

Bonus 3: The October Surprise. To keep it all simple, our goal-setting process avoids tedious formal weekly reviews and obsessive measurement. The Vision sheet is the compass that guides you in all you do. The ROT sheet maps out what you're doing for the coming year and where you're headed.

But no road trip is complete without paying some attention to vehicle maintenance and the road ahead. Enter the **October Surprise**. As Guy realized, October is the perfect time to make course corrections for the year, as well as to implement all those little ideas for improvement that you've collected in your journal.

At the beginning of the month, have an informal meeting at a local retreat (or if it's just you in the firm, camp out in the coffee shop). Look at how things are going so far. Are you where you want to be? And most importantly, how is your system functioning? Are there things that can be fixed or improved? What ideas from your journal can you implement now? Get used to the idea of having just one month when improving the system takes precedence over all but the most critical client work. It takes a leap of faith to do this. However, that's exactly the advantage—almost no other firm will do it. And the compounding effect of having one month each year dedicated to improvement will give you competitive advantages that seem like magic.

What have you got to lose?

CHAPTER 11

Buy-In
General Adoption Tactics and Challenges Unique to Law Firms

November

Carson set the table for Thanksgiving dinner with eight plates, one for each member of Carson's family, two for Guy and Kumiko, and one each for Ambrose and Briana. "Pam!" Carson shouted into the kitchen. "What's the ETA on the turkey?"

"Chill out, honey," Pam said. "You can't rush perfection!"

Carson tried to relax as Pam directed, but it wasn't easy. There was a lot to be excited about. Over the last two months, the Gray Firm had moved solidly into the black. And better even than the financial news was the spirit of optimism and purpose that now pervaded the firm.

So much had changed in the last year. Carson recalled sitting in his dining room with Pam and the kids last Thanksgiving, wondering what bad news awaited him at K&M after the holiday. His worst fears had been realized when K&M sacked him, and he remembered his feeling of hopelessness when, several weeks later, he was still out of work.

Then he'd run into Ambrose by chance doing his modest Christmas shopping. Carson remembered accepting Ambrose's offer mainly because he had no other prospects. Even worse than the feeling of being displaced from his old firm, though, had been his first few weeks at Gray Firm, when he'd felt like a fraud to Ambrose as his efforts to revive the firm went nowhere. It was only a matter of time before he would blow his second chance—and possibly take one of the city's most revered lawyers down in the process.

All that had changed with his second "chance" encounter—meeting Guy in the bike shop. And just like the old days when Guy had coached Carson to racing championships, Guy's outside-the-box methods, dogged persistence, and faith in Carson had paid off. Carson's initial skepticism at Guy's contention that a law firm was like a factory had eroded as Carson began to realize that the firm really was just a system that turned raw material in the form of cases into results for the client and money for the firm. The shift to a systems mindset had allowed Carson to optimize the firm's Cycle Time, the average value of each Case Unit, and—most importantly—their Throughput Rate.

Once the Gray Firm had stopped trying to be everything to everyone and found its niche as "Lawyers for Workers," its intake of quality cases, just as Guy had predicted, eventually increased. It was crazy to think that turning away other cases had somehow led to getting more of what they wanted, but somehow it had. And their reputation for expertise in the employment arena—which had always been there with Ambrose but never was capitalized on before—was making them the go-to firm for aggrieved workers. Not only that, but it seemed to be increasing the settlement value that they could command. Defense firms respected them (and maybe even feared them a little). That was good, too.

The biggest increase in profitability, however, had come with their improvements to their process and the consequent increase in Throughput Rate. Carson understood now how Throughput Rate was affected by Cycle Time, which was in turn impacted negatively by internal constraints and longer Wait Times. And how narrowing their practice area had been critical not only to getting the right kinds of cases, but had allowed the firm to harness the power of repetition and standardization. With their virtual Kanban, checklists, and written procedures in place, everyone at the firm finally understood exactly what they were supposed to be doing, and things just flowed forward. New constraints were always popping up, of course, but they were no longer hidden. And rather than seeing them as problems, Carson saw them now for what they were—yet another opportunity to make incremental improvements.

Speaking of improvement, the firm's October Surprise, which had initially seemed a somewhat terrifying and dangerous idea because the "real" work would not get done, had in fact been one of the most professionally satisfying months of Carson's entire career. The employees loved the break in routine and, even more, the fact that their ideas for improvement had been valued as much as any partner's. Ever since October, the receptionist, secretaries, and paralegals had been showing up at Carson's door after spotting a new constraint, or with ideas for improvement. It was like a giant game of "Where's Waldo?" except with tangible rewards for the bottom line. The whole culture of the firm, thought Carson, has changed. But how exactly had that happened?

The doorbell rang and Pam opened it to the herd of guests. After exchanges of handshakes and hugs, everyone sat down to the serious business of eating. After the blessing and first few satisfying bites, Carson raised his glass and said, "I'd like to propose a toast."

Even though it felt unnecessarily ceremonial among friends, Carson felt like this situation called for something special. He stood and said, "A year ago I sat here with Pam and our kids at this table, trying to celebrate all we had to be thankful for. And we had many wonderful things. But still, I sat here sorry for myself, feeling like a safe was dangling by a thin wire right over my head. And the very next day, when K&M fired me, I felt like that safe had fallen and driven me down into a deep pit."

Carson continued, "I'm not sure if it was fate, or luck, but somehow during that dark time I ran into two of the men I admire most in the world. First, Ambrose, who, for reasons only he knows, took a chance on me. And just when I was feeling that his faith was misplaced, I found Guy, who came back to coach me one more time, through my hardest trial." Carson started to choke up a little bit, and unsure how to conclude, said simply, "Gentlemen, friends . . . from the bottom of my heart . . . thank you."

Glasses clinked and Carson sat back down. Guy said, "I appreciate that, Carson. I want to say two things to you. First, Ambrose and I have been around a long time. As I'm sure Ambrose would agree, there are few things more satisfying at our stage of life than being able to pass on what we've learned to the next generation. I want to thank *you* for that." Ambrose raised his glass in agreement.

Guy continued, "Second, give yourself some credit, Carson. Not only were you willing to give 100 percent of your effort to the cause, but you were receptive to everything I told you. Even when the things I told you seemed counterintuitive, you were willing to try. That kind of openness has to be in place before any real change can ever be made."

Carson remembered his resistance to Guy's suggestions. He'd been pretty skeptical. And even when he overcame his own skepticism, getting buy-in from the other members of the firm had taken time. Even now, with employees excitedly showing up at his office door with improvement suggestions, he was unsure of when and how that shift had occurred. He said, "Yeah, Guy. Funny thing is, I don't even remember when we finally became open to change. Or how I got myself or the employees there."

Guy responded, "Remember my Churchill quote? 'Never let a good crisis go to waste'? Well, you all had a real crisis. But crises are valuable—sick as it sounds—because no one can deny the fact that there's a problem. It's a short hop from there, usually, to define what exactly the problem is. Then to discuss what the solution should be and how to make it happen."

"What do you do when you don't have an obvious crisis?" asked Ambrose. "I hate to admit it, but everyone in town knew I was in a tailspin. But I've seen other firms that seem fine and then just evaporate one day. And others that die a slow, drawn-out death where no one really realizes there is a problem until it's too late. How do you get everyone on board with necessary changes then?"

"Hmmmm. OK," said Guy. "Not exactly the traditional Turkey Day banter I was expecting, but since you asked, let's talk about that. But before I begin—Carson—you have a 70-mile training ride tomorrow, so go easy on that stuffing. Now, about buy-in . . ."

If you're the king or queen of a small law firm, and what you say is the law of the land, some of this chapter is not for you. Read the Kim Jong-Un section on authority and start getting your firm nice and Lean.

If you do not have ultimate authority, hopefully we can help you make inroads with your Lean adoption. Buy-in is not easy, and effecting change is not for the faint of heart.

Rolling out Lean techniques is like planning a wedding: No matter what you do and no matter how good your intentions, you are going to infuriate someone. If you are going to move forward with change in your organization, know that as exhilarating as it will be for some, it will be equally dreadful and threatening for others.

We must pause here to rain on your parade a little. The best ideas don't always win. Just because something is a clearly better way of doing things doesn't mean it will carry the day. After all, humans are involved, and we tend to make questionable decisions.

History is littered with examples of inferior solutions winning out. For instance, the QWERTY keyboard was specifically designed to force people to type as slowly as possible because it was created in an age when fast typists broke typewriters. If you've seen an old typewriter, you may recall that keys struck the ink ribbon via long metal shafts, and when people typed too quickly, the keys would get stuck and tangled. Solution? Make people type as slowly as possible.

In 1936 August Dvorak came up with an alternate design that sped things up. The new layout increased the percentage of English words typed from the home row from 36 percent to 70 percent. Less finger movement leads to fewer errors and less physical strain, so the new layout was better for work and health. Unfortunately, the Dvorak design only retains a cult following, and one can only speculate at the unfathomable amount of collective wasted time and physical strain because of its lack of adoption.

The same phenomenon happened when the inferior VHS technology beat out Betamax to dominate the home video market. In another disastrous example, Bolivian villagers resisted purifying their contaminated drinking water when urged to do so by aid workers.

When you roll out positive change in your law firm, you are going to run into people who want no part of it. They may perceive a threat to their jobs, either from the automation that might replace their responsibilities or from the accountability that a new system may bring. Transparency and clarity may sound like a good thing, but for some people who bumble along under the radar, you are turning their world upside down. They may not be able to keep up, and they know it.

Before you rush to roll out new ideas in any organization, take some time to strategize your moves. You don't want to kill a project dead in its tracks, and you don't want to deal with personnel issues if you don't have to.

- ✔ **DO:** Recognize that the best solutions don't always win.
- ✔ **DO:** Take time to plan how you're going to roll out changes to create a Lean law firm.
- ✘ **DON'T:** Rush. Plan your moves deliberately.

USE AUTHORITY IF POSSIBLE, AND DON'T LET PEOPLE POISON THE WELL

If you are the main partner in a small firm, or if your fellow partners are on board, you have the authority to create change. But don't stop reading this chapter yet, because there are a lot of pitfalls.

If you're in charge, the most important way to implement change is with a solid project plan that emphasizes execution, standardization, and consistency. You need to identify which innovations you are going to roll out and in what order. Doing everything at once is not likely going to work, but you might want to start with the items that will get you on the road to organizational health: retrospective meetings, tracking a couple of Key Performance Indicators (KPIs), and focusing on your collections and Throughput Rate.

Don't be shocked if not everyone on the team survives the transition, whether through your choice or theirs. Even if you are Kim Jong-Un Lawyer, you are likely to get resistance. If all else fails, and you're stuck with someone who refuses to go along with the plan—and worse, is poisoning the well—you might have to remove that person from your organization. As unpalatable as it may seem, replacing staff you thought was completely indispensable, but was destructive to your law firm, is a good change for everyone and likely overdue. In other words, this could be your opportunity to clean house.

Firing is difficult, if not seemingly impossible in certain cases; you often have spent years with these staff members, and you know their spouses and families. However, is this fair to the other families that rely on you? If your organization cannot grow, or if the other people on your team are suffering because of someone, you are obligated to make a move.

Some people have such deep knowledge of your systems and processes that it seems like losing them would be a disaster. And you're right, it probably would be—for a month. First of all, by having a person in your firm with so much power, you are creating a weakness for the organization. What if they don't show up for work one day? What if they get hit by the proverbial bus? What if they go to Burning Man, meet some of the Rainbow People, and decide to live in Ocala National Forest?

Second of all, no one is indispensable. If you lose your back-office person or a paralegal, a call to an accounting or paralegal temp agency will help staunch the bleeding that very day or the next. This will give you time to find the help you need, and often you will end up hiring the temp.

Ask yourself this: Will your clients receive better service or representation without someone on staff? If the answer is yes, it's time to step up as a leader and make a tough decision.

- ✘ **DON'T:** Be afraid to make a personnel move if the resource is negatively affecting your firm.
- ✔ **DO:** Introduce changes slowly, and recognize that people are threatened by change.

> **When the Obstacle Is a Partner**
>
> Firing is not always an option. If you have a stubborn partner, you have an issue on your hands, and the question becomes, "What kind of firm do I want to run, and is this firm the right place for me?" The partner issue is a tough one, but it is a cold, hard truth that needs to be confronted head-on. If you feel that you can get the firm where you need it to be in spite of your partner, perhaps you have a workable situation.
>
> But if you are dealing with someone who refuses to improve the firm's operations, maybe it's time to think about building an organization that supports your vision.
>
> Family can also complicate things. If your partners are family members who have equal if not more authority than you, and you cannot leave because of the tear in your social fabric, you are in a difficult situation. I would encourage you to gently probe any assumption to see if a split would be as disastrous as you fear. But if you are stuck where you are, rush to a bookstore and pick up a copy of Crowley and Elster's *Working with You Is Killing Me*.

UNDERSTAND THE TECHNOLOGY ADOPTION LIFECYCLE

The theory of how new ideas are adopted is an academic one, and it is referred to as the *diffusion of innovations*, a topic pioneered by Everett Rogers in his seminal 1962 book of the same name. Popular authors such as Malcolm Gladwell and Seth Godin have been regurgitating his ideas to the masses ever since.

You may have heard about early adopters, an expression that has entered our lexicon. The term comes from Rogers' work and is part of the *technology adoption lifecycle*.

You may have seen this curve:

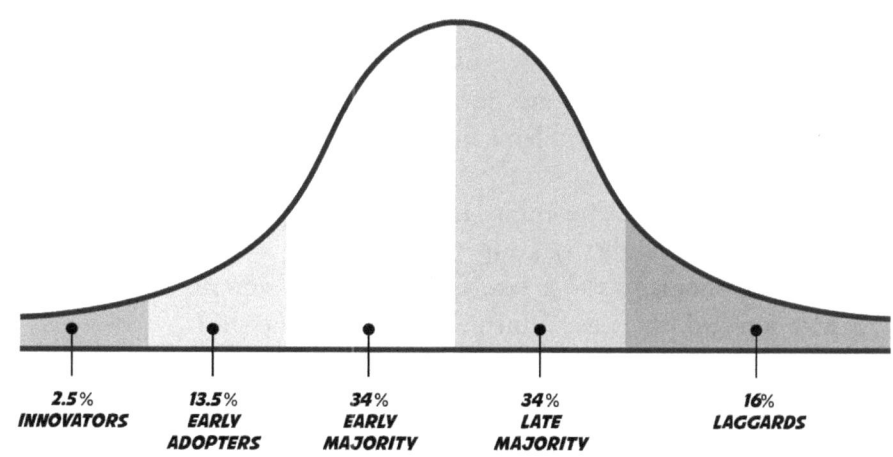

This model is helpful for anyone looking to sell an innovation to an organization, which includes you. If you're looking to optimize a business, you will be constrained by the people inside the organization and their willingness to embrace innovation. The technology adoption lifecycle helps model what to expect.

About 2.5 percent are *innovators*. These are the people willing to take risks that may ultimately fail. They maintain their relationships with other innovators and have the best knowledge of advances happening in their field. If you're an early reader of this book, there's a chance you fall into the innovator category, at least for Lean techniques in the field of law.

Early adopters count for 13.5 percent of the population. They are willing to take risks if they see substantial rewards from them. Usually, early adopters are very influential, and their opinion counts heavily in their peer group. For this reason, they are often a sought-after demographic by people looking to effect change.

The *early majority* will eventually get on board with an innovation. They account for 34 percent of the community. Socially, their status is not as high as that of early adopters or innovators. They are not opinion leaders. It takes them a while to come around to the conclusions reached by the innovators and early adopters. However, it is critical to make the innovation adoption leap from early adopters to early majority. The gap between these two populations is explored by Geoffrey Moore in his business classic *Crossing the Chasm*.

The *late majority* folks take a lot of time to hop on board and adopt an innovation. They are risk-averse and clock in at 34 percent of the community. Most people will have already adopted a technology or innovation by the time these guys do. They tend to be very skeptical of new ideas, but eventually they will go along with the crowd. Socially in an organization, their status is typically lower than that of the early majority.

Laggards are the last to adopt, and often they do not adopt willingly or at all. These are the people who only switched to touch-tone phones once rotary dialers were phased out. They tend to be older and more socially isolated. They account for 16 percent of the population. The good news for a change agent is that laggards are not very influential. The bad news is that they can cause significant problems in the rollout of an innovation.

- ✔ **DO:** Recognize that diffusion is largely a social process and may have little to do with the validity of your initiative.
- ✔ **DO:** Actively identify who is likely to be an early adopter of Lean in your organization and likely to be influential among the staff.
- ✔ **DO:** Identify where folks will fall on the adoption curve to get a sense of how readily they will embrace or resist innovations.

Successful versus Failed Diffusions

What Rogers found was that innovations were adopted largely via social channels. It wasn't good enough to have a compelling argument or a superior way of doing things. What was more important was that the right people in the community embraced the innovation. If that happened, widespread adoption would follow.

If you can persuade the thought leaders in your organization, the ones who have influence and social standing, you are likely to succeed. The popular, nonacademic authors mentioned above, Gladwell and Godin, discuss these individuals and their importance. In *The Tipping Point*, Gladwell talks about "salesmen" and "mavens" as those who gather and disperse information; in *The Purple Cow*, Godin discusses "sneezers" who spread ideas virally.

The takeaway from this principle is that you're going to need two simultaneous approaches to get your ideas adopted across your law firm: First, you're going to need the information track, in which you present the factual evidence that your ideas will result in a more profitable, better law firm. Second, you need to plan an influence track, where you identify the people in the firm whom you think could help spread the word and champion the cause, so that eventually everyone falls in line.

✔ **DO:** Have two tracks for your adoption plan: an informational plan and a social influence plan.

USING PERSONAS TO MODEL BEHAVIOR

A persona is an idealized sketch of a real-life person in a given role or situation. Personas help businesses decide how to approach those individuals. They are used in marketing to try to understand the purchasing process for different people. Software designers employ personas to try to understand different usage scenarios.

In our case, it is worth exploring three difficult personas we have repeatedly seen in law firms as they adopt new technologies. There's a chance these personas will seem familiar to you, and it's important to think about how to deal with them.

✘ **DON'T:** Confuse personas with stereotypes. The former are behavioral in nature and used to model reactions to situations.

✔ **DO:** Not only flesh out personas but identify ways that you can work with them.

Back Office Betty

Back Office Betty keeps the lights on in a law firm. She pays the bills, generates the invoices, runs payroll, and manages QuickBooks (the accounting software).

Betty runs a tight ship and gets her job done. However, she can intimidate the staff, including the senior partners, who can be clueless about numbers and totally reliant on her. Even though she technically doesn't have senior rank, she has a position of authority because she controls the finances.

She has done things her way for years and is married to her routine, including the software she uses to get her job done. In the past, this has caused friction as some associates want to run more modern time-keeping and practice management software that Betty refuses to work with.

Typically, Betty is very risk-averse and may have a few friends on staff, but she is likely not the most popular or social person. She is not a great person to spread a message, but if you can get her on board, she will help implement your decisions. The danger is that her tendencies may make her a very likely candidate to be your principal stonewaller.

Unfortunately, Betty is not often the most accountable person when it comes to responsibility. She will deflect blame and throw systems or other people under the bus to cover herself.

How to Deal with Betty

When you're converting to a Lean process, Betty does not necessarily need to be involved in everything. If you're putting together KPIs, she should be able to pull the data you're looking for and may be invigorated by the attention to numbers.

If you're making a change to any system that will affect Betty, get her involved early on. Be tough and insistent, though—she needs to know that the status quo is not acceptable but you value her input as you move forward. She is likely not a laggard, but because of her risk-averse nature, she falls in the late majority of adopters.

Betty will be wary of anything that could possibly replace her. For instance, if she spends two entire days running your invoices and you implement a practice management system that gets the job done in 30 minutes, she will feel that her job is threatened, and you may have a fight on your hands.

If you are *not* looking to replace her with automation, make that very clear at the beginning and throughout the process. If automation will affect her, explain that you want to make her life easier so that together you can go deeper into the company's performance. She is going to help you take the firm to the next level.

Make sure that Betty is involved in the vetting process for any new financial software and that she will be able to perform her job functions. It is critical that you manage her expectations that workflow will probably have to change, which she will resist, but the focus has to be on the end result that is important to you. The last thing you want to do is see Betty derail an implementation that has gone on for six months. We've seen it, and it is not something you want to go through.

Make it clear to Betty that the organization is going to improve its efficiency, and you need her on board to help you implement the changes. Playing to her authoritative instincts and involving her on the inside track may help minimize her natural recalcitrance.

One caveat: Be aware, no matter how trusted, of any financial professional who fights too hard on oversight of their process. This might be (repeat: *might be*, not *is*) a warning sign that something sketchy is going on.

Stubborn Stuart

Stubborn Stuart has been at the firm for 170 years. He parried with Lincoln on the Illinois circuit back in the day and shared a room with Stephen Douglas. He is venerated for his wisdom and experience and still drinks whiskey in his office from a crystal decanter. Because of his relationships and esteem, he is a pillar of the community and confers a great reputation upon the firm.

Stuart is an old-school lawyer. In the world according to Stuart, things have been done a certain way for decades and there's no need for them to change now. The courts move at a certain pace and so should attorneys. He believes talk of disruption is overblown; the profession has a long, storied history, and ultimately, it's all about representing your client.

The business side of law is not of interest to Stuart. While he's happy to bring on new clients, for him, it's all about the relationships. The detailed, financial side of the law is better left to someone else. He will check in with Betty to get updates on where he is with billing. Stuart goes about his work and jots down notes, but an administrative assistant helps with calendaring, tracking time, and retrieving files.

Stuart is a laggard. When computers first started appearing in law offices he was aghast, and he did not believe they should be on the desks of attorneys. Moreover, Stuart is extremely risk-averse. A lifetime of looking at the worst possible things that could happen to people has made him very hesitant to make any sudden moves. Plus, his reliance on precedent from his legal training and experience render him unable to blaze any new trails.

How to Handle Stuart

Don't hold out hope that Stuart will change personally. Your goal should be for Stuart to not interfere with your efforts, and ideally, to eventually appreciate the fruits of your efforts. Plus, requiring Stuart to attend a standup meeting might physically kill him.

Trying to persuade Stuart that the law firm should adopt Lean methodologies is going to get you nowhere fast. Instead, position the initiatives as necessary for better client service. For example:

> Modern clients have different expectations now—they will work with lawyers who can provide timely information and will jettison those who don't.
> Clients are demanding different billing structures as alternatives to the billable hour, and you need to be able to implement these and know if your pricing is fair to both parties.
> Most states and the U.S. government require e-filing, so not having a paperless office is terribly inefficient. Additionally, the constant moving back and forth between paper and electronic documents introduces risk of human error.

You can also leverage FUD (fear, uncertainty, and doubt), since Stuart is so risk-averse. Angling things as dangerous threats may sound manipulative, but it will work. For example:

> You can argue that if the firm doesn't adopt some of these measures, such as going paperless or collecting credit cards, you are going against the recommendation of your state bar's practice management advisors, who work with disbarred and bankrupt lawyers every day.
> You can also sprinkle in the concern of legal trend-spotters, who note that in the UK, nonlawyers can now own law firms. If this development is part of a larger trend, it will open the door to competition with people who actually know how to run a business. You need to be prepared in case this happens in the United States as well.
> Argue that you may be paying people too much for their work. You don't know for certain who the top performers are, and you need better reporting.
> We have bad habits and are leaving oodles of cash on the table.

Stuart is also likely to not want to upset Betty. There's a chance she's intimidated him in the past, and he doesn't want to deal with that. Make it clear that he won't have to handle her.

IT-Guy Irving

Poor Irving. He's a living caricature. When he's not quoting *Star Wars*, he's snickering at people who don't know the difference between POP and IMAP e-mail protocols.

Irving simply loves digital technology. He reads about it and invests his own dollars in it. Tech is as much a hobby as it is a job. In fact, it may be a true passion. He looks forward to the latest announcements by Apple, Google, and Microsoft. He likes setting up systems and tinkering with them, finding them genuinely fascinating.

Irving is an early adopter of technology. At the same time, automation threatens him. When he has a server to maintain, he has a job. When that server is moved to the cloud, his usefulness at the firm may eventually be called into question. So Irving is caught between the allure of shiny new cloud-based technologies and the concerns of his paycheck. It can be more lucrative for Irving to maintain an old-school client-server-based system that needs a lot of maintenance, and thus income.

Irving is also cautious. He has heard the stories of peers who made a poor technology decision and got canned. For this reason, Irving lives by the credo that "no one ever got fired for hiring IBM," which means that he will tend to gravitate toward brand names people recognize. This playing-it-safe philosophy is especially pronounced with IT managers on staff as opposed to consultants.

Irving is typically a social outsider at the firm. In a small-firm context he is likely a part-time consultant. That said, Irving is very much an influencer, and he has the ear of everyone when it comes to technology. However, Irving's self-esteem is often tied up in his intelligence and technical know-how. Therefore, he may be very suspicious of ideas that are not his own when it comes to tech.

How to Handle Irving

Removing Irving's leverage is key. Do not fear Irving or allow him to hold you hostage to technology concerns. There are lots of people who can do what he does, and he can be replaced. Even if you're in a distant location, IT work can be performed remotely: One of our firms is in American Samoa and uses a technical consultant in Ohio.

Yes, systems can be complex, but a good engineer or technician can understand them with time. No one is irreplaceable, no matter what anyone would have you believe. Furthermore, Irving will likely not violate the law by harming your systems in any way.

The message to Irving needs to be that to modernize is inevitable and you'd love him to come along for the ride. Get him involved in the search for systems. Make sure he knows you're going to do your own research, but stroke his ego by saying you want his opinion on everything. What Irving will be especially helpful with is thinking about and identifying the impact to the other systems in your office.

Let him know he's going to be the point person on your tech transition. Come up with a financial incentive or bonus to drive the behavior you want. You could budget a bonus of $500 to $1,000 for the complete rollout and training of a new system, if hit by a certain deadline and without sacrificing quality. The work itself, migrating data from one system to another, may be enough of a driver for Irving, either financially or from a sheer interest perspective.

Important: Take the advice of your IT consultant, but when it comes to software, make sure you do your own research on your technology needs. A lot of people who specialize in legal technology have affiliate deals with software providers. They may be incentivized monetarily to get you on a specific system, so you need to understand the relationship between the consultant and the software provider. You don't want to be shoehorned into a system because of someone else's economics.

EMBRACE TESTED PERSUASION TECHNIQUES

There is good news for those of us who are fascinated by human nature and eager to make a buck: The field of behavioral economics has yielded us a treasure trove of proven techniques for directing human behavior.

As much as we think we are free, independent thinkers, we are subject to our biology and are not as immune to manipulation as we would like to believe. Have you ever left a stadium wearing the same color shirt as 50,000 people? Bought something because there were only two left in stock? Done shots with your friends against your better instincts? Humans share certain fundamental behaviors that cross cultural boundaries. This reality means that we can use techniques to help advance our agendas, including goading the stubborn and reluctant toward our goal of getting Lean.

- ✘ **DON'T:** Abuse persuasion techniques. They are very powerful. Use them for good.
- ✘ **DON'T:** Be obvious when you use a persuasion technique. Others who are trained in them will know exactly what you are doing.
- ✔ **DO:** Realize that these principles actually do work.

> **The Granddaddy of Influence Books**
>
> I maintain a belief that all professionals should read *How to Win Friends and Influence People* by Dale Carnegie. It's a business classic with eternal truths that has stood the test of time, or at least the last 80 years.
>
> Not only does *How to Win* cover the basics of influence, like convincing people your idea was their idea and weaponizing your smile, it is a delightful anecdotal romp through early 20th century American history and characters.

You can go very deep with behavioral economics. The "Dan" authors of Daniel Pink, Daniel Kahneman, and Dan Ariely are great sources of information and have written a number of popular books. For our purposes, I'd like to cover the basics of psychology professor Robert Cialdini's work, whose *Influence: Science and Practice* is considered a classic of the genre. To be honest, it's worth reading this bestseller as a consumer just to be aware of these techniques so they can't be used against you.

The important thing to note is that Cialdini's work has been tested both in laboratory settings and in the real world. The experiments themselves are fascinating to read about. Cialdini espouses the idea that humans have "click-whirr" behavior, meaning we are as automatic and predictable as cueing and playing a cassette tape, for those readers who remember what that is.

Specifically, he outlines the following six principles of influence, which can be used for evil or good.

Reciprocation

The principle of reciprocation is simple: "We should try to repay, in kind, what another person has provided for us. If a woman does us a favor, we should do her one in return; if a man sends us a birthday present, we should remember his birthday with a gift of our own," according to Cialdini.

Humans are programmed to give, receive, and repay. When you do something positive for someone, they feel an obligation to return the favor. You see reciprocity employed in politics, when legislators trade favors for backing each other's bills. It's used in supermarkets, when good will is earned by giving out product samples. Charities send us return-address labels to prod us to donate.

Using reciprocity is powerful, and it can be used to advance your Lean law firm agenda. Helping someone out with a problem at work can result in them standing behind you when you implement daily standups or other techniques.

Commitment and Consistency

Humans desire consistency in their own and others' behavior. We love it when you can rely on someone and their actions match their words. Once people put a stake in the ground and make a commitment, they will continue to back that stance, even if it means wading deeper into territories that are not in their own interest. On the flip side, inconsistency and hypocrisy are viewed with hostility. As Cialdini points out, "We fall into the habit of being automatically consistent even in situations where it is not the sensible way to be."

Consider John Kerry's failed 2004 presidential bid. The biggest attack against him was that he was a "flip-flopper" and changed his mind about his political positions.

To see how commitments can be used for influence, consider this sales technique: A car salesman might ask a potential customer, seemingly innocuously, if she would buy a vehicle if the price were right. If the prospect says yes, then a trained salesman can throw the commitment back in her face at a later time and lead her toward a purchasing decision. "Well, you agreed that the price I offered is right, and earlier you told me you would buy the car if that were the case."

This can help in changing minds in a Lean law firm: "Couldn't we agree that we're not collecting as much of our billables as we should?" or "Wouldn't it be more convenient if we got rid of the paper files?" Getting people to make these small concessions and put a stake in the ground can be leveraged later.

Social Proof

The social proof principle states that "we determine what is correct by finding out what other people think is correct," according to Cialdini. Basically, humans want to act the way other humans act. We rely on each other to guide our own behavior.

This is why television executives continue to add laugh tracks to sitcoms. Research suggests viewers think jokes are funnier with other people laughing. Companies love to boast that more people are using their product than others—it makes us feel we are making a validated choice. Services with user reviews like Yelp, Amazon, and AllRecipes are valued not just for the ratings they give of a product or service, but by the number of people that reviewed it.

Lawyers tend to be very precedent-oriented by training. That's how they evaluate the strengths of a case. For this reason, social proofing works very effectively with them. Pointing out that other law firms use some of the techniques in this book, or that the movement itself has enough steam to even merit a book in the first place, is a great way to get your ideas to be considered seriously.

Liking

Humans much prefer to work with people we find likeable over those we find disagreeable. In fact, Cialdini cites a lawyer to lead off the chapter. "The main work of a trial attorney is to make a jury like his client," according to Clarence Darrow.

If you are choosing between two cars and you cannot make a decision, will you give the business to the saleswoman you got along with or the saleswoman who rubbed you the wrong way? Detectives use the good cop/bad cop routine to extract information and concessions. (Hint: It's not the bad cop that gets the information.) Tupperware recognized the liking principle and turned it into gold by organizing parties and having people purchase containers from their friends. Salespeople ask customers for referrals so that when they call upon a prospect, they can say, "Your friend said I should get in touch with you."

There are a lot of techniques to become more likeable, and you'll find you have more persuasive powers if you embrace them. If you're unpleasant to be around, it's going to be more difficult to get others on board with your initiatives.

Authority

Humans are overwhelmingly obedient to authority. That's a good thing for the most part, as it keeps society functioning in an orderly manner, but as history shows, it can be manipulated for very nefarious purposes.

Two of the most famous experiments in behavioral studies demonstrate the power of authority over people. The Stanford prison experiment, which was made into a movie, demonstrated that students acting as prisoners were completely subservient to their peers acting as guards, putting up with humiliation and abuse. In another seminal work, Stanley Milgram showed that under the watchful eye of an authority figure wearing a white lab coat and holding a clipboard, volunteers would administer electric shocks to people, even when they heard screams.

You don't have authority just because you're in charge of an organization. Bookkeepers like Betty have a lot of authority because they control a precious resource: the firm's money. IT-Guy Irving has authority because he has mastered the arcane art of digital technology. Job titles, clothes, and professional appearance all convey authority. Mustering up as much authority as you can will help in any situation where you want to direct human behavior.

Scarcity

The scarcity principle states that the less able we are to obtain something, the more we want it. "Opportunities seem more valuable to us when they are less available," writes Cialdini. Furthermore, people are "more motivated by the thought of losing something than by the thought of gaining something of equal value." In other words, if somebody is going to lose something, their desire starts to become a powerful urge.

You see scarcity in action with how we value commodities, be they silver, gold, or baseball cards. It is used in retail all the time by using the limited-number and deadline techniques: There are only so many left and the offer expires tonight, so you need to act now. Censorship is also powerful. People are attracted to things that are banned. The fear of losing things drives auction prices higher and higher. We seem to just value something more when it seems like it's harder to get.

For our purposes in driving adoption, one use of the scarcity principle is using progressive disclosure to pique interest in Lean techniques. For example, by teasing with a limited amount of information about KPIs, and hinting that more powerful ones exist, you will drive curiosity. Scarcity works more in selling goods and services than it does in general persuasion, but it is a good tool to know about.

CHAPTER SUMMARY

If you're in a fortunate enough position to be the absolute boss, adoption is a lot easier. You can skip the persuasion and go straight to the project rollout. For most people, implementing change in an organization is difficult and comes with a likelihood of failure. Buy-in and adoption are critical and are largely driven by social forces within your organization. Understand the technology adoption lifecycle and try to understand who the early adopters, early majority, late majority, and laggards are. Think about the influencers in your organization and whom you need to get on board. For the ones who are tricky, learn a little bit about personas to model behavior and plot how you are most likely to win them over.

Cialdini's work on influence is worthy of study and contemplation as you seek to win people to your side. His identified principles of reciprocity, social proofing, commitment, likability, authority, and scarcity are born from academic rigor and are universal across cultures.

Epilogue

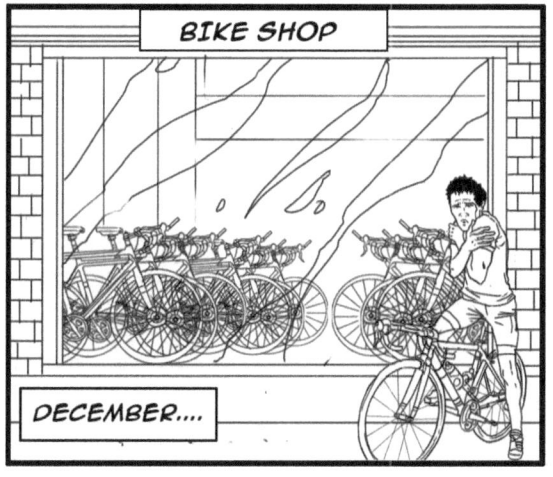

December

Carson was freezing in his cycling clothes as he waited for Guy outside the bike shop. Guy had said he had a couple of final surprises for Carson, and he told him to come dressed for training to the bike shop. Carson had a pretty good idea that the surprise involved some kind of torturous training. But he didn't mind. He was logging more miles every week, and if it continued he'd be in shape soon to compete in the Master's division at State Cup. His hands moved to his middle. All traces of his paunch were gone now, but he was still getting used to its absence. He felt better, he realized, than he had in many years.

    A van emblazoned with C^2 logos finally pulled up, and Guy jumped out attired, like Carson, in cold-weather cycling gear. "Looking lean and mean, Carson!" said Guy. "Come give me a hand over here."

Carson followed Guy to the back of the van. Guy opened the doors and pulled out a racing bike covered in a paper sheet. "Surprise number one," Guy said, and theatrically tore the sheet off the bike.

Carson had never seen anything quite so beautiful in all of his years as a bike geek: jet-black glossy paint, matte black finished components, and blue and black checkerboard rims with the C^2 logo inversely printed on each square. Small white script on the top tube read simply, "Tsunami 7."

"It's a prototype, of course," said Guy. "One of two in the world. Like it?"

"It's the most beautiful bike I've ever seen, Guy."

"Good," said Guy. "Merry Christmas. It's yours."

Carson stood speechless.

Guy chided, "It's not much good if you just stare at it. Get on. Let's ride." Guy pulled a matching Tsunami 7 from the van. "Here's the other one in the world."

They mounted their bikes and started pedaling. The pace built steadily over the first few miles over smooth asphalt and rolling terrain. The Tsunami 7 was a revelation. Guy was apparently feeling it, too. Still a powerful rider, Guy started pushing the pace. It was going to be a long 100 miles.

Finally they came to a long, open, straight stretch of road and fell back to a conversational speed. Guy said, "I have another surprise for you. But this one's a present for me. Kumiko and I are moving to Japan. At least for a while."

Guy glanced at Carson and read the surprised look on his face. "Don't look so shocked, Carson."

Carson finally managed to ask, "What about C^2? Who will run it?"

Guy laughed. "Not you! What? Did you think I was going to pull a Willy Wonka on you? No chance." Carson laughed as Guy continued, "The beauty of a systems-based business—and one of its hallmarks—is that it can run without you. And incidentally, if you ever decide to sell it, that's essential. I haven't decided about that yet, of course. I may never sell it. But on the other hand, I might, if I can find a buyer who will be true to Dad's vision. But the point is, if you can create something that can exist without your physical presence, that's a sign you're on the right track."

"What about our meetings, Guy? I still have lots of questions," Carson said.

Guy replied, "You should never run out of questions. And you should never stop experimenting to find the answers. Surviving means being willing to adapt. Much of what I've taught you are what I consider universal principles of business; however, some of what you've learned may become obsolete at some point. Be willing to experiment."

They came to a fork in the road and Guy suddenly veered to the right fork, surprising Carson again. "Where are you going, Guy?"

Guy replied, "I've got to get home and start packing, so I'm cutting my ride to 25 miles. But you need to ride the whole 100 today."

Guy continued shouting over his shoulder. "You're not getting rid of me this easy, Carson. I'm going to e-mail your training schedule to you and follow up on Skype. We can talk business then, too. But I've taught you all I can, now. You have to take it from here, Carson. You can do this." As Guy disappeared pedaling into the distance, Carson looked up the road into the hills he was approaching. He picked up the pace. "You're right, Guy," he thought. "I *can* do this."

Index

A
A/B testing, 110–112
Action, in AIDA model, 107
Advertising, online, 117–118
AIDA model, 107
Alignment, 144
Annual goal setting, 194–203
Annual Planning and Goal-Setting Meeting, 149
Ariely, Dan, 219
As late as possible (ASLAP), 91
Authority, 210–211, 221–222
Average Case Unit Value (ACUV), 20, 30, 35, 43, 47, 60–61, 75, 89, 93, 196–197, 201
Average Cycle Time, 65, 75
Average Net Case Value, 60–61, 75
Average Reaction Time, 65–66, 75
Avvo, 121–122
Awareness, in AIDA model, 107

B
Backlog, 26
Back Office Betty, 214–215
Balance Sheet, 72–73
Baseline, 54
Behavior modeling, 213–218
Big data, 108–109
Billable time tracking, 135
Billing standardization, 133–134
Block, defined, 28
Bottleneck, defined, 28
Brand Basket, 26
Business acceleration, 171–178
Business continuity, 138
Buyer personas, 112–113
Buy-In, 26

C
Call tracking number, 111
Carnegie, Dale, 219
Carpenter, Sam, 193
Case, 27
Case Unit, 27
Cash Balance (CQ), 54–58, 74
Cash management, 59
Cash Pipeline (CP), 55–58
Cash Position (CQ), 54–58, 74
Cash Pu, 74
Changeover, 26, 41, 47
Checklists, 130–131. *See also* Standardization
Cialdini, Robert, 219
Click-Through Rate, 119
Client
 defined, 27
 in law firms vs. manufacturing, 37
Client intake, 132–133
Cloud-based software, 182–183
Collection, 167–169
Collection Percentage, 57–59, 69–70, 74–75
Commitment, 220
Consistency, 220
Constraint
 defined, 27
 external, 27
 internal, 27–28

Content marketing, 111–112. *See also* Marketing
Conversion Rates, 115
Core customers, 112–113
Cost per Click, 119
Cycle Time (CT), 20, 28–29, 36, 43–45, 47, 57–58, 60–62, 75, 81–84, 87–89, 91–93, 195–196, 198–199, 201, 206. *See also* Average Cycle Time
Cycle Time for Case Unit, 45

D
Daily Standup Meeting, 145–147
Dashboards, 73–74, 109–110
Deadlines, 52–53, 75, 91
Deadline Tracking, 66–67
Desire, in AIDA model, 107
Devices, 181–182
Diffusion of innovations, 211, 213
Display Advertising, 118–119
Document assembly, 166–167
Document creation, with templates, 137–138
Document filing, 135–136
Document management systems (DMSs), 137
Document naming, 135–136
Document storage, 163–166
Dvorak, August, 209

E
Early adopters, 212
Early majority, 212
E-billing, 59
Efficiency, 162–171
E-mail, 138
Employees, 37. *See also* Utilization Rate
Excel, 73–74
External constraint, 27

F
Facebook, 118
Filing, 135–136
Financial statements, 71–73
Firm Collection Percentage (FCP), 57–59, 74
Focus, 179–180

G
Gawande, Atul, 131
Generalists, 106

Goals, results vs., 192
Goal setting
annual, 194–203
dangers of, 190–191
Goldratt, Eliyahu, 25
Google Analytics, 114–115
Google Display Advertising, 118–119
Google Places, 121–122
Google Remarketing Advertising, 119
Google Search Advertising, 118

H
Harding, Ford, 106

I
Impressions, 119
Income Formula, 20, 29, 34, 42–43, 47, 195, 197
Individual Collection Percentage, 69–70, 75
Information Advantage, 160–161
Innovators, 212
Intake, client, 132–133
Interest, in AIDA model, 107
Internal constraint, 27–28
Inventory, 47. *See also* Work in Process (WIP)
Invoicing, 167–169
IT-Guy Irving, 217–218

J
Just-in-Time (JIT), 29, 52–53

K
Kahneman, Daniel, 219
Kaizen, 29, 129
Kanban Board, 29, 64, 87–88, 142–143, 154–156, 173–174
Kanban Cards, 174–175
Kanban system, 21–22
Key Performance Indicators (KPI)
baseline, 54
defined, 29
quantity, 54–64
reviewing, 149–150
staff-related, 68–71
tracking software, 171–173
Keyword Ranking, 117

L
Laggards, 212
Landing pages, 120

Late majority, 212
Leads, 62–63, 75. *See also* Prospects
Lean Manufacturing, 25
Liking, 221
Little's law, 43–46

M
Marketing. *See also* Online marketing
   A/B testing in, 110–111
   basic concepts, 106–108
   big data and, 108–109
   buyer personas in, 112–113
   call tracking numbers in, 111
   content, 111–112
   core customers in, 112–113
   dashboards in, 109–110
   in Lean firms, 109
   monthly review and, 110
   numbers game, 108–109
   offline, 122–123
   online, 114–122
   sales funnel and, 106–108
   software, 176–178
Matter, 27
Matter setup, standardization of, 134–136
Meeting rhythms, 145–149
Monthly Retrospective Meeting, 147–148
Monthly review, 110
Monthly Searches, 117
Muda, 30, 162–163. *See also* Waste
Multitasking, 29, 41, 179–180

N
Naming, of documents, 135–136
Net Promoter Score (NPS), 67–68
New Clients per Month, 63–64, 75
New Leads Per Month, 62–63, 75
New Visitor, 115
Numbers Ninja, 53–54

O
October Surprise, 150, 190, 202, 207
Offline marketing, 122–123. *See also* Marketing
One-page summaries, 152
Online advertising, 117–118
   Facebook in, 118
   Google Search Advertising in, 118

Online marketing, 114–122. *See also* Marketing
   advertising and, 117–118
   Avvo in, 121–122
   Google Display Advertising in, 118–119
   Google Places in, 121–122
   Google Remarketing Advertising in, 119
   landing pages in, 120
   search engine optimization in, 115–117
   social media in, 120–121
   website design in, 116
   website in, 114–115
   Yelp in, 121–122
Opportunities, 92–93
Optimization, of active work, 93
Origination by Individual, 70–71, 75
Outcome Goals, 188, 191–192, 195
Output, 36, 47

P
Paperless, 163–166
Passwords, 181
Personas, 213–218
Personnel problems, with technology, 178–179
Persuasion techniques, 218–222
Physical security, 138
Pink, Daniel, 219
Poison the well, 210–211
Position, 51
Practice management software, 169–171
Process
   catalog, 132–138
   defined, 29
   mapping, 96
   standardization, 131
Production Advantage, 160–161
Productivity, 38
Pronovost, Peter, 131
Prospects, 92
Pull Scheduling, 29

Q
Quarterly Meetings, 153–154
Queue, 80–81, 84, 86, 88–89, 91–92

R
Reaction Time, 28–29, 60, 65–66, 92
Reciprocation, 219
Referring Sources, 115
Remarketing Advertising, 119

Remote communication software, 175–176
Results, goals vs., 192
Retrospective, 152–154
Return on investment (ROI), 108–109
Revella, Adele, 113
Rodgers, Everett, 211

S

Sales Funnel, 106–108
Saunders, Paul, 155
Scanning, 163–166
Scarcity, 222
Search engine optimization (SEO), 115–117
Security, physical, 138
Security, technology and, 180–182
Security practices, 181–182
Social media, 120–121. *See also* Facebook
Social proof, 220–221
Spreadsheets, 73–74
Staff-related KPIs, 68–71
Stage/Kanban, 64, 75
Standardization
   of billing, 133–134
   of client intake, 132–133
   of document creation, 137–138
   of document filing, 135–136
   of document naming, 135–136
   of matter setup, 134–136
   of processes, 131
   tips, 139
Statement of Cash Flow (SOCF), 71–72
Storage, document, 163–166
Strategic Objective, 193
Stubborn Stuart, 215–216
SWOT analysis, 92–93, 150–152
Synergy, 144
System(s)
   conceptualization, 85–87
   thinking, 42
   visualization, 87–88
   working, 90

T

Task Goals, 188, 191–192, 200–201
Technology, 38
   adoption lifecycle, 211–213
   business acceleration and, 171–178
   cloud-based, 182–183
   concerns and considerations, 178
   efficiency and, 162–171
   focus and, 179–180
   Information Advantage and, 160–161
   multitasking and, 179–180
   personnel problems and, 178–179
   Production Advantage and, 160–161
   security and, 180–182
   waste reduction and, 162–171
Templates, document creation with, 137–138
Theory of Constraints, 25–26
Threats, 93
Throughput Rate, 20, 29, 43–47, 60, 64–66, 75, 81, 89, 92–93, 97, 196–197, 199, 206
Toyota Production System (TPS), 25, 88
Tracking billable time, 135

U

Unique Visits, 115
Utilization Rate, 69, 75

V

Value Stream Mapping, 88–90
"Vanity metric," 63
Vision, 192–193
Visual Controls, 30

W

Waiting for No Reason (WNR) Time, 28, 84, 88, 90, 93, 95, 197
Wait Time, 20, 28, 90–91, 93
Waste, 30
Waste reduction, 162–171
Waste types, 163
Website, in online marketing, 114–115
Website design, 116
Weekly Meetings, 153–154
Whitney, Eli, 25
Womack, Ames, 25
Work in Process (WIP), 27, 30, 43–46, 59–60, 63, 75, 81, 84, 88, 195–196, 198–199, 201

Y

Year over year (YoY), 63
Yelp, 121–122